Safety-Critical Systems Journal

Compilation Volume 2

2023

This collation page left blank intentionally.

Edited by John Spriggs
Cover design by Alex King

Published by the Safety-Critical Systems Club 2023

Individual papers copyright as explicitly stated in the first page footer of each paper

All other material © Safety-Critical Systems Club C.I.C. 2023

www.thescsc.org

SCSC-187

ISBN: 9798878623216

This collation page left blank intentionally.

Contents

About this Volume 6

Important Note 6

About the Publisher 7

Vol. 2 Iss. 1 (2023): Safety-Critical Systems eJournal Winter Issue 9

Editorial to the 2023 Winter Issue 11

Papers

The Boeing 737 MAX 8 Crashes: System-based Approach to Safety — A Different Perspective — Sanjeev Appicharla 13

Safety Assessment of Point Merge Operations in Terminal Airspace: An IEC 61508 Viewpoint — Derek Fowler, and Octavian Nicolas Fota 35

The Terminological Analysis Method SemAn and its Implementation — Peter Bernard Ladkin, Lou Xinxin, and Dieter Schnäpp 65

Vol. 2 Iss. 2 (2023): Safety-Critical Systems eJournal Summer Issue 125

Editorial to the 2023 Summer Issue 127

Papers

Reducing the Risk of a Software Common Mode Failure — Rob Ashmore, Mark Hadley, and James Sharp 129

An IEC 61508 Viewpoint on the Safety Assessment of Railway Control Systems — Derek Fowler, and Alasdair Graebner 145

Chasing the Black Swan — Malcolm Jones 195

About the Safety-Critical Systems eJournal 211

Copyright and Disclaimer 212

Letters to the Editor 212

Index of Authors 213

Index of Titles 214

About this Volume

This is the annual print compilation volume of all the issues of 2023 of the Journal of the Safety-Critical Systems Club (SCSC): ISSN 2753-6599 Volume 2.

The mission of the Safety-Critical Systems eJournal is to publish high-quality, peer-reviewed articles on the subject of systems safety. When we talk of systems, we mean not only the platforms, but also the people and their procedures that make up the whole. Systems Safety addresses those systems, their components, and the services they are used to provide. This is not a narrow view of system safety, our scope is wide and also includes safety-related topics such as resilience, security, public health and environmental impact.

Issue 1 and Issue 2 of Volume 2 were first issued on line as SCSC Publication Numbers SCSC-183 and SCSC-186; they are accessible as https://scsc.uk/scsc-183 and https://scsc.uk/scsc-186 respectively.

Important Note

While the authors and the publishers have used reasonable endeavours to ensure that the information and guidance given in this work is correct, all parties must rely on their own skill and judgement when making use of this work and obtain professional or specialist advice before taking, or refraining from, any action on the basis of the content of this work. Neither the authors nor the publishers make any representations or warranties of any kind, express or implied, about the completeness, accuracy, reliability, suitability or availability with respect to such information and guidance for any purpose, and they will not be liable for any loss or damage including without limitation, indirect or consequential loss or damage, or any loss or damage whatsoever (including as a result of negligence) arising out of, or in connection with, the use of this work. The views and opinions expressed in this publication are those of the authors and do not necessarily reflect those of their employers, the SCSC, or other organisations.

About the Publisher

This journal is published by the Safety-Critical Systems Club (SCSC). The SCSC is a "Community Interest Company" (CIC), which is a special type of limited company that exists to benefit a community rather than private shareholders. The SCSC has:

- A 'community interest statement', explaining our plans;
- An 'asset lock' — a legal promise stating that our assets will only be used for our social objectives;
- A constitution; and
- Approval by the Regulator of Community Interest Companies.

Our community is that of Safety Practitioners. As a distinct legal entity the SCSC has more freedom and can legitimately do things such as make agreements with other bodies and own copyright on documents.

The SCSC began its work in 1991, supported by the UK Department of Trade and Industry and the Engineering and Physical Sciences Research Council. Since 1993 it has organised the annual Safety-Critical Systems Symposium (SSS) where leaders in different aspects of safety from different industries, including consultants, regulators and academics, meet to exchange information and experience, with the content published in a proceedings volume. The Club has been self-sufficient since 1994, and became a CIC in 2021.

The SCSC supports industry working groups. Currently there are active groups covering the areas of: Assurance Cases, Autonomous Systems Safety, Data Safety, Multicore and Manycore Safety, Ontology, Safe AI, Safer Complex Systems, Safety Culture, Security Informed Safety, Service Assurance, and the Systems Approach to Safety of the Environment. These working groups provide a focus for discussions within industry and produce new guidance materials.

The SCSC maintains a website (thescsc.org, scsc.uk), which includes a diary of events, working group areas and club publications. It organises seminars, workshops and training on general safety matters or specific subjects of current concern. It produces a regular newsletter, Safety Systems, three times a year and also a peer-reviewed journal. The journal is published on-line, as the Safety-Critical Systems eJournal, and comprises two issues a year, with an annual print volume: ISSN 2754-1118 (Online), ISSN 2753-6599 (Print).

SCSC Mission: To promote practical systems approaches to safety for technological solutions in the real world.

Where:

- "systems approaches" is the application of analysis tools, models and methods which consider the whole system and its components;
- "system" means the whole socio-technical system in which the solution operates, including organisational culture, structure and governance; and
- "technological solutions" includes products, systems and services and combinations thereof.

The Aims of the SCSC are:

1. To build and foster an active and inclusive community of safety stakeholders:
   a. "safety stakeholders" include practitioners (in safety specialisms and other disciplines involved in the whole lifecycle of safety related systems), managers, re searchers, and those involved in governance (including policy makers, law makers, regulators and auditors)
   b. from across industry sectors, including new and non-traditional areas
   c. recognising the importance of including and nurturing early career practitioners
   d. working to remove barriers to inclusion in the community
2. To support sharing of systems approaches to safety:
   a. enabling wider application
   b. supporting continuing professional development
   c. encouraging interaction between early career and experienced practitioners
   d. using a variety of communication media and techniques to maximise coverage
   e. highlighting the lessons which can be learned from past experience
3. To produce consistent guidance for safety stakeholders where not already available.
   a. "consistent" meaning the guidance is consistent within itself, and with other guidance provided by SCSC; although SCSC will also aim to co-ordinate with external guidance this is more difficult to achieve
4. To influence relevant standards, guidance and other publications.
5. To work with relevant organisations to provide a co-ordinated approach to system safety.
6. To minimise our environmental impact wherever possible.

SCSC Membership may be either corporate or individual. Membership gives full web site access, the hardcopy newsletter, other mailings, and discounted entry to seminars, workshops and the annual Symposium. Corporate membership is for organisations that would like several employees to take advantage of the benefits of the SCSC. Different arrangements and packages are available. More information can be obtained at: scsc.uk/membership.

Also available is a short-term Publications Pass which, at very low cost, gives a month's access to all SCSC publications for non-members. Contact alex.king@scsc.uk for more details.

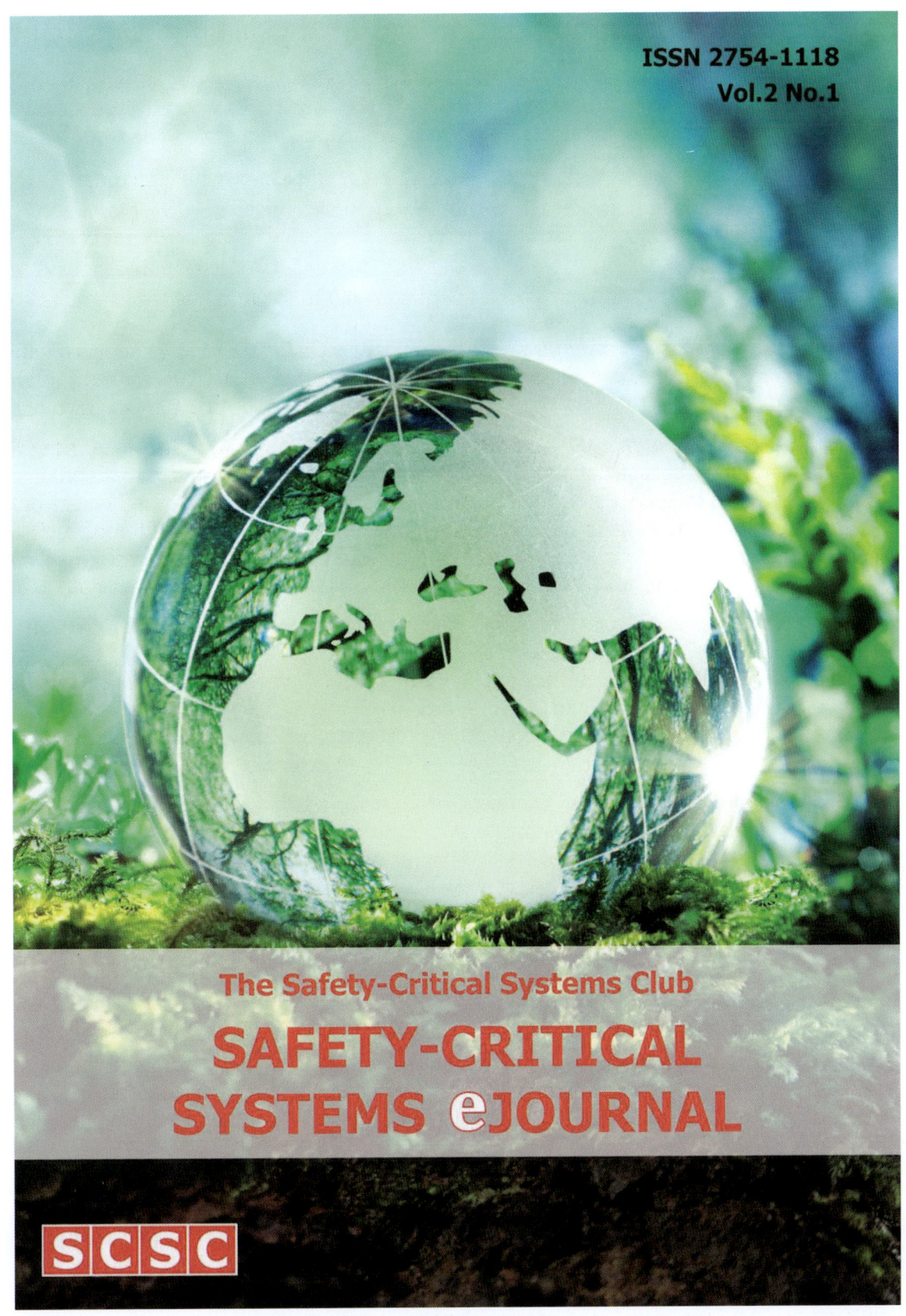

Issue 1 Cover

This collation page left blank intentionally.

Editorial to the 2023 Winter Issue

Welcome to the first issue of the second volume of the Safety-Critical Systems eJournal, which is published by the Safety Critical Systems Club (SCSC).

We have a new cover image for this volume, designed by Alex King. It has an environmental theme to mark the Club's new Working Group, which started up last Summer. The Systems Approach to Safety of the Environment Working Group is intending to apply Systems Safety practices to systems that are embedded within the natural environment, while focussing on that environment. The group aims to produce clear guidance on how engineered systems should be developed and managed throughout their entire lifecycle so as to preserve, protect and enhance the environment. If you would like to join, or find out more about this group, please go to their page on the SCSC website: https://scsc.uk/ge.

This issue contains three papers:

- Sanjeev Appicharla (UK), in *"The Boeing 737 MAX 8 Crashes: System-based Approach to Safety — A Different Perspective"*, contends that, despite all the literature on considering human and organisational factors in safety assessment, fewer researchers and practitioners than hoped actually do this as a matter of course. He concludes that we should be advancing models that include human, technical *and* organisational factors, *and their interactions*, when assessing the risks posed by complex systems.
- Derek Fowler (UK) and Nicolas Fota (France) build upon Derek's paper in the last issue, on using IEC 61508 in the Transport Sector, by providing a worked example, *"Safety Assessment of Point Merge Operations in Terminal Airspace — An IEC 61508 Viewpoint"*. Point Merge is a systemised method for sequencing air traffic arrival flows that was developed by the EUROCONTROL Experimental Centre in Brétigny.
- Peter Bernard Ladkin, Lou Xinxin, and Dieter Schnäpp (Germany) present a method for the semantic analysis of electrotechnological definitions appearing in IEC standards: *"The Terminological Analysis Method SemAn and its Implementation"*. The method is accompanied by a software tool, the SemAn Analyser, which provides outputs in a pretty-printed and annotated format that retains the symbol-for-symbol syntax of the original text of the *definiens*.

My thanks go to the authors for contributing their papers, and also to the peer-reviewers (at least three per paper) for suggesting improvements. Apologies to those reviewers who made some recommendations that were not taken up.

The editorial to the first issue of this journal said, *"You may find some of this material controversial, or you may think that it does not go far enough. Subsequent issues of this journal will have provision for readers' letters to the Editor responding to individual papers."* Such a letter was published in the last issue, which itself prompted some correspondence. Apparently, it is accepted practice that letters for publication to journal editors should be between 300 and 800 words long, and someone even suggested that the maximum should be 400 words. The published letter was over 1600 words; twice as long as people seem to expect. Not wanting to be quite so constrained, I have now adopted a limit of (about) 1000 words (not counting title, attribution or references). That would take up two pages of this journal. Note that a letter should ideally address a single concern with few, if any, external references.

John Spriggs, SCSC Journal Editor

January 2023

This collation page left blank intentionally.

The Boeing 737 MAX 8 Crashes

System-based Approach to Safety — A Different Perspective

Sanjeev Appicharla

System Safety Researcher

Abstract

This review article presents in a brief manner the lessons learnt from the Boeing 737 MAX 8 crashes using the System approach to safety perspective. Learning the right lessons from past accidents is a huge challenge from the organisational learning perspective; as Professor James Reason cautioned us, "Being blessed with both uninvolvement and hindsight, it is a great temptation for retrospective observers to slip into a censorious frame of mind and to wonder at how these people [i.e. those involved in design and development, safety assurance of these planes] could have been so blind, stupid, arrogant, ignorant or reckless" (Reason 1990, p.214). To distinguish it from the classical approach to safety, the "System approach" perspective used in the paper additionally includes human and organisational aspects. Drawing upon a brief review of case studies published by Chizek (2020) and Daniels (2020), this paper highlights the need to conduct accident case study analysis based upon the concept of System approach to safety. Such an approach will focus attention on two basic kinds of failures, namely, active and latent failures conditions. Latent failure conditions relating to human and organisational factors in particular refer to fallible decisions made at the higher levels of a socio-technical system; these were defined by Reason (1990, 1993). That identification of latent failure conditions, and addressing them, is a continuing challenge for both System safety research and System safety practice domains is also noted.

1 Introduction

From a systems engineering perspective, incorporating System safety, Human factors and Organisational factors (H & OF) into a comprehensive assessment process with a dynamic model to help implement pro-active risk management methods, is a research challenge posed to researchers and practitioners alike as noted, *inter alia*, by Rasmussen et al. (1994), Reason et al. (2006), and Leveson (2011).

The FAA Human Factors Team (1996) made some recommendations to improve aviation safety, including: *"In accident/incident investigations where human error is considered a potential factor, the FAA and the National Transportation Safety Board should thoroughly investigate the factors that contributed to the error, including design, training, operational procedures, the airspace system, or other factors. The FAA should encourage other organizations (both domestic and foreign) conducting accident/incident investigations to do the same. This recommendation should apply to all accident/incident investigations involving human error, regardless of whether the error is associated with a pilot, mechanic, air traffic controller, dispatcher, or other participant in the aviation system"*.

© Sanjeev Appicharla 2023.
Published in the Safety-Critical Systems eJournal by the Safety-Critical Systems Club C.I.C.

As an editor of the book on H & OF concerns, Gilbert (2020) noted the idea has been largely accepted in academia as well as in business that the main vulnerabilities in industrial safety come from human and organisational factors. Despite this acceptance, the H &OF perspective is not, in general, integrated into system safety as part of the systems engineering activity (Appicharla 2006) (Appicharla 2022b).

The system safety concept calls for a risk management strategy based on identification and analysis of hazards, with application of remedial controls using a systems-based approach (System safety 2007). The system safety discipline involves the application of special technical and managerial skills to the systematic, forward-looking identification and control of hazards throughout the life cycle of a project, programme, or activity (Roland and Moriarty 1990) (FAA Safety Team n.d.). System safety engineering using techniques of systems engineering analyses a (socio-technical) system as an interacting set of elements generating hazards is described by Roland and Moriarty (1990).

Appicharla (2006) noted that a complex system or a situation may be approached from three perspectives:

1. the technical perspective (science, technology);
2. the organisational perspective (social, informal, or formal); and
3. the personal perspective (Individual, self).

To manage the complexity of the situation, all three perspectives need to be taken into account. Insights from each perspective cannot be obtained from other perspectives. Technical perspectives can be based on several models and data interpretations: "realities." From a systems point of view, all three perspectives need to be properly taken into account.

Assessing the safety of complex systems is of vital importance to stakeholders in many industry sectors, such as railway transportation, aviation, and other industries, where there is a likelihood that accidents can happen. These accidents may result in loss of lives and/or cause damage to property and the environment. Further, this approach is different from traditional safety strategies for simpler systems, which rely on control of conditions and causes of an accident based either on epidemiological analysis or as a result of investigation of individual past accidents (Rasmussen et al. 1994, Chapter 6) (System safety 2007).

This tendency to omit H & OF concerns from risk assessments and accident analysis can be seen from papers discussing two Boeing 737 MAX 8 accidents published by the Safety Critical System Club (Daniels 2020) (Daniel and Tudor 2022). Also, Appicharla (2022b) critiqued Chizek (2020) for omission of H & OF concerns and failing to identify latent failure pathways to both accidents.

At the end of Sub-section 4.4 of their paper "Software Reliability and the Misuse of Statistics", in the section on Requirements Engineering, Daniel and Tudor (2022) state:

Finally, in the two recent Boeing 737 MAX accidents on 29 October 2018 and 10 March 2019, the Manoeuvring Characteristics Augmentation System (MCAS) software implemented its requirements correctly, but the requirements caused full nose down trim to be applied following an Angle of Attack sensor failure (Daniels 2020). As Nancy Leveson has said, "Software-related accidents are usually caused by flawed requirements". It therefore follows that our efforts should be focused on writing better requirements. Formal methods can help with writing better requirements by using formal requirements languages with unambiguous semantics and formal methods tools that can ensure the requirements are complete and consistent.

The author's objections to the above claim and arguments made about the two Boeing 737 MAX 8 accidents are threefold, as set out in the subsequent sections.

1. The first objection is that they did not pay attention to the H & OF called "latent failure conditions" that contribute to accidents[1] (Appicharla 2006) (Appicharla 2022b). The theme of paying attention to H & OF concerns through accident causation models is taken up in a greater detail herein at Section 2. Following from the first hypothesis is the corollary that systems engineering activity and its contribution to latent failures conditions is to be noted as well. This theme is taken up in Section 3.
2. The second objection is that that learning lessons from past accidents is not easy if such lessons learning exercise is subject to biases on the part of accident analysts or investigators, and this theme is discussed, inter alia, by Reason (1990), Leveson (2004b), and Johnson & Botting (1999). A dynamic model is introduced to show who how unsafe outcomes are produced using the control systems theory whilst discussing this objection in Section 4.
3. The third objection is related to the theme of estimating probabilities of unsafe outcomes and related biases in risk assessments. Biases in risk assessments and accident analysis emerge when companies seek to follow the ISO 31000 risk management standard as part of the systems engineering activity (ISO 31000:2018) (ISO/IEC/IEEE 15288:2015) (Conrow et al. 2021). This theme is taken up in Section 5.

2 Identification of Causal Factors

From a systems engineering perspective, the scope of accident analysis is the socio-technical system of which humans form a part directly, or indirectly through organisations, and interact either for utilisation or developing engineering systems through activities of thinking, problem solving, decision making and rely upon standards, models, methods, and frameworks to engineer acceptable systems (Rasmussen et al. 1994, p. xi) (ISO/IEC/IEEE 15288:2015).

Tozer and Wharton-Street (1993), drawing upon James Reason sponsored research, discussed the need for identifying latent failure conditions, as attention was focussed on active failures of front-line staff, but these staff are the inheritors of latent failures, not the source. They developed REVIEW, showing the sixteen distinct Railway Problem Factors[2]. The results of application of the REVIEW in the Australian railway sector were published by Edkins and Pollock (1996). However, the privatisation of British Railways is assumed to have impeded further developments on the application of pro-active safety risk management.

Tozer and Wharton-Street, (1993) discussed four shortcomings of the British Railways Safety Management System:

1. Current limited amount of feedback from ground-level staff.
2. Different perceptions of safety at each level of organisation.

---

[1] This objection is to details of the Daniels (2020) paper; Daniels and Tudor (2022) concentrate on whether one can quantify software reliability.

[2] The Railway Problem Factors are Training, Tools and equipment, Materials, Design, Staff communication, Rules, Supervision, Working environment, Staffing and rostering, Staff attitudes, Housekeeping, Planning, Departmental communication, Management, Contractors, Maintenance.

3. A general failure of management to recognise latent problems until accidents happen.
4. A reactive assessment of accidents.

Appicharla (2006) took up the concern of latent failure conditions and reactive approach to safety management and this is a continuing research theme for the author. With variety of theories, models and techniques being available for organisations to select from, it is understandable that under the concept of "Satisficing Behaviour" (Appicharla 2010) organisations may fail to integrate their knowledge base to inform their processes for accident prevention. An example of this lack of integrated knowledge base can be seen from the Network Rail (2016) Safety Central web page, Prevention through Engineering and Design. We find there that two different approaches, one at the level of disciplinary process level such as CDM Regulations[3] and another at the company level mandatory processes, the CSM-RA Regulation[4], are presented in the same graphic as providing input apart from the inputs from System safety engineering and Safety by Design Groups to the Prevention through Engineering and Design approach. Further, the web page describes the activity of Prevention through Engineering and Design is based on STAMP[5] related concepts and the concept of Szymbersk's Time-Safety Influence Curve, but extended to cover the asset whole-life and not just change phase. Various concepts and accident models are confused within the lifecycle activity on the web page, probably leading to an impasse in making progress in identifying and addressing the latent failure conditions.

In 2006, the author was surprised to learn that Airbus had applied a system approach at the aircraft level *for the first time* in the aviation industry, and thereby affirming a fly-fix-fly approach was the norm in the industry (Lawrence 2006, p.9) (Roland and Moriarty 1990).

Appicharla (2022b) suggested that the concept of System safety had its beginning with Bell Labs in the form of Fault Tree Analysis, and was adopted by Boeing dating back to 1962 (Ericson 2005). The aviation industry is a pioneering industry in terms of System safety techniques and its adoption of Fault Tree Analysis in the nineteen sixties led to its adoption by the nuclear industry, and subsequently by UK railways (Ericson 1999) (Ericson 2005) (Rasmussen 1981) (Leihton and Denis. 1993). However, integrating H & OF concerns was noted as a problem in the aviation industry by the FAA Human Factors Team (1996). The UK Human Factors Integration Defence Technology Centre[6] raised the HF concern as well (HFIDTC 2006). Despite these Guidance notes and recommendations, the practitioners' apparent lack of interest in H & OF concerns is a common theme in the accident literature (Reason et al. 2006) (Gilbert 2020). That Roland and Moriarty (1990) trace the history of System safety back to 1947 is to be noted.

A research paradigm effort to include all levels of a socio-technical system in system safety activity over the last few decades developed into what is called "Unbounded thinking" or "Systems thinking" or "System approach to safety" (Rasmussen et al. 1994) (Rasmussen 1997) (Appicharla 2010) (Leveson, 2011).

Jens Rasmussen (1997, Figure 1) developed a risk management framework integrating all the levels of socio-technical system involved in generating system hazard. Leveson (2011, Figure 2) presents an example of a hierarchical safety control structure involving all stakeholders in generating the system hazard. Leveson (2009) (2011) claims that chain of

---

[3] The Construction (Design and Management) Regulations 2015 — UK legislation
[4] The Regulation on a Common Safety Method for Risk Evaluation and Assessment — EU legislation
[5] Systems-Theoretic Accident Model and Processes
[6] The UK Human Factors Integration Defence Technology Centre (HFIDTC) is a virtual centre of excellence funded by the MOD which undertakes research to develop and evaluate processes methods and tools

events is included at all levels of system; Rasmussen (1997, Figure 1) is a limitation and her model overcomes this limitation. However, Leveson (2019) noted, while not required to start a CAST[7] analysis, identifying the proximate events preceding the loss may sometimes be useful in starting the process of generating questions that need to be answered in the accident investigation and causal analysis. Therefore, in light of the above discussions, the author's first objection is that the case study analysis of Boeing 737 MAX 8 accidents by Daniels (2020) does not capture all related causal factors.

The author's contention is that the contribution of all stakeholder organisations involved, all disciplines including systems engineering, software engineering and their contribution together with all other relevant causal factors to the accident flights as per the various levels of socio-technical system are required as per the System approach to safety. The question of subjective rule to where to stop in the search of causal factors in the accident investigation is addressed by Rasmussen (1997) includes all levels of a socio-technical system.

Sub-section 2.3 of the ICAO website "Safety Management System Implementation" (ICAO 2022) states on Accident Causation, thus:

> *Safety risks can be generated by active failures and latent conditions. The concept of accident causation is an active field of study, and many types of models exist to illustrate the events taking place leading up to an accident.*

As noted in the quotation above, Reason (1993) argued that modern high-hazard, low-risk systems (such as nuclear power, and chemical plants or contemporary 'fly by wire' commercial aircraft) are prone to breach of several defences due to unlikely combinations of two basic kinds of failures. These are known as active and latent failures or resident pathogens. Definition of these concepts are presented later in the section.

Appicharla (2006) accepted the idea that complex systems can suffer from 'organisational accidents': Complex system(s) are defined as integrated composites of components of people, processes, assets, procedures, rules, and organisations. Complex systems always suffer from latent failures (errors in the original) which pose greatest threat to the safety of the system. These failures combine with the active failure to give rise to what are known as 'organizational accidents' (see Figure 1, derived from (Reason, 1993)).

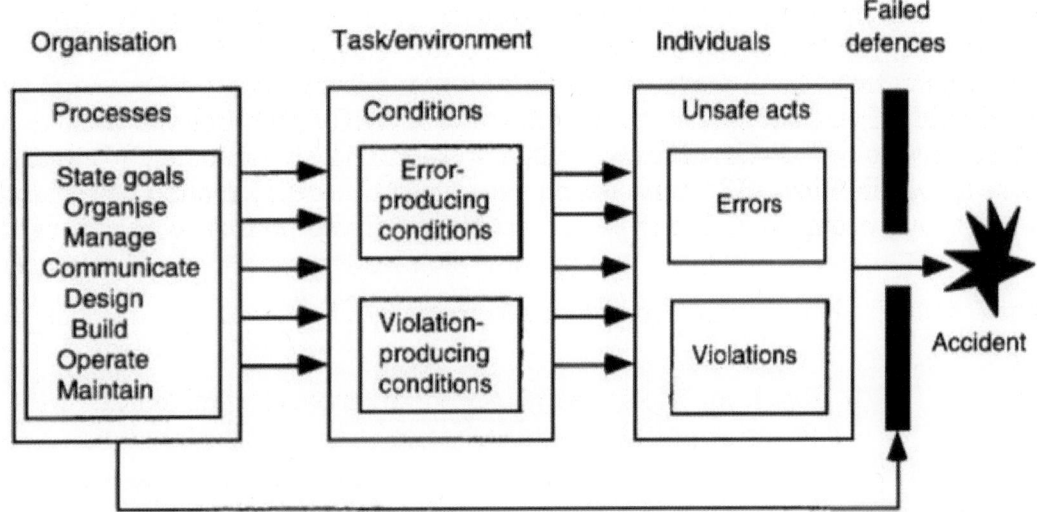

Figure 1 ~ Common Elements in the Development of Accident

---

[7] Causal Analysis based on System. Theory

The model of accident causation shown in Figure 1 is called the Swiss Cheese Model Mark II model by James Reason et al (2006). From the ICAO website quotation above, Reason's (1993) model of accident causation, and use of Swiss Cheese Model to investigate the 2002 Überlingen air accident and publication of the results in the EUROCONTROL Agency report, implies that both ICAO and EUROCONTROL accept the Swiss Cheese Model of Accident Causation as a framework for explanation.

James Reason, *et alia*, (2006) presented the history of Swiss Cheese Model and extended it to include international regulatory frameworks, and discussed the criticisms of the model and explanation of the Überlingen air accident in an open access article. Reason (1993) explained the development of the Swiss Cheese Model in terms of general pattern of accident causation advanced by Heinrich's (1931) "dominoes" model, the Bird & Germain (1985) model, and a fourth element of failed or absent defences was added to these models. Johnson (1973) focussed on management as being responsible for the planning of the context within which accidents unfold, that is, he stressed the role of 'less than adequate' management decisions and developed MORT, the 'Management Oversight and Risk Tree' tool, for accident analysis. Jens Rasmussen (1997), a cognitive systems engineering expert, commented on relations of the MORT technique and the Swiss Cheese Model to accident analysis, thus: *"The combination of the two basic views that (1) accidents should be understood in terms of an energy related process and (2) hazard management therefore should be directed towards planning of the release route"*. Later Reason (1990) has focused analysis on management errors and organisational factors, such as 'resident pathogens making organisations vulnerable to accidents'.

The definitions of active and latent failure conditions are presented hereafter. These are presented here as the author learned that some professional systems engineers in the UK railway domain were not aware of these concepts[8].

Definition: James Reason (1993) defined **Active Failures**: unsafe acts committed by those at the "sharp end" of the system (pilots, air traffic controllers, ships' crews, train drivers, [signallers], control room operators, maintenance crews, and the like). They are the people who are at the human-system interface whose actions can do, and sometimes have immediate consequences. These may be acts of omissions or commissions on the part of front-line operatives.

Definition: James Reason (1993) defined **Latent Failures**: usually fallible decisions taken at the higher-level echelons of the organisation whose damaging or adverse consequences may lie dormant within the system for a long time, only becoming evident when they combine with local triggering factors (i.e. active failures, technical failures, atypical system states, etc.) to breach a system's defences.

In the safety research domain, we find that despite the criticism of the Swiss Cheese Model by Nancy Leveson, discussed by Reason et al. (2006), researchers continue to use the concept of latent failure conditions. For example, Swuste et al. (2020) stated on the theme of latent failures, thus: *"The origin of latent failures lies in the company's organisation and in its decision-making processes. Decision making within an organisation is determined by the context and limitations of the decision-makers, who tend to recycle known solutions for technical problems"* (Halpern 1989). These latent failures are present in a system for a long period of time without causing problems, but are activated in combination with other system failures, breaking through barriers. The psychologist

---

[8] In July 2022, communication with the UK INCOSE Railway Industry Group Chair revealed this fact prior to the INCOSE RIG Annual General Body Meeting. After explaining the meaning of the latent failure conditions or "resident pathogens" in systems engineering activity, the author addressed the AGM to consider the role of "resident pathogens" in systems engineering activity.

Reason described these latent failures using a medical metaphor: *"resident pathogens caused by designers, procedure writers, and top managers representing the 'blunt end' of an organisation"*.

Reason (1993) noted that apart from the lifecycle errors in the system development and design processes that may occur[9], there would be cultural factors of competence, commitment, and cognizance that are impacted by the quality of decision making.

- Competence factor deals with organisational capability to meet the safety goals. Elements of such competence are related to the organisation processes and standards for systems engineering process and their application. Ericson (2005) describes the hazard identification and analysis techniques used by system safety professionals.
- Commitment relates to the motivation and resources for the pursuit of the safety goals in terms of either meeting regulatory targets or pursue leadership status in overcoming the hazards inherent in design and operations. Safety Management Policy, together with the ways and means to pursue the safety objectives define the motives. Most importantly, capability and commitment must be tailored to cognizance of hazards.
- Cognizance of hazards must include managerial attention to latent failure conditions contributed by means of human and organisational factors and their contribution to accidents. Senior managers must look beyond the active failures to understand the resident pathogens in organisational and management practices.

James Reason (1990, p.53-96) drawing upon the insights of economists, such as Daniel Kahneman and Herbert A. Simon and related human error research, developed a conceptual framework — the Generic Error Modelling System, "GEMS" — within which to locate the origin of basic human error types. Using Jens Rasmussen's skill-rules-knowledge classification of human performance, Reason (1990) mapped the three error types of slips and lapses, rule-based mistakes, and knowledge-based mistakes in the form of failure modes at the three levels of human performance a problem solver is likely to face, and determined their cognitive origins. Using these failure modes of skill-rules-knowledge-based mistakes, it is feasible for an accident analyst, using the data derived from the accident reports, to locate the cognitive origins of active and latent failures within this error classification system.

The quality of decision making and role of risk-based decision-making play in the organisational context was examined, *inter alia*, by James Reason (1990) and Charles Perrow (1999). Reason (1990, Chapters 2 & 3), Perrow (1999, Chapter 9), and Kahneman (2012b, Chapter 31) all discuss the role of risk policy, risk assessment, ways and means to address the problems of decision making. These referenced texts may be consulted to understand in a greater detail the sources of errors (biases and their sources) in decision making process in the industrial setting.

In this section, two types of failures, active failures and latent failures in terms of cultural factors, and their contribution to the development of accidents were briefly presented.

---

[9] Perrow (1999, p. 77) uses a DEPOSE (Design, Equipment Procedures, Operators, Supplies and materials, and Environment) framework to identify the potential sources of failures.

3   Systems Engineering Activity and Contribution to Latent Failures

Daniels and Tudor (2022) claim that behaviour specified by the requirements of the Boeing 737 MAX 8 caused full nose down trim to be applied following an Angle of Attack (AoA) sensor failure. Further, as noted in the introductory section, drawing upon Nancy Leveson's quote, they suggest improving the requirements engineering approach, because the software implemented requirements correctly, but this led to accidents. To illustrate their perception of this phenomena, they discuss two run-away accidents as well as the Boeing 737 MAX 8 crashes.

The Boeing 737 MAX 8 crashes, as per the ICAO classification of accidents, fall into the category of "Loss of Control in Flight" (Appicharla 2022b). Further, a previous paper by Daniels (2020, Sub-section 8.3.3) failed to recognise the Human-MCAS Interface failure but suggested how display of good airmanship skills by the ETH 302 accident flight crew could have saved the aircraft and its passengers. Analyses by Daniels (2020) and by Daniels and Tudor (2022) seems to contradict the concepts of System safety and ideas advanced by Leveson (2004a) (2011) as well as the official reports. This theme is taken up in the paragraphs to follow to illustrate the idea that safety of software is to be examined in the context of its use.

The abstract of Leveson (2004a) states:

> *The ... most important step in solving any problem is understanding the problem well enough to create effective solutions. To this end, several software-related space-craft accidents were studied to determine common systemic factors. Although the details in each accident were different, very similar factors related to flaws in the safety culture, the management and organization, and technical deficiencies were identified. These factors include complacency and discounting of software risk, diffusion of responsibility and authority, limited communication channels and poor information flow, inadequate system and software engineering (poor or missing specifications, unnecessary complexity and software functionality, software reuse without appropriate safety analysis, violation of basic safety engineering practices in the digital components), inadequate review activities, ineffective system safety engineering, flawed test and simulation environments, and inadequate human factors engineering...*

Further, official reports cited the inadequate MCAS operations and design. For example the NTSB (2019) questioned the role of *"unintended MCAS operation"* and assumptions made by Boeing regarding MCAS operation. The NTSB reviewed sections of Boeing's system safety analysis of the stabilizer trim control that pertained to the MCAS on the Boeing 737 MAX 8 planes. The NTSB Review showed that the specific failure modes that lead to *"uncommanded MCAS activation"* were not simulated (such as an erroneous high AoA input to the MCAS) in the safety validation tests. This omission led to non-consideration of consequences of these failure conditions, i.e. additional flight deck effects (such as the IAS DISAGREE and ALT DISAGREE alerts, and stick shaker activation.

Firesmith (2010, p.115) discusses interactions between various team members participating in danger analysis. The author does not agree with the idea of abuse analysis used by Firesmith (2010) but accepts that, even from traditional safety engineering perspective, such a hazard analysis at Boeing Commercial Airplanes business division would have revealed the problems with the MCAS design and operations. But, from an organisational perspective, the economic imperative to compete on costs with Airbus may have resulted in a less than adequate safety culture perspective, and organisation dynamics may have driven the decision towards setting up of the latent failure pathway (Appicharla 2022b).

The JATR (2019) stated: *"The MCAS design was based on data, architecture, and assumptions that were reused from a previous aircraft configuration without sufficient detailed aircraft-level evaluation of the appropriateness of such reuse, and without additional safety margins and features to address conditions, omissions, or errors not foreseen in the analyses"*. This finding has implications for inter-operable systems in the railways, but that is out of the scope of this paper.

Moreover, Johnston and Harris (2019) accept the idea that MCAS software played a role. They argued on the contribution of software to the crashes, thus:

> *The initial analyses suggest that the MCAS software system was poorly designed and caused two plane crashes. But this is a complex situation, involving many people and organizations. In addition, other pilots had successfully struggled against the MCAS system and safely guided their passengers to their destination. Four contributing factors, observed in the Boeing case, have also been observed in other catastrophic software failures. They are poor documentation, rushed release, delayed software updates, and humans out of the loop.*

The report produced for Peter A. Defazio, Chair of US Committee on Transportation and Infrastructure and Rick Larsen, Chair of Sub-Committee on Aviation, stated that: *"Boeing's software supplier, Collins Aerospace, also falsely believed that Boeing had communicated the AoA Disagree alert issue to its 737 MAX customers"* (US House Committee on Transportation and Infrastructure 2020, p.23).

In the following paragraphs, we look at important systems engineering tasks and their possible contribution to accidents, if not performed adequately.

Bahill and Henderson (2005) identified Requirements Development, Requirements Verification, Requirements Validation, System Verification, and System Validation as important systems engineering tasks. In their examination of twenty-three 'famous failures', they used the following 'definitions' to generate a classification system:

Requirements Development: A functional requirement has to define what, how well, and under what conditions one or more inputs must be converted into one or more outputs at the boundary being considered in order to satisfy the stakeholder needs. Besides functional requirements, there are dozens of other types of requirements. Requirements Development includes:

(1) eliciting, analysing, validating, and communicating stakeholder needs,

(2) transforming customer requirements into derived requirements,

(3) allocating requirements to hardware, software, bio ware, test, and interface elements,

(4) verifying requirements, and

(5) validating the set of requirements.

There is no implication that these five tasks should be done serially, because, like all systems engineering processes, these tasks should be done with many parallel and iterative loops.

Verifying Requirements: Proving that each requirement has been satisfied. Verification can be done by logical argument, inspection, modelling, simulation, analysis, [audit,] expert review, test, or demonstration.

Validating Requirements: Ensuring that

(1) the set of requirements is correct, complete, and consistent,

(2) a model can be created that satisfies the requirements, and

(3) a real-world solution can be built and tested to prove that it satisfies the requirements.

If Systems Engineering discovers that the customer has requested a perpetual-motion machine, the project should be stopped…

Verifying a System: Building the system right: ensuring that the system complies with the system requirements and conforms to its design.

Validating a System: Building the right system: making sure that the system does what it is supposed to do in its intended environment. Validation determines the correctness and completeness of the end product and ensures that the system will satisfy the actual needs of the stakeholders.

As per the above definitions, the report to the US House Committee on Transportation and Infrastructure. (2020, p.119) noted that MCAS did not meet its own design requirements. The Boeing Aerodynamics Stability & Control Requirements included:

- "*MCAS shall not have any objectionable interaction with the piloting of the airplane.*" (US House Committee on Transportation and Infrastructure 2020, foot-note 708)
- "*MCAS shall not interfere with dive recovery.*" (US House Committee on Transportation and Infrastructure 2020, foot-note 709)

Based on the admission of John Hamilton, then-Chief Engineer for the Boeing Commercial Airplanes division, that one of the above two design requirements were not met, the House Committee Report (ibid) concluded that MCAS was poorly designed, not adequately tested, and had received flawed oversight by the FAA.

Thus, the MCAS verification and validation contained mistakes in addition to the mistakes in Requirements development and Validating requirements of MCAS design at Collins Aerospace (US House Committee on Transportation and Infrastructure 2020).

Contrary to a claim by Daniels (2020) that the FAA ODA Organisation *was not* a contributor to the Boeing 737 MAX 8 crashes, the report produced for the US House Committee on Transportation and Infrastructure (2020) states that the FAA ODA Organisation Delegation Act *was* a contributor. Also, Leveson et al. (2019) observed:

> *For example, one possible factor that can be hypothesized as being part of the cause of the B737 MAX losses is that the past success of Boeing in promoting safety and a lack of adequate resources provided by Congress helped to convince the FAA to relax the oversight in the DER [Designated Engineering Representative] process, essentially changing it into a self-certifying process for Boeing. This process was probably fine at first but degraded over time by pressures on the company that conflicted with safety. It is this type of change that usually precedes an accident — the system slowly and inadvertently changes to one where an accident is inevitable. Basically, the system migrates slowly toward a state of higher risk. Doesn't that provide a more useful causal explanation than "the pilot zigged when he/she should have zagged"?*

Appicharla (2022b) noted that organisational dynamics playing out between the system safety engineers and the business unit management in the examination of hazard controls and this dynamic contributing a latent failure pathway to future accident scenarios; this was not studied by Johnston and Harris (2019). Therefore, given the evidences regarding the Boeing Aerodynamics Stability & Control Requirements, NTSB (2019) findings, JATR (2019) findings, and (in the context of Leveson (2004b) having introduced a new accident model to explain accidents based on control theory to replace the chain of event models), the hypothesis of improving the Requirements Engineering activity alone by Daniels and Tudor (2022) and Daniels (2020 is untenable. Further, such blame actions on a single discipline or organisation or aircraft crew cannot help us learn from adverse events is noted by the Ergonomics and Human Factors society (CIEHF 2020). The argument to support this hypothesis are further discussed in Sections 4 and 5.

Appicharla (2022b) modelled the evidence(s) from the report produced for the US House Committee on Transportation and Infrastructure (2020) using the hybrid Swiss Cheese Model (Reason 1990) and the MORT technique (Johnson 1973). From a systems engineering perspective, the model showed following latent failures at the regulatory and systems integrator levels:

- The FAA's and Boeing's lack of leadership to enforce positive safety culture,
- Boeing's efforts to describe MCAS as simply an extension of the existing speed trim system was an effort to "*give shade and cover*" to the notion that MCAS in the 737 MAX 8 was not new,
- Boeing's reliance upon production pressures, failure to classify single point failures as safety-critical events, and failure to communicate risk to the airlines/operators based on less than adequate risk assessments, dismissal of warnings from the engineers,
- FAA regulatory failure to implement its own Human Factors team recommendations show that the commitment, capability, and competence of decision takers in all organisations involved was less than adequate, and
- The way the work objectives were set by Boeing and FAA shows that the senior managerial levels attitude towards duty of care towards their customers in the aviation industry by the FAA, Design Organisation and even Airlines/Operators was less than adequate.

McDermott, *et alia*, (2020) discussed the need of addressing cognitive biases in systems engineering teams. As an example, they briefly discussed the Space Shuttle Challenger accident as an example of randomness bias in engineering domain. Engineers' intuition regarding the correlation of seal failure with the low temperature at the time of launch could not be translated into the data to support the decision to delay the launch as per Appicharla (2012), McDermott et al. (2020).

4 Learning The Right Lessons From Past Accidents

My second objection to Daniels (2020) is that learning lessons from past accidents is not easy if such lessons learning exercise is subject to biases on the part of accident analysts or investigators, and this theme is discussed by Leveson (2004b), Johnson and Botting (1999), to name just a few academics in the System Safety discipline.

Synthesizing the work on the Swiss Cheese Model of accident causation and the MORT technique cited in the previous section, Sanjeev Appicharla (2022a) published a cybernetic risk model (see Figure 2, derived from that paper) adapted from Reason (1990) and Kahneman (2012a), and used it to study the Boeing 737 MAX 8 crashes.

The model assumes the knowledge base of controls system theory and introduces the "Heuristics and Biases" as disturbances in a control system theoretic representation. Further, the author's intention is to highlight the fact that a cognitive system approach to risk management is feasible conceptually. Due to space limitation, full results of the study cannot be presented here. Appicharla (2022b) may be consulted for the process used to derive the following results.

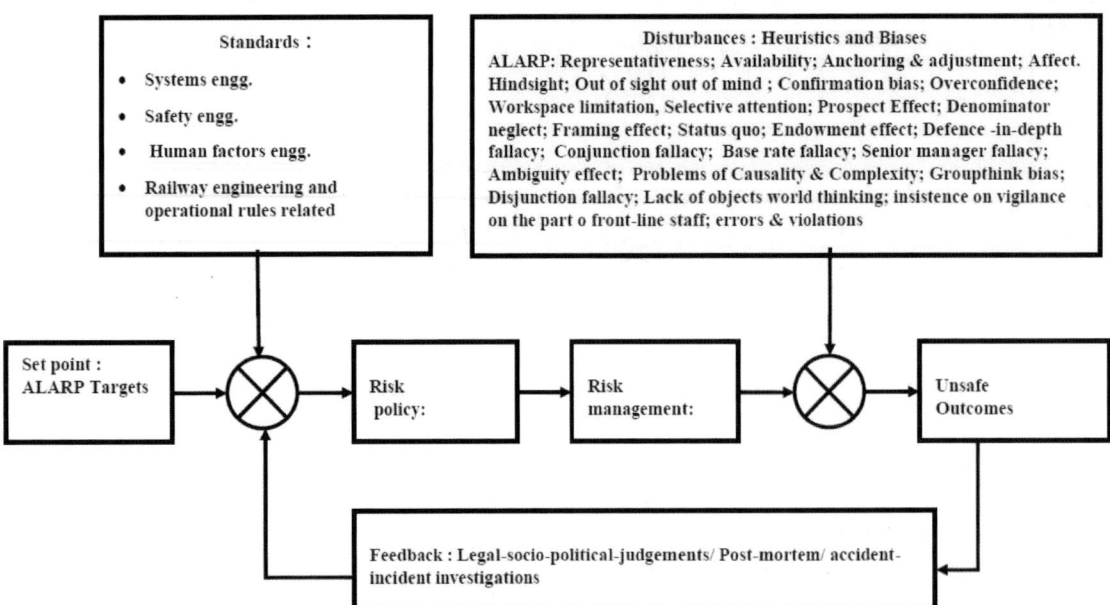

Figure 2~ Cybernetic Model of Risk Management

The following high level latent failures in the Boeing 737 MAX 8 crashes were identified using the cybernetic risk management model of Figure 2. Appicharla (2022b), drawing upon a management article by Sandra Sucher and Shalene Gupta (2021), presented a more-nuanced picture of the regulatory environment and the stakeholders involved with their contributions to what is called in risk literature as "system" or "organisational" accident (Perrow 1999, p. 70) (Reason, 1997) (Leveson, 2004a). The latent failures investigated at Boeing Board level and inadequate feedback from past accidents were:

- Boeing 737 MAX 8 airplane was a complex system product and an outcome of a safety culture prevailing at Boeing Commercial Airplanes that did not pay sufficient attention to the biases in its Engineering Review and Safety Review Boards.
- The Boeing board had five committees (Audit; Finance; Compensation; Special Programs; and Governance, Organization & Nominating). Audit oversaw risk, but its charter focused on financial risk, and it had no mandate to discuss safety. Moreover, the committee had no mechanism for receiving alerts from whistle-blowers. Several different airlines, including Southwest, JetBlue, and Delta have board committees specifically established to address safety. Boeing did not establish a board committee to address safety until 4th April 2019, which was six months after the first crash in Indonesia, and nearly a month after the second crash in Ethiopia. Instead, safety issues were reviewed by a "Safety Review Board" run by employees, which had neither a mandate nor a mechanism for reporting to the board. Meanwhile, the Boeing board was not even aware that the Safety Review Board existed until after the 737 MAX 8 had been grounded in 2019.
- Research shows that when there is an impending disaster, up to 70% of people enter a state of denial call the "normalcy bias". It is called "normalcy" because our desire to flee from disaster goes so deep that when a terrible event occurs our first instinct is to deny reality instead of dealing with it. And it's a "bias" because it interferes with our ability to imagine the scale and impact of a situation that we have never encountered before. Boards need to mitigate for the normalcy bias.
- Boards are fiduciaries, which means that their duty is to protect other people's interests, generally defined as consisting of a duty of care, a duty of loyalty, and some legal scholars would argue, a duty of candour. The responsibilities of boards that include

approving a company's strategy, budgets and plans and monitoring progress against them; approving the company's capital structure, major expenditures, and Merger & Acquisition activity; appointing the CEO and approving senior executive compensation; ensuring risks to the company are identified and managed; ensuring compliance with legal and community requirements; and establishing ethical standards for the company. Operationalizing these duties is harder than it sounds, and Boeing's fall from grace offered management lessons other boards can learn from.

- If Dekker (2009) had made his investigation into the Turkish Airlines TK1951 accident[10] public when he shared them with the academic community, then the Boeing and FAA business management level may have had a chance to reflect upon the single sensor-based architecture that was chosen. This document on the Turkish Airlines crash was made public only after the second 737 MAX 8 accident by the New York Times investigation. Therefore, the non-availability of Professor Dekker's report (Dekker 2009) became a contributory factor to the Boeing 737 MAX 8 accidents. That Boeing's decision to allow MCAS to operate off a single AoA sensor has been roundly criticized by a wide range of aviation safety experts is noted in the report produced for the US House Committee on Transportation and Infrastructure (2020, footnote 100).

Swuste et al. (2020) noted on the nature of cognitive system, thus:

> *Automation[11] does not decrease the incidence of major accidents but changes their nature. An example is the Turkish Airlines [TK1951] crash at Schiphol in 2009, caused by a conflict between the automated systems of the aircraft and pilots. Complexity is also caused by the different time scales of departments within a company, which are essential for the process or production. For example, workers, operators, drivers, and pilots have a time horizon of a few minutes in control rooms and cockpits. All operational problems and process disturbances at this level must be solved within a short period of time, adjusting process parameters, and detecting failing process components.*

Further, Daniels (2020) did not apparently use any accident models such as the Swiss Cheese Model (Reason, 1993), or consider the role of bias play in accident investigations (CIEHF 2020), apply systems thinking in the like manner of the Systems-theoretic model of Leveson (2004), or any other formal accident investigation model recommended by IEC 31010:2019 to investigate the causal and contributory causes. Daniels (2020) relied upon his own subject matter expert judgement. However, there is extensive risk literature available on the matter of applying the subjective matter expert judgement and limitation of such expertise (Kahneman 2012a), (Kahneman 2012b). Further, the application of the Swiss Cheese Model by Lawton and Ward (2005) enabled the Ladbroke Grove Inquiry to go beyond the single causal factor of SPAD caused by an active error on the part of train driver to several latent factors in the operational and management side of the organisation (HSC 2000).

Lawton and Ward (2005) argued that the net result of a systems-based analysis is a more comprehensive understanding of the crash in order to provide a more effective strategy for preventing future crashes by addressing all levels of factors and the critical interactions among them. Leveson (2004b) argued that a new approach is needed to human error is needed beyond the Swiss Cheese Model. However, Haddon-Cave (2009) used a hybrid model of bow-tie model (a fault and event tree model) and the Swiss Cheese Model to gain a more comprehensive understanding of the Nimrod Crash in Afghanistan.

---

[10] This accident was to a Boeing 737-800

[11] Sheridan and Parasuraman (2006) may be consulted regarding definition of automation and automation related incidents and accidents.

Subsequently, CIEHF (2017) expressed concerns with current practices of bow-tie analysis. Further, the CIEHF Working Group noted that the Swiss Cheese Model has found widespread application and is still used globally as a means of thinking about safety management (CIEHF 2017). It has however been developed and elaborated in many directions: while the core ideas continue to have great value and are easily understood, variations of the model are now in widespread use. Leveson (2019) argued against the use of chain of event models for their inability to represent process errors. For example, Leveson et al. (2019) state, thus:

> *Can we really explain the B737 MAX accidents with a simple chain of events, with the pilot actions highlighted along with perhaps the MCAS design as the only actions worthy of attention? Competitive pressures, regulatory policies, basic design features are not 'events', so they don't appear in the chain of events and therefore can be dismissed without consideration by those who find it convenient to ignore these factors?*

The Daniels and Tudor (2022) citation of Nancy Leveson was out of context, was done without giving reference to her paper, and is based on the premise that, "*Software-related accidents usually caused by flawed requirements*" and concluded erroneously that "*requirements engineering needs improvement*". This is a classic error in logic where the conclusion does not follow from premise as noted by Kahneman (2012b) and Leveson (2019) clearly rejects the conclusion can be seen from the previous paragraph as well.

CIEHF (2020) discussed, in their white paper, system engineering principle #4 thus: "*Most adverse events in socio-technical systems are systemic. They arise through the relationship and interactions between numerous functional elements involved in delivering the overall purpose of the system (Reason 1997)*".

Omission bias and confirmation bias on the part of Daniels and Tudor (2022) through their neglect of MCAS design requirements as stated in the Boeing Aerodynamics Stability & Control Requirements, and affirming Nancy Leveson's hypothesis of "*Software-related accidents usually caused by flawed requirements*", without considering the interaction between the regulatory and regulated organisations (See Section 4). Review the literature; it is clear that the learning of lessons from Boeing 737 MAX 8 accidents has been less than adequate.

5 Probability Distribution Model in Probabilistic Risk Assessments

My third objection is related to measure of risk in risk assessments. Daniels and Tudor (2022) cite Mandelbrot and Hudson (2004) who claim thus:

> *...the mathematical models used were flawed and that it was mistaken to assume that the normal distribution was a useful model for tracking price changes in the stock markets. Most economists responded that independence and normality are just assumptions that help simplify the mathematics. However, the inappropriate application of the normal distribution underestimated the probability that many borrowers would default on their subprime mortgages at the same time.*

Estimation of probabilities of rare or adverse events is not an easy task. Measuring risk in terms of F-N[12] curve statistics (Evans 2003), or in terms of Normal distribution curve applied to the stock market movements are fallible in nature. That point estimation of risk

---
[12] F-N curves are graphs relating the probability per year of causing N or more fatalities (F) to N.

can lead to erroneous perception of risk is noted by Rasmussen (1981). Despite these facts, the above claim by Daniels and Tudor (2022) is erroneous as taken up in this section.

As regards 2008 financial crisis, it is a mistake on the part of Daniels and Tudor (2022) to draw conclusion based just two factors to explain the crisis: (1) of inappropriate application of the normal distribution; and (2) many borrowers would default on their subprime mortgages at the same time, without considering all other factors that contributed to the 2008 financial crisis.

Disciplines of cognitive psychology, economics, social psychology, and statistical analysis relying upon the two-system model of human thinking provide a better explanation of 2008 financial crisis where collective blindness to risk and uncertainty developed. Kahneman (2012b, p. 262 & Chapter 24) may be consulted for psychological factors of planning fallacy, optimism bias, overconfident forecasts, and how risk-taking phenomenon emerged in the financial industry. David Hand stated that the probabilities of 25 standard deviation events that occurred in August 2007 were better predictable using the Cauchy distribution (Hand 2015, Chapter 7). It is true that Mandelbrot (2005) uses the fractal model of risk to better represent the risk phenomenon, but science cannot be limited to fitting statistical curves to the data[13] in a parsimonious manner without considering the social and organisational factors involved (Kahneman 2012a), (Gilbert 2020). Further, Gaussian normal distribution is used in physics and the reference cited in the footnote may be consulted.

Future Nobel laureate Eugene Fama (1965) commented on the Mandelbrot's hypothesis, thus: "*In light of this* [stable Paretian distribution] *discussion we see that Mandelbrot's hypothesis can actually be viewed as a generalization of the central-limit theorem arguments of Bachelier and Osborne to the case where the underlying distributions of price changes from transaction to transaction are allowed to have infinite variances. In this sense, then, Mandelbrot's version of the theory of random walks can be regarded as a broadening rather than a contradiction of the earlier Bachelier-Osborne model*".

Further evidence that Daniels and Tudor (2022) concept of risk measurement needs improvement comes from the research on F-N curves by Professor Andrew Evans for a UK HSE Research project. Using the putative model of risk, Andrew Evans placed a constraint on the use of F-N curves for taking decisions on the risk (Evans 2003). Weakness of bow-tie (fault and event tree) based models in their treatment of human errors was highlighted by (Reason,1990). CIEHF (2017) concerns were noted in the Section 4 may be recalled here.

Moreover, Daniels and Tudor (2022) do not pay attention to concepts of organisational leaning and psychological safety (Edmondson et al. 2005)[14]. The role played by the concept of bounded rationality and satisficing behaviour (Simon 1979) in risk management was noted in the SCSC Newsletter (Appicharla 2010). Contrary to rational human cognition, the tendency of firms is to settle for satisfactory option than choose an optimal course of action is to be recognised. Less than adequate awareness of emergent property of system safety using the analogy of water that has properties to support life and at the same time has the hazard potential to cause floods and devastation was discussed in the context of ALARP risk-based decision taking. And the role of less than adequate interaction between technical understanding, decision maker's risk preferences and organisational viewpoint that form three components of a firm to trigger hazard potential

---

[13] For discussions on the roots of science, Chapters 1 and 34 of Penrose (2004) may be consulted. Penrose, R. (2004). *The Road to Reality: A complete guide to the laws of the universe*. Jonathan Cape, Random House, London.

[14] This is understandable, considering that it is a paper concentrating on the reliability of software.

and it was argued that action to prevent the drift into the unsafe operating zone is necessary to keep risk level tolerable.

In terms of the main lesson for their organisation and management, senior management and boards must pay attention to fiduciary duty of care towards their customers and staff (Appicharla 2022b). Further, understanding and modelling of automation-human interaction is challenging in nature due increased automation (Sheridan and Hennessey 1984) leading to greater complexity (Perrow 1999), and systems are prone to latent failures apart from fallible managerial decisions due to host of factors such as less than adequate understanding of human automation interaction (Bainbridge 1997), systems becoming opaque (Rasmussen 1988), computer being at the centre of action (Moray 1986), increased use of multiple automatic safety devices (Rasmussen and Pedersen,1984) leading to less than adequate human supervision of automated systems, maintenance related omissions (INPO 1983), and the operator in the control room takes up co-ordinating activity during emergencies and temporal judgements may be prone to error (Javaux and De Keyser 1998) (Reason,1990). The study of automation-human interaction is an active research area in search of an objective function of human automation interface property (Bolton et al. 2013).

From the foregoing paragraphs, it can be concluded that improvement of the requirements engineering practice or using the right probability distribution to model the risk phenomenon may be necessary but not sufficient solutions because there are several other cognitive biases (see Figure 2) that may impact decision making in an adverse manner. Therefore, the risk management discipline needs to take a system approach to safety.

6 Conclusion

In conclusion, we should be advancing models that include human, technical *and* organisational factors, *and their interactions*, when assessing the risks posed by complex systems.

Note that the concept of System-based approach to safety management is not new and goes back at least seventy years (Roland and Moriarty 1990). See also Ericson (2005) and Appicharla (2006; 2010; 2022a; 2022b).

Acknowledgments

The author thanks the editor and peer reviewers for many useful suggestions on the earlier drafts of the paper. The author also expresses gratitude to professors from his college, Karnataka Regional Engineering College, Surathkal, India.

Figure 1 herein was derived from Reason (1993), the copyright holder of which is Springer-Verlag Berlin Heidelberg.

References

Appicharla S. K. (2006). *System for Investigation of Railway Interfaces*. 2006 1st IET International Conference on System Safety. London. pp. 7-16. https://ieeexplore.ieee.org/document/4123683.

Appicharla S. (2010). *Letters to Editor - Tolerability of Risk: ALARP. Safety Systems*. The Safety-Critical Systems Club Newsletter. SCSC-112. May 2010, 19(3), pp. 8-10.

Appicharla S. (2012). *Analysis and Modelling of NASA Space Shuttle Challenger Accident using Management and Oversight Risk Tree (MORT)*. 7th IET International System Safety Conference (p. 8). Edinburgh: IET. Retrieved 7th May 2013 from https://ieeexplore.ieee.org/document/6458956

Appicharla, S. K. (2022a). *From Nobel Prize (s) to Safety Risk Management: How to Identify Latent Failure Conditions in the Railway Safety Risk Management Practices*. 13th World Congress on Railway Research (WCRR) (p.6). Birmingham: (Proceedings volume is still under development at time of writing; a pre-print is available at https://www.researchgate.net/publication/361230614_From_Nobel_Prizes_to_Safety_Risk_Management_How_to_Identify_Latent_Failure_Conditions_in_the_Railway_Safety_Risk_Management_Practices).

Appicharla S. (2022b). *Lessons Learnt from Boeing 737 MAX 8 Crashes as Safety Data: Needles in the Haystack*. International System Safety Conference ISSC-2022 Safety Data: Needles in the Haystack, August 18th, 2022, Cincinatti, Ohio (Proceedings volume is still under development at time of writing; a pre-print is available at https://www.researchgate.net/publication/362833335_Lessons_Learnt_from_Boeing_737_Max_8_Crashes_as_Safety_Data_Needles_in_the_Haystack).

Bahill A. T., and Henderson S. J. (2005). *Requirements Development, Verification, and Validation Exhibited in Famous Failures*. Systems Engineering, 8(1), Retrieved 30th March 2012 from http://sysengr.engr.arizona.edu/publishedPapers/FamousFailures.pdf.

Bainbridge L. (1997). *The change in concepts needed to account for human behavior in complex dynamic tasks*. Systems, Man and Cybernetics, Part A: Systems and Humans, IEEE Transactions on. 27(3), pp. 351 - 359. DOI:10.1109/3468.568743

Bird F. E., and Germain G. L. (1985). *Practical Loss Control Leadership*. Loganville, GA: International Loss Control Institute, Inc.

Bolton M. L., Bass E. J., and Siminiceanu R. I. (2013). *Using formal verification to evaluate human-automation interaction: A review*. IEEE Transactions on Systems, Man, and Cybernetics: Systems, 43(3), pp. 488-503. https://ieeexplore.ieee.org/stamp/stamp.jsp?arnumber=6472094

CIEHF. (2017). *Human Factors in Barrier Management*. White Paper. The Chartered Institute of Ergonomics & Human Factors (CIEHF). Retrieved 5th September 2022, from: https://ergonomics.org.uk/resource/human-factors-in-barrier-management.html

CIEHF. (2020). *Learning from Adverse Events*. White Paper. The Chartered Institute of Ergonomics & Human Factors (CIEHF). Retrieved 5th September 2022 from https://ergonomics.org.uk/resource/learning-from-adverse-events.html

Chizek M. (2020). *Tutorial: 737 MAX Case Study - Lessons for Safety Professionals*. 38th International Systems Safety Conference. St. Paul, MN 55114. Retrieved 31st March 2021 from https://system-safety.org/store/viewproduct.aspx?ID=17536206.

Conrow E., Madachy R., Roedler G., and Turner R. (2021, May 19th). *Risk Management*. Retrieved 9th December 2022from https://www.sebokwiki.org/wiki/Risk_Management.

Daniels D. (2020). *The Boeing 737 MAX Accidents*. Proceedings of SSS'20, the Twenty-eighth Safety-Critical Systems Symposium, York, UK. Accessed 9th November 2021 from https://scsc.uk/rp154.1:1.

Daniels D., and Tudor N. (2022). *Software Reliability and the Misuse of Statistics*. Safety-Critical Systems eJournal 1(1), SCSC-174, Safety-Critical Systems Club, January 2022. Available from https://scsc.uk/r174.3:1. Accessed 14th July 2022.

Dekker S. (2009). *Report of the Flight Crew Human Factors Investigation Conducted for the Dutch Safety Board into the Accident of TK1951, Boeing 737-800 near Amsterdam Schiphol Airport, February 25, 2009*. Lund University. Retrieved 15th May 2022 from https://www.onderzoeksraad.nl/en/media/inline/2020/1/21/human_factors_report_s_dekker.pdf

Edkins G. D., and Pollock G. M. (1996). *Pro-active safety management: Application and evaluation within a rail context*. Safety Science, 24(2), 83-93. Retrieved 9th April 2021, https://www.sciencedirect.com/science/article/abs/pii/S0925753596000276

Edmondson A., Ferlins E., Feldman L., and Bohmer R.(2005). *The Recovery Window: Organizational Learning Following Ambiguous Threats*. In Farjoun M., and Starbuck W. (Editors). *Organization at the Limit: Lessons from the Columbia Disaster*. pp. 220–245. Wiley-Blackwell.

Ericson C. A. (1999). *Fault Tree Analysis – A History*. Retrieved 12th May 2022, from https://ftaassociates.files.wordpress.com/2018/12/C.-Ericson-Fault-Tree-Analysis-A-History-Proceedings-of-the-17th-International-System-Safety-Conference-1999.pdf

Ericson C. A. (2005). *Hazard Analysis Techniques for System Safety*. First Edition. New Jersey: Wiley & Sons. ISBN 0-471-72019-4

Evans A. W. (2003). *Transport fatal accidents and FN-curves: 1967-2001*. UK HSE Research Project 073. Health & Safety Executive. Retrieved 28th July 2021 from https://www.hse.gov.uk/research/rrpdf/rr073.pdf

FAA Human Factors Team. (1996). *The Interfaces Between Flightcrews and Modern Flight Deck Systems*. Federal Aviation Administration Human Factors Team Report. Retrieved May 15th, 2022, from https://www.tc.faa.gov/its/worldpac/techrpt/hffaces.pdf.

FAA Safety Team. (n.d.). *System Safety Process*. Retrieved 12th December 2022, from https://www.faasafety.gov/gslac/alc/libview_normal.aspx?id=6877.

Fama E. F. (1965). *The Behavior of Stock-Market Prices*. The Journal of Business, Vol. 38, No. 1 (Jan. 1965), pp. 34-105. Retrieved 20th September 2022 from https://www.jstor.org/stable/2350752

Firesmith D. G. (2010). *Engineering Safety- and Security-Related Requirements for Software-Intensive Systems*. One-Day Tutorial 32nd International Conference on Software Engineering, 4th May 2010. Retrieved 10th December 2022 from https://resources.sei.cmu.edu/asset_files/presentation/2010_017_001_23269.pdf

Gilbert C. (2020). *What Is the Place of Human and Organisational Factors in Safety? An introduction*. Retrieved 28th February 2022 from https://link.springer.com/content/pdf/10.1007%2F978-3-030-25639-5.pdf.

Haddon-Cave C. A. (2009). *The Nimrod Review: An independent review into the broader issues surrounding the loss of the RAF Nimrod MR2 Aircraft XV230 in Afghanistan in 2006*. London: The Stationery Office. Retrieved 25th December 2019 from https://assets.publishing.service.gov.uk/government/uploads/system/uploads/attachment_data/file/229037/1025.pdf

Halpern J. J. (1989). *Cognitive factors influencing decision making in a highly reliable organization.* Industrial Crisis Quarterly, 3(2), pp. 143–158. https://doi.org/10.1177/108602668900300204.

Hand D. (2015). *The Improbability Principle: Why coincidences, miracles and rare events happen all the time.* London: Penguin. ISBN 9781448170661.

Heinrich H. W. (1931). *Industrial accident prevention; a scientific approach.* First Edition. McGraw-Hill, New York, 1931.

HFIDTC. (2006). *Cost Arguments and Evidence for Human Factors Integration.* UK Human Factors Integration Defence Technology Centre. Wiltshire: Systems Engineering & Assessment Ltd.

HSC. (2000). *The Ladbroke Grove Rail Inquiry: Part 1 Report of The Rt Hon Lord Cullen PC.* Health & Safety Commission (HSC). Accessed 1st October 2022 from https://www.jesip.org.uk/wp-content/uploads/2022/03/Ladbroke-Grove-Rail-Inquiry-Report-Part-1.pdf.

ICAO. (2022). *Safety Management Implementation.* ICAO, The International Civil Aviation Organization. Uniting Aviation website accessed 26th September 2022 from https://www.unitingaviation.com/publications/safetymanagementimplementation/content.

IEC 31010:2019. *Risk management — Risk assessment techniques.* ISO 31010, Edition 2. International Electrotechnical Commission. Geneva.

INPO. (1983). *An Analysis of Root Causes in 1983 Significant Event Reports* (INPO 84-027), plus addendum. Institute of Nuclear Power Operations. Atlanta, GA.

ISO/IEC/IEEE 15288:2015. *Systems and software engineering — System life cycle processes.* ISO/IEC/IEEE 15288, Edition 1. International Organization for Standardization and International Electrotechnical Commission. Geneva. Institute of Electrical and Electronics Engineers. New York 2015.

ISO 31000:2018. *Risk management — Guidelines.* ISO 31000, Edition 2. International Organization for Standardization. Geneva. Retrieved July 17th, 2022, from https://www.iso.org/standard/65694.html.

JATR. (2019). *Boeing 737 MAX Flight Control System, Observations, Findings, and Recommendations.* Joint Authorities Technical Review. Retrieved 4th September 2020 from U.S. Federal Aviation Administration website: https://www.faa.gov/news/media/attachments/Final_JATR_Submittal_to_FAA_Oct_2019.pdf.

Javaux D., and De Keyser V. (1998). *Complexité et conscience de la situation.* Rapport final SFACT/DGAC.

Johnson C. W., and Botting R. M. (1999). *Using Reason's Model of Organisational Accidents in Formalising Accident Reports.* Retrieved 9th September 2022 from https://link.springer.com/article/10.1007/s101110050037.

Johnson W. G. (1973) *The Management Oversight And Risk Tree – MORT.* United States Atomic Energy Commission. Retrieved 25th January 2023 from https://www.nerc.com/pa/rrm/ea/CA_Reference_Materials_DL/MORT%20Bill%20Johnson%20for%20AEC%201973%20SAN8212.pdf.

Johnston P and Harris R. (2019). *The Boeing 737 MAX Saga: Lessons for Software Organizations.* Retrieved 1st October 2022 from https://embeddedartistry.com/wp-content/uploads/2019/09/the-boeing-737-max-saga-lessons-for-software-organizations.pdf.

Kahneman D. (2012a). *Of 2 Minds: How Fast and Slow Thinking Shape Perception and Choice [Excerpt]*. Scientific American, June 15. Retrieved 18th September 2022 from https://www.scientificamerican.com/article/kahneman-excerpt-thinking-fast-and-slow/

Kahneman D. (2012b). *Thinking, Fast and Slow*. London: Penguin Books.

Lawton R., and Ward N. J. (2005). *A systems analysis of the Ladbroke Grove rail crash*. Elsevier Accident Analysis & Prevention, 37(2), 235-244. Retrieved 18th May 2022 from https://www.sciencedirect.com/science/article/abs/pii/S0001457504000879

Lawrence B. M. (2006). *A380 Aircraft Safety Process*. 2006 1st IET International Conference on System Safety. London. pp. 96-115. Retrieved 4th September 2020 from https://ieeexplore.ieee.org/document/4123694

Leihton C. L., and Denis C. R. (1993). *Risk assessment of a new high-speed railway*. IMA Journal of Management Mathematics, 5(1), pp. 211-225. Retrieved 22nd April 2021 from https://academic.oup.com/imaman/article-abstract/5/1/211/804267

Leveson N. G. (2004a). *The Role of Software in Spacecraft Accidents*. Journal of Spacecraft and Rockets, 41(4), 564-575. Accessed 1st October 2022 from http://sunnyday.mit.edu/nasa-class/jsr-final.pdf.

Leveson N. G. (2004b). *A New Accident Model for Engineering Safer Systems*. Safety Science, 42(4), 237-270. Retrieved 15th May 2019 from http//sunnyday.mit.edu/accidents/safetyscience-single.pdf.

Leveson N. G. (2009). *Engineering a Safer World: Systems Thinking Applied to Safety*. Retrieved 12th December 2022 from http://sunnyday.mit.edu/safer-world.pdf

Leveson N. G. (2011). *Applying Systems Thinking to Analyse and Learn from Events*. Safety Science, 49(1), 55-64. Retrieved 1st December 2021 from http://sunnyday.mit.edu/Safety-Science-Events.pdf.

Leveson N. G. (2019). *CAST Handbook: How to Learn More from Incidents and Accidents*. MIT. Retrieved 25th August 2021 from http://sunnyday.mit.edu/CAST-Handbook.pdf.

Leveson N. G., Straker D., and Malmquist S. (2019). *Updating the Concept of Cause in Accident Investigation*. International Society of Air Safety Investigators (ISASI), The Hague. Retrieved 18th September 2022 from http://sunnyday.mit.edu/ISASI-Cause.pdf.

Mandelbrot B. B. (2005). *Parallel cartoons of fractal models of finance*. Annals of Finance 1, 2005. pp. 179–192. Retrieved 18th September 2022 from https://link.springer.com/article/10.1007/s10436-004-0007-2

Mandelbrot B. B., and Hudson R. L. (2004). *The (Mis)Behavior of Markets: A Fractal View of Risk, Ruin and Reward*. New York: Basic Books.

McDermott T. A., Folds, D. J., and Hallo L. (2020). *Addressing Cognitive Bias in Systems Engineering Teams*. INCOSE International Symposium, 30(1), 257-271. Retrieved 23rd May 2021 from https://doi.org/10.1002/j.2334-5837.2020.00721.x

Moray N. (1986). *Monitoring behavior and supervisory control*. In K. R. Boff, L. Kaufman, & J. P. Thomas (Eds.), *Handbook of perception and human performance*, Vol. 2. *Cognitive processes and performance*. (pp. 1–51). John Wiley & Sons.

Network Rail. (2016). *Prevention through Engineering and Design*. Safety Central. Retrieved 11th December 2022, from https://safety.networkrail.co.uk/safety/prevention-through-engineering-and-design

NTSB. (2019). *Assumptions Used in the Safety Assessment Process and the Effects of Multiple Alerts and Indications on Pilot Performance.* Safety Recommendation Report ASR-19-01. The National Transportation Safety Board. Retrieved 8th March 2020 from https://www.ntsb.gov/investigations/AccidentReports/Reports/ASR1901.pdf

Perrow C. (1999). *Normal Accidents; Living with High-Risk Technologies.* Princeton: Princeton University Press. Second Edition. ISBN 9780691004129

Rasmussen J. (1988). *Coping Safely with Complex Systems.* American Association for Advancement of Science, Annual Meeting, Boston, February 1988; In: Risø-M-2769, https://backend.orbit.dtu.dk/ws/portalfiles/portal/137538338/COPESAF.PDF

Rasmussen J. (1997). *Risk management in a dynamic society: a modelling problem.* Safety Science. 27(2-3), pp. 183-213. Retrieved 4th July 2020 from http://sunnyday.mit.edu/16.863/rasmussen-safetyscience.pdf.

Rasmussen J., and Pedersen O. M. (1984). *Human Factors in Probabilistic Risk Analysis and in Risk Management.* In: Operational Safety of Nuclear Power Plants. Vol. 1, pp. 181-194, IAEA, Wien, 1984.

Rasmussen J., Pejtersen A. M., and Goodstein L.P. (1994). *Cognitive Systems Engineering.* New York: John Wiley and Sons, Inc.

Rasmussen N. C. (1981). *The application of probabilistic risk assessment techniques to energy technologies.* Ann. Rev. Energy. 1981. 6:123-38. Retrieved 12th May 2022 from https://www.annualreviews.org/doi/pdf/10.1146/annurev.eg.06.110181.001011

Reason J. (1990). *Human Error.* Cambridge: Cambridge University Press. doi:10.1017/CBO9781139062367.

Reason J. (1993). *The Identification of Latent Organizational Failures in Complex Systems.* In: Wise J.A., Hopkin V.D., Stager P. (editors) *Verification and Validation of Complex Systems: Human Factors Issues.* NATO ASI Series, Vol 110. pp. 223-237. Springer, Berlin, Heidelberg. https://doi.org/10.1007/978-3-662-02933-6_13.

Reason, J. (1997). *Managing the Risks of Organizational Accidents.* Chapter 1: *Hazards, Defences and Losses.* Retrieved 22nd August 2020 from https://www.taylorfrancis.com/

Reason J., Hollnagel E., and Pariès J. (2006). *Revisiting the "Swiss Cheese" model of accidents.* EUROCONTROL Experimental Centre (EEC). 2006-017EEC Note 2006/13. Available via https://www.eurocontrol.int/publication/revisiting-swiss-cheese-model-accidents Accessed 24th January 2023.

Roland H. E., and Moriarty B. (1990). *System Safety Engineering and Management.* Second Edition. New York: John Wiley & Sons, Inc. Retrieved 25th December 2007 from https://onlinelibrary.wiley.com/doi/book/10.1002/9780470172438.

Sheridan T. B., and Hennessy R. T. (1984). *Research and Modelling of Supervisory Control Behavior. Report of a Workshop.* National Research Council, Washington. Retrieved 25th January 2023 from https://apps.dtic.mil/dtic/tr/fulltext/u2/a149621.pdf.

Sheridan T. B., and Parasuraman, R. (2006). *Human-automation interaction.* Reviews of Human Factors and Ergonomics, Volume 1, Issue 1, pp. 89-129. Retrieved 25th January 2023 from https://doi.org/10.1518/155723405783703082I

Simon H. A. (1979). *Rational decision making in business organizations.* The American Economic Review. 69 (4), pp. 493–513. https://www.jstor.org/stable/1808698

Sucher S. J., and Gupta S. (2021). *What Corporate Boards Can Learn from Boeing's Mistakes*. Harvard Business Review, 2nd June 2021. Retrieved 2nd December 2021 from https://hbr.org/2021/06/what-corporate-boards-can-learn-from-boeings-mistakes

Swuste P., van Gulijk C., Groeneweg J., Zwaard W., Lemkowitz S. and Guldenmund F. (2020). *From Clapham Junction to Macondo, Deepwater Horizon: Risk and safety management in high-tech-high-hazard sectors: A review of English and Dutch literature: 1988–2010*. Elsevier Safety Science Vol. 121 January 2020, pp.249-282. Accessed 1st October 2022 from https://doi.org/10.1016/j.ssci.2019.08.031

System safety. (2007). *System safety*. Version ID: 931313550. In Wikipedia. https://en.wikipedia.org/wiki/System_safety Retrieved 15th March 2020.

Tozer S., and Wharton-Street D. (1993, October). *Development of pro-active system for measuring organisational safety health in a railway environment*. Retrieved 11th December 2022, via: https://www.sparkrail.org/Lists/Records/DispForm.aspx?ID=19944.

US House Committee on Transportation and Infrastructure. (2020). *Final Committee Report: The Design, Development & Certification of the Boeing 737 MAX*. US House of Representatives. Washington DC. Retrieved 20th September, 2020, from https://transportation.house.gov/imo/media/doc/2020.09.15%20FINAL%20737%20MAX%20Report%20for%20Public%20Release.pdf.

Safety Assessment of Point Merge Operations in Terminal Airspace

An IEC 61508 Viewpoint

Derek Fowler[1] and Octavian Nicolas Fota[2]

1. Independent Safety Engineering Consultant, Reading, UK
2. EUROCONTROL Innovation Hub, Brétigny, France

Abstract

An article entitled "An IEC 61508 Viewpoint on System Safety in the Transport Sector", in Volume 1, Issue 2, of the Safety-Critical Systems Club eJournal, proposed a way of thinking about the safety assessment of transportation systems that is based on the fundamental principles of international functional-safety standard IEC 61508. Now, in this article, the example of Point Merge — a systemised method for sequencing arrival flows developed by the then EUROCONTROL Experimental Centre and first deployed in Oslo in 2011 — is used to outline how an IEC 61508 approach to safety assessment could be applied to the Air Traffic Management sector in general.

1 Introduction

IEC 61508 (IEC 2010) is probably the most widely-accepted, international generic standard on functional safety. Although its ancestry can be traced back to process industries, the intention behind the standard has always been to provide a solid, comprehensive basis for adaptation, as necessary, to meet the needs of a wide range of industry sectors.

Fowler (2022), proposed 'a way of thinking' about the assessment of the various safety-related systems deployed in the Transport sector — especially commercial-aviation and rail applications — based on the key principles and safety lifecycle set out in IEC 61508-1 and IEC 61508-4.

This article now takes an example application, from the Air Traffic Management (ATM) sector, of an operational concept for sequencing arrival flows in Terminal airspace, known as Point Merge, and uses it to outline how an IEC 61508 approach to safety assessment could be applied effectively to the ATM sector, and what the results thereof might look like, starting from the viewpoint of the traffic in the airspace being "virtual Equipment Under Control".

It is important to note that it is *not* the intention herein to prescribe IEC 61508-compliant processes for ATM applications — rather, it is to use the IEC 61508-1 lifecycle cycle model to shape thinking about system safety assessments away from a mindset that *"focussed too much on system reliability and not enough on system functionality, contrary to, inter alia, the most basic principles of the international functional-safety standard IEC*

61508" (Fowler 2022). *Nor* is it the intention to carry out a detailed compliance assessment of any existing ATM safety standards against IEC 61508 — the latter is left to readers with a sector-specific interest, and for whom the findings of Fowler (2015) might be relevant.

Like Fowler (2022), the scope of this article is limited to the following, initial phases of the IEC 61508 safety lifecycle, which result in the specification of detailed *functional safety requirements*[15] and *safety integrity requirements* necessary and sufficient for the subject safety-related systems to achieve a tolerable level of risk:

- Concept (Phase 1);
- Overall scope definition (Phase 2);
- Hazard and risk analysis (Phase 3);
- Overall safety requirements (Phase 4);
- Overall safety requirements allocation (Phase 5);
- Safety -related System (SRS) Safety Requirements Specification (Phase 9)[16];
- Other Risk-reduction Measures (ORRM) Safety Requirements Specification (Phase 10).

As we work herein through these lifecycle phases for Point Merge, it might appear that some of the steps could be simplified by, for example, subsuming them into other steps. Indeed, IEC 61508 allows for this to be done, where applicable, but, for the purposes of this paper, we decided to adhere exactly to the lifecycle detailed in Fowler (2022), except where indicated otherwise below.

2   Operational Context

Arrival procedures in Terminal airspace have historically involved open-loop vectoring of aircraft by Air Traffic Controllers. However, since the 1990s, Area Navigation (RNAV) procedures have gradually been introduced to systematise operations in most areas. A major drawback of both of these techniques, however, is that, under conditions of high traffic flows, their use tends to favour capacity at the cost of low flight efficiency and high environmental impact.

Therefore, the then EUROCONTROL Experimental Centre[17], Brétigny, France developed Point Merge operations (EUROCONTROL 2021) as a new method for integrating arrival flows, safely and efficiently, by combining the systematic use of lateral guidance by the aircraft's flight management system (FMS), with continuous descent approaches (CDAs), even at high traffic throughput.

Point Merge operations make use of Precision RNAV (P-RNAV)[18] procedures in terms of airspace design and functionality in the aircraft, but applied in a very specific way for arrival traffic in Approach airspace. The main difference between radar-vectoring (or

---

[15] The term *functional safety requirements* was coined in Fowler (2022) in preference to the (arguably ambiguous) IEC 61508 term of *safety functions requirements*; it covers safety requirements for both functionality (what has to be done) and performance (how well it has to been done).

[16] IEC 61508 phases 6 to 8 are concerned only with the planning of subsequent lifecycle phases and so are outside the scope of this paper

[17] Now called the EUROCONTROL Innovation Hub.

[18] Or equivalent

conventional P-RNAV) operations[19] and Point Merge operations is that in the former, arrivals are typically merged on to a line, whereas in the latter, they follow predefined routes until they are merged on to a point, known as a Merge Point.

Point Merge was first deployed in Oslo in 2011 and now operational at 37 or more airports across 4 continents, where it has been shown to provide significant potential benefits in terms of flight efficiency and the environment.

The question for the remainder of this paper is, however, would its introduction to a hypothetical airport be safe, and how would we demonstrate this, if we were to follow the IEC 61508 safety lifecycle?

3 Safety Assessment

3.1 Concept (IEC 61508-1 Phase 1)

3.1.1 Aim

The aim of this phase is to gather as much information about what IEC 61508 calls the *Equipment Under Control* (EUC), its *Environment*, and the *EUC Control System*, as necessary and sufficient to enable the other safety lifecycle activities to be satisfactorily carried out.

It is important to note that, as an enabling activity, this would be a precursor to, but not form part of, the safety assessment *per se* and would require substantial operational and system-engineering specialist input, relevant to each specific application. In practice, such material may be found in a typical Concept of Operations document.

3.1.2 EUC

As with other ATM applications, we can understand the EUC as being, in general, the flow of aircraft through the airspace, during landing or taking off, and/or taxiing on the airport surface — in this case, it is the flow of arrival traffic through Approach airspace, until each aircraft intercepts the Instrument Landing System (ILS) Glidepath beam for its final descent to the runway. This understanding is consistent with the core IEC 61508 principle that the EUC is the main source of hazards, which Safety Related Systems (SRSs) are required to mitigate in order to achieve a tolerable level of risk.

The key inherent properties of the EUC that we will assume for this Point Merge example are as follows:

- traffic is a mix of commercial jets / turbo-props and general aviation;
- arrivals per year: 100,000;
- maximum sustained arrival rate: 28 per hour;
- average arrival flight time in Approach airspace: 12 minutes;

---

[19] For example in "tromboning", where P-RNAV routes define a complete path from the Initial Approach Fix (IAF) to the final approach fix (FAF), including an extended down-wind leg, base leg, and initial approach path, but aircraft are vectored off the downwind leg to merge on to the runway extended centreline.

- on average, at least 95% of aircraft in the main arrival flow are certified and approved for P-RNAV approaches;
- aircraft wake-turbulence category mix is dependent on time of day; during peak times it averages 1.5% super; 25% heavy; 65% medium; 8.5% light.

3.1.3 Environment

IEC 61508 defines the environment in terms that include its physical, operating, legal and maintenance properties.

The environment properties for Point Merge operations are assumed to be as follows, the list covering most of the key points necessary for the safety assessment:

- Airspace Parameters and Flight Rules:
  - applies to Approach airspace / Approach control phase, corresponding to Approach arrival sectors, typically between the IAF and the FAF or transfer to the Tower;
  - all traffic operates under Instrument Flight Rules.
- Transition Altitude is 18,000 ft, well above the highest part of the Point Merge structure.
- Adjacent Airspace / Operations:
  - adjacent surrounding airspace is En-route;
  - airport served by the Point Merge structure has two, parallel, main runways (26L and 26R), one for landing and one for take-off (interchangeable), with ILS Cat II.
- Climate and Terrain:
  - climate is temperate, liable to dense fog in winter and occasional heavy thunderstorm activity in summer; prevailing winds are westerly;
  - terrain is generally undulating but with high mountains starting at 35 nautical miles South-west of the runway.
- Environmental Constraints: for the purposes of this paper, we will assume that no particular environmental constraints apply to Point Merge operations.

3.1.4 EUC Control System

Given the above interpretation of the EUC itself, we can understand the EUC Control System as being a functional system, encompassing people, procedures and equipment, and comprising, in general:

- The usual Air Traffic Services (ATS) and facilities to be found at a typical busy airport, irrespective of the specific type of Approach operations in place; and
- The Flight Crew actions related to flying the P-RNAV routes and following the ATS procedures and instructions, together with airborne equipment supporting the execution of those actions.

It is important to emphasise that, in the description of the EUC Control System which follows, the focus is on the business / operational *rationale* for Point Merge, and the text deliberately makes little or no explicit reference to the safety constraints that, of course, must be applied to Point Merge operations — these will be addressed in Phase 3 *et seq*.[20]

The Point Merge configuration applicable to this safety assessment is a single structure, as shown in Figure 1.

The Point Merge structure comprises two continuous P-RNAV routes, linking two IAFs (IAF1 and 2) to the FAF[21] and the start of final descent into a single arrival runway (RWY 26L), with waypoints signified by the star symbols. It includes the following key stages:

- Two Sequencing Legs, which are centred on the Merge Points; the inner Leg (i.e. the one closer to the Merge Point) is, wherever practicable, higher than the outer Leg;
- Two Run-off Legs, each one of which connects the end of a Sequencing Leg to the Merge Point;
- The FAF, by which time the aircraft will have acquired the ILS Glidepath for final approach and landing.

A holding point is provided prior to each Point Merge entry point, for use as required.

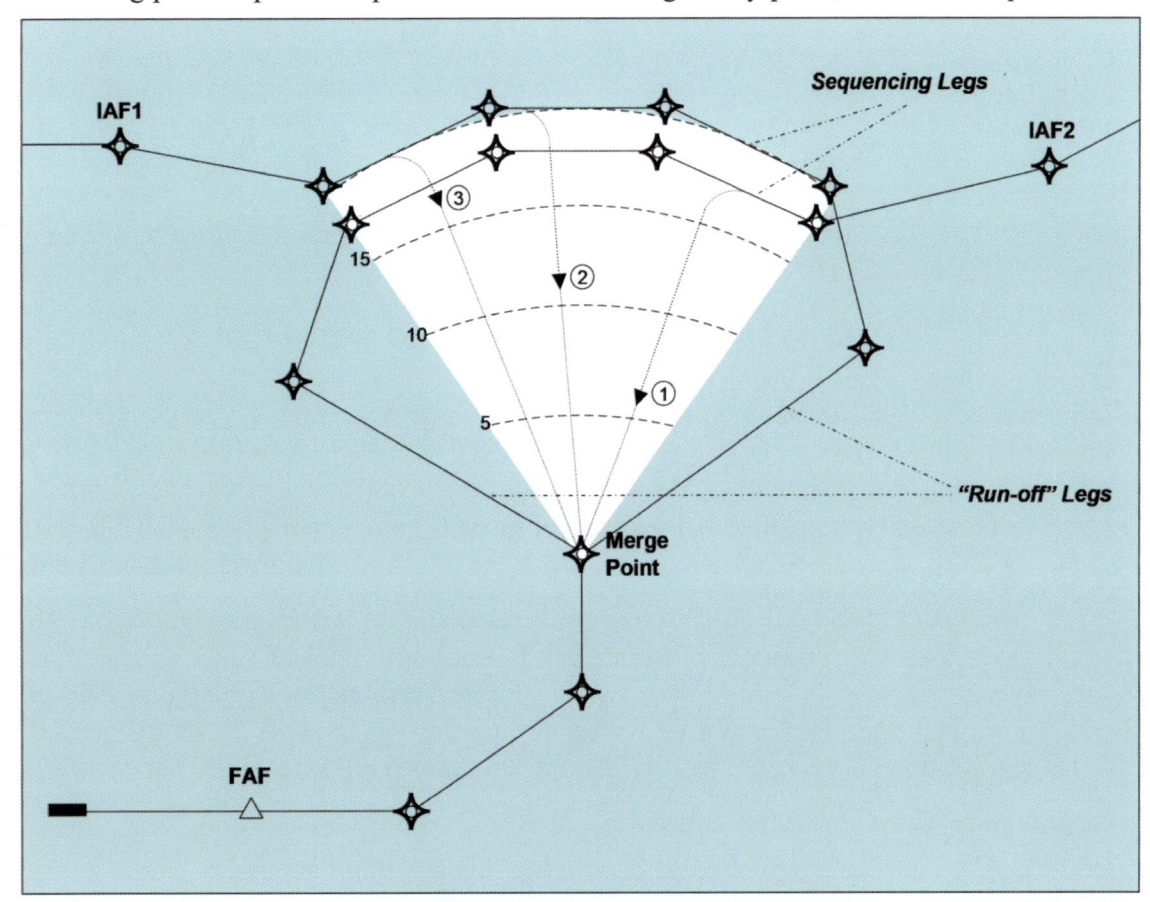

Figure 3 ~ Point Merge Route Layout

The boundary between Approach airspace and adjacent En-route / Terminal airspace sectors occurs before the IAF in each case.

---

[20] It is acknowledged that this distinction might seem somewhat artificial; however, it serves to emphasise the point made, at Sub-section 3.1.1 herein, that this phase is a necessary precursor to, rather than a part of, the safety assessment *per se*.

[21] A dual configuration is also possible, based on an additional, mirror-image structure to the south of the runway centreline, with the two Merge Points linked to a Common Point, which itself has a single route linking it to the FAF.

What we have identified as the "EUC Control System", is required, under *normal* operating conditions[22], to establish and maintain the arrival sequence, within this structure, i.e. to order the arrivals, and *space* them in accordance with the runway metering requirements, so as to maximize runway throughput while taking account of the safety and other needs of individual flights[23]. This is achieved as follows:

- non-arrival traffic in the area is handled as follows:
  - departing traffic (usually from RWY26R) follows standard instrument departure (SID) routes, above the Point Merge structure, to the top of climb;
  - overflying traffic follows conventional Airways route structure;
  - low-level transits of traffic operating under Instrument Flight Rules, and Arrivals to proximate aerodromes, are radar-vectored though Approach airspace, whilst avoiding the Point Merge structure;
- the required aircraft-arrival rate is derived in Approach airspace and fed upstream to adjacent En-route / Terminal airspace sectors as "metering" requirements based on runway capacity and the limited ability of Approach airspace to absorb momentary traffic overloads;
- sequencing and spacing of traffic are established initially in En-route/ Terminal airspace according to the metering requirements, and to an initial estimation of the order of aircraft in the final landing sequence, that would achieve the maximum runway throughput commensurate with the need to maintain adequate spacing between aircraft in the same flow;
- arriving traffic is cleared initially, by ATC[24], to follow standard P-RNAV Terminal airspace arrival routes (STARs) from the top of descent to the IAF;
- prior to reaching its IAF, ATC clears each P-RNAV-capable arrival to continue to follow the remainder of the appropriate P-RNAV route, i.e. down to the FAF but subject to contrary instructions from ATC as necessary;
- aircraft that are not P-RNAV capable (i.e. not equipped or suffering from P-RNAV equipment failure) are vectored along the appropriate Point Merge route, to emulate P-RNAV-capable aircraft, as per the rest of the sequence;
- ATC issues a Direct-to instruction (or a vector, in the case of a non-P-RNAV aircraft) to each aircraft to leave its Sequencing Leg, and head to the Merge Point, once sufficient spacing has been established behind the aircraft immediately preceding it in the overall landing sequence — note that the preceding aircraft might not be on the same Sequencing Leg;
- if the spacing requirements cannot be met before the aircraft reaches the end of the Sequencing Leg[25], the aircraft will, by default, continue on its P-RNAV route (and / or vectors) to the Merge Point — i.e. following the associated Run-off Leg;
- once ATC clears the aircraft to start its descent towards the Merge Point (having ensured safe separation from traffic on the parallel sequencing leg), it will converge vertically (and laterally) with the other aircraft in the flow;
- finally, from the Merge Point to the FAF, there is now only one horizontally-merged flow in which all the aircraft are spaced longitudinally. Along this segment, each

---

[22] i.e. what we want, and expect, to happen in day-to-day operations (Fowler 2022).

[23] The use of the term "space" here includes *implicitly* the need to also apply the required longitudinal separation minima, wherever other separation *modes* are not available. The way in which the various separation modes are applied throughout the Approach airspace is addressed explicitly in Phase 3 *et seq.*

[24] ATC = Air Traffic Control

[25] Or, for example, and aircraft is unable to respond to a Direct-to instruction

aircraft is cleared to continue its descent until it eventually acquires the final-approach path to the runway.

3.2 Overall Scope Definition (IEC 61508-1 Phase 2)

3.2.1 Aim and Objectives

The aim of this phase is to define the scope of the Hazard and Risk Analysis, for Phase 3.

It seeks to achieve that aim through determining the boundary of the EUC / EUC Control System and its Operational Environment and, within those constraints, specifying the scope of the Hazard and Risk Analysis.

This would be particularly important when assessing the safety of a change to an existing operation and/or system so as to identify, and exclude, the unnecessary safety assessment of those elements that are not affected by the change. It should be noted, however, that we can do this only in general terms herein because of the necessarily generic nature of the operational context for which this example safety assessment is being carried out.

3.2.2 Boundary Constraints

For the purposes of the safety assessment of Point Merge operations, the flow of arrival traffic, which constitutes the EUC, is that which lies between the IAF and the FAF, though it might be necessary to consider the conditions for handover from the adjacent En-route airspace and to final approach and landing. The functioning of the EUC Control System and the properties of the Operational Environment are similarly limited spatially.

3.2.3 Scope of the Hazard and Risk Analysis

Within the above constraints, it is *not* intended to address:

- any hazardous event or situation that does not involve at least one arriving aircraft; nor
- hazards associated with failure onboard an aircraft that leads to a loss of control, other than the effects that such events might have on other aircraft in the vicinity.

3.3 Hazard and Risk Analysis (IEC 61508-1 Phase 3)

3.3.1 Aim

The aim of this phase is to determine, and characterise, all the hazards and risks associated with the EUC[26], in the stated Environment, and within the scope already identified in Phase 2.

Note: it is acknowledged that these EUC hazards (and some of the detail that follows, up to and including Sub-section 3.4.3 below), which are not specific to Point Merge operations, might have already been identified and documented adequately in, say, a safety

---

[26] Strictly speaking, IEC 61508 includes "EUC Control System Hazards" here as well. We have taken the view that, for ATM, failures with the EUC Control System are among the *causes* of EUC hazards.

case for the airspace concerned. For the purposes of this paper, however, we do not assume this to be the case.

3.3.2 EUC Hazard Identification

The objective here is to determine the hazards relating to the EUC, within the scope defined in Sub-section 3.2 above.

From the IEC 61508 definition of a hazard, which can be paraphrased as *"a potential **source** of death, physical injury or damage to the health of people or damage to property or the environment"* (Fowler 2022), it follows that we must first identify the types of harmful **outcome,** i.e. accident, that fall within ATM's general sphere of responsibility and specifically within the above scope of Point Merge operations.

Table 1 shows accident types relevant to ATM, in Approach airspace, and has been adapted from ICAO (2011)[27] and, in each case, involves death or serious injury to one or more of those on board.

Table 1 ~ Accident Types Relevant to ATM in Approach Airspace

Accident Type	Description
Mid-air collision (MAC)	All collisions between aircraft (or between an aircraft and an unmanned aerial vehicle or missile), while both are airborne
Controlled Flight into Terrain (CFIT)	Inflight collision with terrain, water, or obstacle without loss of control
Uncontrolled Flight into Terrain (UFIT)	Inflight collision with terrain, water, or obstacle following loss of control, *except* where such loss is caused by failure(s) internal to the aircraft
Abrupt, Violent Manoeuvre (AVM)	Sudden, large, intentional or unintentional departure from the intended flightpath and/or attitude, *except* where such departure is caused by failure(s) internal to the aircraft

The EUC hazards derived from the above, and in relation to what are seen to be credible accident outcomes, are shown in Table **2**. The hazards are (by definition) those that are inherent in aviation, in the stated Operational Environment. It is crucial to note that these hazards apply directly to the EUC (the flow of arrivals through Approach airspace) and exist *before* any form of EUC-hazard mitigation has been applied (Fowler 2022).

The numbers in parentheses in Table **2** refer to the notes that follow the table.

Table 2 ~ EUC Hazards and Precursor States

ID	EUC Hazard Title (1)	Immediate Precursor State (2)	Related Accident(s)
Hp#1	Conflicts between pairs of aircraft 4-D flight trajectories	The trajectories concerned intersect, at the approximately same altitude, and the two aircraft would arrive at the crossing point at approximately the same time	MAC or AVM (3)

---

[27] ICAO (2011) Categories are intended for use in *a posteriori* categorisation of actual occurrences, rather than *a priori* safety assessment — hence the need for some adaptation

ID	EUC Hazard Title (1)	Immediate Precursor State (2)	Related Accident(s)
Hp#2	Aircraft in conflict with terrain or obstacle	Aircraft, under the control of the flight crew (or autopilot), is on a downward trajectory that would bring it in contact with the ground or fixed obstacle, *other* than at a suitable runway touchdown point at an appropriate speed and in an appropriate configuration	CFIT or AVM (3)
Hp#3	Aircraft in conflict with unauthorized areas	Aircraft is on a trajectory that would pass through active restricted airspace without authority	MAC (4)
Hp#4	Aircraft in conflict with severe weather conditions	Aircraft is on a trajectory that would pass through an area of weather conditions that are severe enough for its ability to continue its flight safely to be significantly impaired	AVM or UFIT (5)
Hp#5	Aircraft in conflict with wake turbulence	Aircraft is on a trajectory that would put it in an area of wake turbulence that is severe enough for its ability to continue its flight safely to be significantly impaired	AVM or UFIT (5)

Notes:

1. "Conflict" is used here in its broadest sense – see column 3.
2. IEC 61508 requires that the sequence of events be described for each EUC hazard, but it would be impracticable for ATM, at this stage in the process, because of the number of causal factors involved. What we can usefully do *here* is to describe the immediate precursor to each hazardous event, and leave it to the modelling approach described in Sub-section 3.4.2 below, which does capture how such states are arrived at in the first place, and thus satisfy this IEC 61508 requirement.
3. AVM here is the result of *onboard* actions to avoid an imminent collision
4. Incudes collision with another airborne vehicle and from being hit by some form of munitions.
5. AVM would be the more likely outcome except when the aircraft is closer to the ground and timely recovery from the departure is more difficult.

What we have not said thus far is anything about the probability that each EUC hazardous event would lead to the related accident except, that the probability would, by definition, be finite. That is addressed next, in Sub-section 3.3.3.

3.3.3 EUC Risks

Severity of a hazard could, in general be deduced from the probability that the hazard would lead to the associated accident(s)[28], and the seriousness of the accident in term of the number of fatalities and/or degree and extent of serious injury involved; in ATM, however, the latter has traditionally *not* been considered in *a priori* safety assessments.

In theory, we could then determine either:

---

[28] Otherwise known as the probabilistic "distance" to the accident

- the EUC risks: i.e. by *estimating* the frequency of occurrence of each EUC hazard and combining it with an assessment of the hazard's severity; or
- the tolerable frequency of occurrence for each hazard: i.e. by setting a *target* tolerable level of EUC risk for each hazard and dividing it by the assessed hazard severity.

Fowler (2022) discussed the potential problems of identifying EUC risk, and Sub-section 3.4 below explains why its determination is actually not necessary under IEC 61508, though it is clear that a method of determining hazard severity is needed in *either* case. Unfortunately, in ATM, predicting the outcome of any hazard is not that simple because:

- as shown in Table 2, each EUC hazard has more than one potential, credible accident outcome;
- any given probability of such an outcome would vary according to, *inter alia*, phase of flight, traffic patterns and density;
- the probability and harmful effects would vary between accident types, e.g. between MAC and AVM, notwithstanding the fact that, traditionally, most ATM harmful events are treated as being of the same severity, irrespective of the number of people affected.

Concerns about hazard-severity / risk-classification schemes, in general, are not new; indeed, as long ago as 2006, the then EUROCONTROL Safety Case Development Manual (EUROCONTROL 2018), expressed concerns about the potential misuse of such schemes unless the user understands:

- at what level in the system hierarchy the values are intended to be applied;
- where the probability/frequency values used in the scheme came from and whether they are (still) valid;
- to what operational environment the values apply, eg type of airspace, traffic patterns, traffic density, spatial dimension, phase of flight, etc;
- how the aggregate risk, as specified in ESARR 4[29] for example, can be deduced from analysis of individual hazards, in restricted segments of the total system.

With all of the above issues in mind, Sub-section 3.4 below introduces a more rigorous approach to hazard and risk assessment, which has been developed by the EUROCONTROL Innovation Hub (EIH) for the Single European Sky ATM Research (SESAR) programme (SESAR 2021). It is based on a set of Accident Incident Models (AIMs), one per accident type, from each of which an RCS can be derived. More information on AIMs is provided in SESAR (2018a) and SESAR (2018b) but, essentially, they model the contributions that the ATM functional system makes to aviation safety, both when working as specified, and in the event of failure. The RCSs derived from the AIMs have four key advantages over the more traditional schemes referred to above:

- they are based on real, historical accident and incident data;
- they more accurately capture the progression of a hazardous event through to an accident;
- they provide safety criteria at many levels in the ATM functional-system hierarchy and for specific phases of flight;
- they provide safety criteria that take account of future changes to the ATM functional system and/or operational environment.

---

[29] ESARR 4 was the EUROCONTROL Safety Regulatory Requirement "Risk Assessment and Mitigation in ATM", which has since been overtaken by Single European Sky legislation.

3.4 Overall Safety Requirements (IEC 61508-1 Phase 4)

3.4.1 Aim

The aim of this phase is to produce a specification of the Overall Safety Requirements for each Overall Safety Function in order to achieve the required level of functional safety. These requirements cover both functional-safety and safety-integrity properties.

3.4.2 Introduction

According to IEC 61508, an Overall Safety Function is the highest-level abstraction of the "*Means of achieving, or maintaining, a safe state for the EUC, in respect of a specific hazardous event*", and therein lies a problem — the relationships between accidents and hazards (as explained above) is "many-to many" and so is the relationship between EUC hazards and the safety functions that are intended to mitigate them.

This can be illustrated by expressing the three layers of ATM, described in the ICAO Global ATM Concept (ICAO 2005), in the form of a generic Barrier Model[30], as shown in Figure 4 (Fowler et al 2009).

The inputs to the model are the relevant EUC hazards and the barriers, acting in rough sequence from left to right, effectively "filter out" a proportion of the EUC hazards. The final barrier reflects the point that, even when all three layers of ATM have been unable to remove a hazard, there is still a relatively high probability that an actual accident will not result, as indicated by the Providence barrier. This probability depends on a number of factors, including the type of the resulting accident, the volume of the available airspace, the density of traffic therein, and the geometry of the encounter.

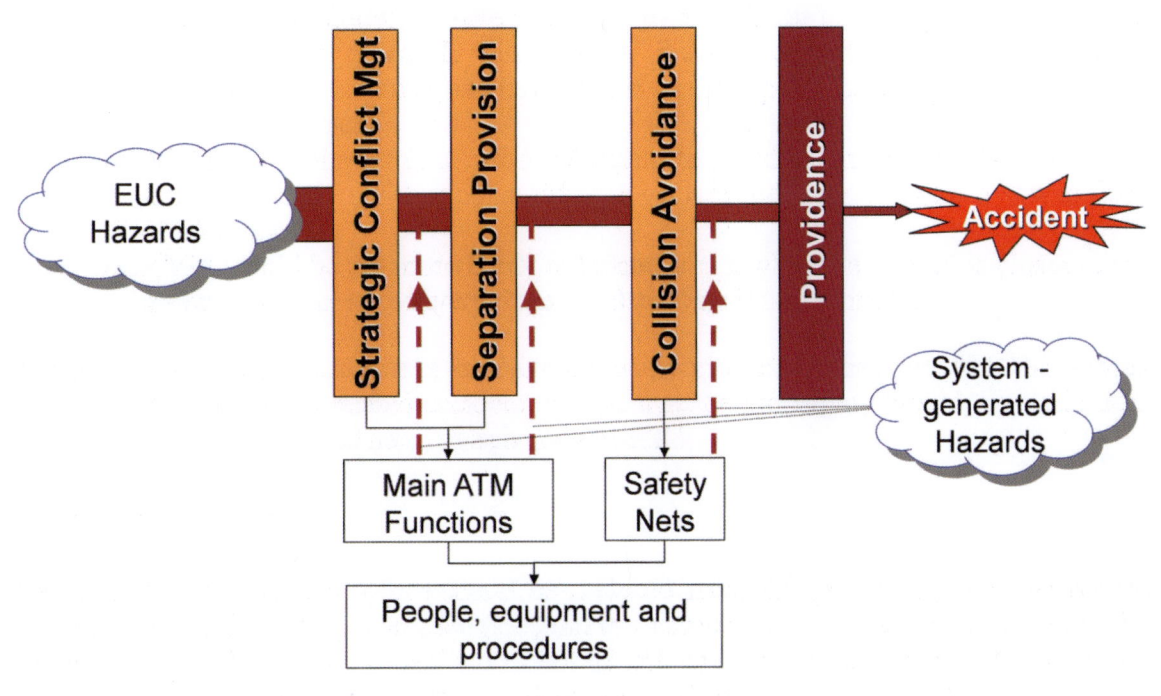

Figure 4 ~ ATM Barrier Model

---

[30] Derived from James Reason's "Swiss Cheese" model (Reason 2000)

The main three barriers are provided by the primary ATM safety functions and ground-based / airborne safety nets, implemented in the elements of the end-to-end ATM system. Of course, these elements can fail to operate, effectively reducing the probability of success of the barrier, or operate incorrectly, giving rise to new, *system-generated* hazards.

Fowler (2022) presented a simple fault tree model of a generic safety function and showed how its safety properties govern its ability to prevent, i.e. to act as single a barrier to, the progression of an EUC hazard through to an accident. That idea, based on a low-demand situation, is extended, in Figure 5 to represent the multi-barrier model of Figure 4.

Apart from its slightly unconventional layout, this model has one very important feature that distinguishes it from most other Fault Trees — i.e. it has an external input (EUC hazards)[31], which enables the computation of the risk of an accident (R_A) from:

- the EUC hazards (those hazards inherent in aviation) and their frequencies (F_U);
- the net probability of success (P_{Sn}) of each barrier in mitigating those risks, taking account of its functionality and performance, and of the probability that it might occasionally fail to operate at all; and
- the frequency (F_{Fn}) with which corrupt-operation failure of each of the main barrier introduces new, system-generated hazards / risks.

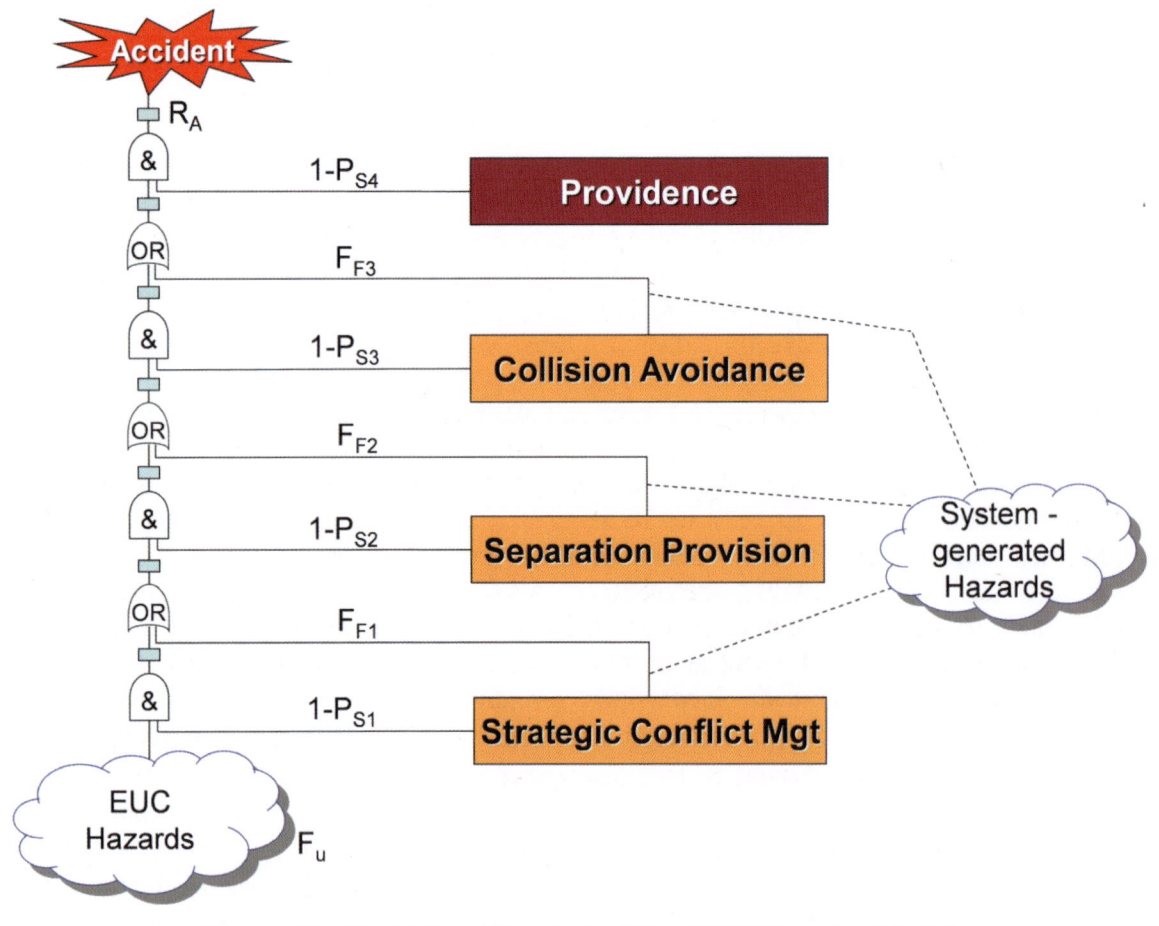

Figure 5 ~ Fault Tree Version of the ATM Barrier Model

---

[31] Without this input, a Fault Tree could model only *failures internal* to the system on which the Fault Tree is based – i.e. it could model only *negative* effects on safety

Alternatively, of course, if we make the top-level risk our target (R_T) then, given F_P and access to historical accident and incident data, we can make informed judgements about what P_{Sn} and frequency F_{Fn} are required to be in order to satisfy R_T.

Thus the model captures the net positive, as well as the negative, contributions of ATM to aviation safety, and it is this form of risk model on which the SESAR Accident Incident (AIM) models (SESAR 2018a) are based.

Of course, the model, as presented here, is purely illustrative and very high-level. In reality, each AIM model is very much more comprehensive, and actually represents the Barrier model as an Event Tree which integrates the Fault Trees dedicated to each Barrier.

In seeking to overcome many of the shortcomings of traditional hazard-severity / risk-classification schemes, discussed in Sub-section 3.3.3 above, the SESAR approach:

- has, at a detailed level, separate models for each phase of flight and accident type;
- uses real accident and incident data to populate the model with the required probability and frequency values; and
- is capable of modelling the interdependencies between barriers, including lower-level common-cause and common-mode failures, that are implied in Figure 4.

The remainder of this sub-section follows the above principles embedded in the AIM.

3.4.3 Overall Safety Function Identification

The objective here is to identify a set of Overall Safety Functions, based on the EUC hazardous events derived from the hazard and risk analysis of Phase 3. Notwithstanding the minor problem that the IEC 61508 view, of a one-to-one relationship between EUC hazards and Overall Safety Functions, does not work for ATM, the three ATM barriers (or "layers" (ICAO 2005)) fit the role of Overall Safety Functions quite nicely, and are shown in Table **3**.

Table 3 ~ Overall Safety Functions

ID	Overall Safety Function Title	Related EUC Hazards
OSF#1	Strategic Conflict Management (SCM)	Hp#1, Hp#2, Hp#3, Hp#4, Hp#5
OSF#2	Separation Provision (SP)	Hp#1, Hp#2, Hp#3, Hp#4, Hp#5
OSF#3	Collision Avoidance (CA)	Hp#1, Hp#2

3.4.4 Overall Safety Function Required Functional Properties

This step involves the determination of the required functional properties of each of the above Overall Safety Functions. The resulting Overall Safety Requirements (OSRs) are based on the *reference* operational scenario described in Sub-section 3.1.4 above and cover those items that are necessary and sufficient to ensure the safety of Point Merge operations.

In order to avoid, and / or mitigate the consequences of, the hazards shown in Table 1, the functional properties shown in Table 4 are required of the respective Overall Safety Functions. It should be noted that these requirements are objective based — i.e. they express what the OSF have to achieve rather than what they have to do.

Table 4 ~ **Overall Functional Safety Requirements for Normal Operations**

Reqt. ID	Requirement Description	Related EUC Hazard
OSF#1	**Strategic Conflict Management**	
OSR1.1	Arrival rates into Point Merge airspace shall not exceed the capacity of the P-RNAV routes or runway	Hp#1, Hp#5
OSR1.2	Crossing traffic and departures shall be segregated strategically from the Point Merge structure	Hp#1
OSR1.3	The Point Merge structure shall be segregated strategically from all restricted airspace	Hp#3
OSF#2	**Separation Provision**	
OSR2.1	All aircraft in Approach airspace shall be separated from each other, by either: the greater of the radar-separation minima and the wake-turbulence minima, horizontally; or by 1000ft vertically	Hp#1, Hp#5
OSR2.2	At all points along each route, from IAF to FAF, aircraft shall remain above the altitude of all close terrain/obstacles and/or be adequately separated laterally from such terrain/obstacles	Hp#2
OSR2.3	Point Merge operations shall cease in the event of severe weather posing a threat to the safety of arriving traffic flow in the Point Merge structure	Hp#4
OSF#3	**Collision Avoidance**	
OSR3.1	When the associated *separation mode* has been compromised, *mid-air* collision-avoidance action shall be taken in accordance with current operational procedures	Hp#1
OSR3.2	When the associated *separation mode* has been compromised, *terrain/obstacle* collision-avoidance action shall be taken in accordance with current operational procedures	Hp#2

3.4.5 *Determine the Safety Integrity Requirements for each Overall Safety Function*

This step involves the determination of the SIRs required of each of the above Overall Safety Functions, to achieve a tolerable level of risk overall. Two points are stressed in Fowler (2022):

- IEC 61508 states that the SIRs, at this level, must be specified in terms of either:
    - the risk reduction required to achieve the tolerable level of risk; or
    - the tolerable [EUC] hazardous event rate to achieve the tolerable level of risk; and
- according to IEC 61508, SIRs at this "overall" level are *not*, despite their name, properties of the OSF to which they relate — they actually specify a *target* amount of EUC risk reduction that the OSF has to meet, and could be seen to correspond to the more appropriately termed *safety criteria* in ATM.

Here, the SESAR AIM approach has two big advantages over IEC 61508 Phase 4, as follows:

- it derives SIRs that *are* properties of the OSFs themselves; and
- those properties accord directly, and fully, with the concept of Safety Integrity as defined in IEC 61508 — viz:

"the probability of a ... safety-related system satisfactorily performing the specified safety functions under all the stated conditions, within a stated period of time"

There is not the space in the context of this paper to provide a worked example for Point Merge but, in principle, we can see from Figure 5 above how, given sufficient relevant real-world accident data, a realistic value of EUC hazard rate and a risk tolerability level for, say, a MAC accident, the following three SIRs could be derived for each ATM barrier:

- probability of successful mitigation of the input hazard, in the absence of failure internal to the barrier;
- frequency or probability of failure internal to the barrier[32]; and
- frequency of corrupt operation of the barrier.

3.5 Overall Safety Requirements Allocation (IEC 61508-1 Phase 5)

3.5.1 Aim

The aim of this phase is to allocate to SRS(s) and/or ORRM(s), the functional safety requirements and safety integrity requirements, which were derived for the corresponding overall safety function in Phase 4.

3.5.2 Discussion

IEC 61508 gives prominence to the distinction between SRSs and ORRMs — partly, it would seem because, once identified, the latter measures fall outside the scope of the Standard.

For ATM in general, ORRMs could include non-functional, safety-related items such as airspace /route structure and runway / taxiway layout, for which specific design & development standards exist in most cases. However, given the close interaction between ATC and, say, P-RNAV route structures in the SP barrier for Point Merge, it was decided that there was little additional value in the distinction, in this case[33]. Therefore, Table 5 shows the allocation of the OSFs from Table 4 on to what might be interpreted generically as SRSs[34], within an ATM "system of systems".

Table 5 ~ Allocation of Overall Safety Functions for Point Merge

OSF/OSR ID	Safety-related System
OSF#1	**Strategic Conflict Management**
OSR1.1	Demand & Capacity Balancing (DCB)

---

[32] Depending on whether the barrier operates continuously, i.e. at a high demand rate, or at a low demand rate, respectively.

[33] We considered whether ORS1.2 should be allocated to ORRMs since the segregation of transits / overflights and departures depends on risk-reduction measures which fall mainly outside of the scope of Point Merge. Whereas this would have merit as a way of managing such measures, it would have added non-essential complexity to this paper, which we chose to avoid.

[34] These are based on what ICAO (2005) terms *"ATM operational concept components"*.

OSF/OSR ID	Safety-related System
OSR1.1	Departure Synchronisation (DS)
OSR1.1	Arrival Sequencing & Spacing (ASS)
OSR1.1	Airspace Organisation & Management (AOM)
OSR1.2	
OSR1.3	
OSF#2	**Separation Provision**
OSR2.1	ATC Pre-tactical Conflict Management ~ air-to-air (ATC-PTCM-AA)
OSR2.2	ATC Pre-tactical Conflict Management ~ air-to-ground (ATC-PTCM-AG)
OSR2.1 OSR2.3	ATC Tactical Conflict Management ~ air-to-air (ATC-TCM-AA)
OSR2.2	ATC Tactical Conflict Management ~ air-to-ground (ATC-TCM-AG)
OSR2.2	Airborne Tactical Conflict Management ~ air-ground (AB-TCM-AG)
OSF#3	**Collision Avoidance**
OSR3.1	ATC mid-air collision-avoidance (ATC-MACA)
OSR3.2	Airborne mid-air collision-avoidance (AB-MACA)
OSR3.2	ATC terrain collision-avoidance (ATC-TCA)
OSR3.3	Airborne terrain collision-avoidance (AB-TCA)

The ICAO Global ATM Concept (ICAO 2005) uses the term "strategic" to mean "in advance of tactical" whilst recognising that "a continuum exists from the earliest planning of the user activity through to the latest avoidance of the hazard". In respect of the use of P-RNAV routes, with various altitude constraints, to effect separation, it is debatable whether that is strategic or tactical, or lies on the continuum somewhere between the two; we concluded that the latter was the case and coined the term "pre-tactical", within Separation Provision, to capture this in Table **5**.

Furthermore, where pre-tactical separation is provided, by the P-RNAV route structures of Point Merge, we envisage that ATC monitoring of aircraft compliance with the P-RNAV route parameters would be provided within the two (ATC-TCM) barriers, in advance of Collision Avoidance.

3.6 Safety Requirements Specification (IEC 61508-1 Phases 9 and 10)

3.6.1 *Aim*

In IEC 61508, the respective aims of Phases 9 and 10 is to develop safety requirements for the "SRSs" and "ORRMs" identified in Phase 5, in terms of their Functional Safety Requirements (FSRs) and the SIRs, in order to achieve the required functional safety under all *normal*, *abnormal* and *failure* conditions.

Given that, in the case of Point Merge above, we have viewed the distinction between SRSs and ORRMs as being of limited value, we have thus combined Phases 9 and 10 together in this sub-section.

3.6.2 Overview

It is important to note here that IEC 61508-1 places great emphasis on the need for a description of the workings of the SRS at this level, including:

- a description of all the safety functions, how they work together to achieve the required functional safety and whether they operate in low-demand, high-demand or continuous modes of operation;
- the required performance attributes of each safety function — e.g. timing properties and, for more data-intensive applications than possibly envisaged by IEC 61508, data accuracy, latency, refresh rate, and overload tolerance;
- all interfaces that are necessary to achieve the required functional safety;
- all relevant modes of operation of the EUC;
- response of the SRSs to abnormal conditions that might arise in the EUC or its environment;
- all required modes of behaviour of the SRSs — in particular, its failure behaviour and the required response in the event of such failure (Fowler 2022).

In the particular case of Point Merge operations, there are no new SRSs /safety functions; rather, the operational concept is based on existing Approach airspace functions / infrastructure, most of which are elements of the ATM system, i.e. what IEC 61508 terms the "EUC Control System" (see Sub-section 3.1.4 above), and which must be considered to be SRSs in their own right by virtue of their safety significance in Point Merge operations.

The questions that we need to address at this stage, therefore, are *where and when* those safety functions are deployed for Point Merge and would that be safe. To that end, this sub-section comprises four stages, as follows.

Firstly, the development of FSRs using operational scenarios, covering *normal* operations. This will be done initially at two levels (see Sub-section 3.6.3 below):

1. initially, at a relatively abstract level, without reference to explicit elements within the end-to-end ATM system, and

2. then, the lower level of a "*logical*-architecture" representation of the ATM system (i.e. the "EUC Control System")[35].

The former level is focused on *what* needs to be done and uses narrative scenarios to represent a (basic) form of behavioural model of Point Merge, which captures the initial FSRs, for the operational processes involved in a typical flight through the airspace. The latter, however, focusses on *how* this is achieved by the logical elements of the ATM system[36].

---

[35] Whereas IEC 61508 does not distinguish between these two levels, the approach described here has been found by the authors to be a useful approach to the safety assessment of a number of ATM applications

[36] As noted in Sub-section 3.7.2 of Fowler (2022), the IEC 61508 objective here is to "*describe, in terms not specific to the equipment, the required safety properties of the SRS(s)*". Both of these levels of requirements expression respect that objective since neither makes any assumptions about the technology involved in the realisation of the requirements.

Secondly, to show that the FSRs specified for the SRSs would be adequate to meet the risk-reduction required of the barriers / SRSs, in the absence of failure (see Sub-section 3.6.4).

Thirdly, to analyse, in a similar manner, scenarios covering *abnormal* events in order to identify any additional FSRs necessary to maintain a tolerable level of safety during such events (see Sub-section 3.6.5 below).

Fourthly, to analyse scenarios relating to potential failures of the ATM system in order to identify SIRs, and any additional FSRs, necessary to maintain a tolerable level of safety during such failure events (see Sub-section 3.6.6 below).

3.6.3 *FSRs for Normal Operations*

3.6.3.1 Derivation of FSRs for the "Reference" Operational Scenario

In order to derive the initial set of FSRs, the analysis first considers a typical flight through Approach airspace, as a continuum, looking in particular at transitions in the *separation mode* and in the merging of traffic, for the Point Merge structure shown in Figure 3.

For the purpose of analysis, the *subject* aircraft is assumed to be P-RNAV capable and enters the Point Merge structure, in a westerly direction, at IAF1[37]. It is termed the *reference* scenario (designated N0) since it is based on the most likely set of operational and environmental conditions[38].

For each stage in the flight at which something has to be achieved in relation to one or more of the OSRs shown in Table **4** above, the need for an FSR is identified, as shown thus "{FSR#n}" in the text below, and then the corresponding FSRs are detailed (and traced back to the related SRS(s), at Table 10 in Appendix A.

General Conditions: the following conditions apply generally throughout flight in Approach airspace:

- vertical separation at intersections of Point Merge routes with SIDs is provided achieved through aircraft conforming to appropriate published altitude restrictions {FSR#1};
- all other traffic is kept away from the Point Merge structure strategically, or by ATC tactical intervention as and when appropriate {FSR#2};
- the whole Point Merge structure is segregated spatially from Restricted Airspace {FSR#3};
- entire P-RNAV routes (i.e. from IAF to FAF) are designed in accordance with ICAO Doc 8168 Vol II (ICAO 2014) {FSR#4}.

Pre-conditions: the following conditions apply prior to aircraft entering the Point Merge structure at the designated IAF:

- required aircraft-arrival rate is derived in Approach airspace and fed upstream to adjacent En-route / Terminal airspace sectors as "metering" requirements based on

---

[37] The choice here is entirely arbitrary, and the analysis would apply equally to any P-RNAV-capable aircraft entering at the other IAF.

[38] Other scenarios will cover other *normal* conditions, e.g. the cases of aircraft that are not P-RNAV capable, as well as, later in this sub-section, *abnormal* and *failure* conditions.

runway capacity (arrivals and departures) and the limited ability of Approach airspace to absorb momentary traffic overloads {FSR#5 and FSR#6};
- sequencing and spacing of traffic are established initially in En-route/ Terminal sectors according to the metering requirements, and to an initial estimation of the order of aircraft in the final landing sequence, that would achieve the optimum runway throughput commensurate with the need to maintain separation minima/wake turbulence criteria and maintain the required departure flow {FSR#7, FSR#8};
- ATC monitoring of aircraft conformance with all clearances and instructions is carried out throughout each flight, including when aircraft are following the predefined P-RNAV routes that make up most of the Point Merge structure {FSR#9}.

Flight in Approach Airspace: the aircraft proceeds as follows:

- entry into Approach airspace is coordinated with the adjacent upstream sector(s) according to the agreed entry conditions, including the aircraft being stable at the defined altitude prior to Sequencing Leg entry {FSR#10} — this is to reduce the chances of unnecessary ACAS / STCA alerts with opposite-direction aircraft that are approaching the end of the adjacent Sequencing Leg;
- on entry to, and along, the Sequencing Leg (SL1), the aircraft remains in level flight and is vertically separated from each eastbound aircraft on the adjacent, opposite-direction Sequencing Leg (SL2) by all aircraft complying with height restrictions published for the P-RNAV route applicable to its Sequencing Leg {FSR#11};
- spacing from preceding and succeeding aircraft on the same Sequencing Leg is provided tactically by ATC such that the 3 nautical mile longitudinal-separation minimum and wake-vortex criteria are maintained {FSR#12};
- vertical clearance from terrain/obstacles is provided by the minimum altitude specified for each Sequencing Leg's P-RNAV route section {FSR#13};
- once sufficient spacing has been established behind the aircraft immediately preceding it in the overall landing sequence, the subject aircraft is instructed by ATC to leave its Sequencing Leg, on a *Direct-to* towards the Merge Point (MP) {FSR#14} — its position in the final sequence order is thus established;

Notes:

1. If the spacing requirements cannot be met before the aircraft reaches the end of the Sequencing Leg, the aircraft will continue on its P-RNAV route to the Merge Point – see scenario N1 below.
2. The handling of aircraft that are not P-RNAV-capable is discussed in scenario N2 below.

- during the Direct-to section of the flight, the following separation rules apply:
    - in this case, the subject aircraft is on the higher, i.e. inner, Sequencing Leg, and as the aircraft starts to follow the Direct-to, vertical separation from traffic on the *adjacent, i.e. lower, Sequencing Leg* is maintained by ATC instructing the subject aircraft to maintain its altitude until longitudinal separation from the aircraft still on the adjacent Sequencing Leg has been achieved {FSR#15};
    - once the subject aircraft is clear of the adjacent Sequencing Leg *and* longitudinal separation from other aircraft also heading to the MP has been established (see {FSR#15 above}), it can be cleared to descend to the MP;
    - terrain/obstacle clearance is enabled by the minimum altitude of the MP being such that there is no terrain/obstacle that is higher than the MP anywhere in the sector of the circle defined by the MP and its outermost Sequencing Leg {FSR#16};

o unless instructed otherwise by ATC, the aircraft flight crew is responsible for maintaining safe altitude from the start of descent on the "Direct-to" leg until acquiring the ILS glidepath {FSR#17}.

- finally, from the MP to the FAF, there is now only one horizontally-merged flow; along this segment, the aircraft continues its descent, and eventually acquires the Final Approach path.

Table 10 in Appendix A specifies each of the FSRs identified above.

3.6.3.2 Derivation of Additional FSRs for other Normal Scenarios

Other scenarios describing *normal* operations, are usually variations on scenario N0, two examples of which are as follows.

Firstly, scenario N1 in which a non-P-RNAV aircraft requires to join the landing sequence. In this case, all the ATC-related FSRs for operational scenario N0 apply, with the following addition:

> *FSR#18   All non-P-RNAV aircraft shall be vectored along the Point Merge routes to emulate P-RNAV aircraft, whilst being provided with obstacle / terrain clearance by ATC.*

Secondly, scenario N2 in which an aircraft reaches the end of its Sequencing Leg before it had been possible to find a slot for it in the landing sequence[39]. The FSRs for scenario N0 apply, with the following addition:

> *FSR#19   Each Point Merge route shall include a Sequencing Leg Run-off procedure (P-RNAV segments and / or ATC manual procedure) to ensure that an aircraft will automatically continue to the Merge Point, on a predefined vertical profile, in the event that no Direct-to instruction is received before reaching the end of the Sequencing Leg.*

Other *normal* scenarios might include the following:

- planned transitions into, and out of, Point Merge operations;
- planned change of runway (same direction);
- planned change of runway direction;
- onset of strong winds.

In analysing such scenarios, any additional FSRs would need to be identified and specified.

3.6.3.3 Logical FSRs for Normal Operations

Thus far, we have specified, at a conceptual level, *individual* FSRs for the management of conflicts and avoidance of collision for Point Merge operations under normal and abnormal conditions.

What needs to be done next is to describe *how* these FSRs map on to the ATM system and how the system itself needs to behave in order to achieve the desired result.

---

[39] Could also be a mitigation of an ATM system failure – e.g. lost comms

It was decided to carry out such analyses (and the subsequent failure analysis) at the level of the system *logical* design, which describes the main human roles / tasks and machine-based functions of the system but in a manner that is entirely independent of the eventual *physical* implementation of that design — to this extent it conforms to the associated provisions of Phase 9 of the IEC 61508.

A typical set of elements of the Logical Model that would be appropriate to Point Merge is shown in Table 6. The list is not exhaustive in that elements not specifically affected by Point Merge, e.g. are required to simply perform their normal functions, are excluded at this stage. The type of element is also shown, and is designated as MF (machine function), HR (human role) or a set of Data.

Table 6 ~ Logical Elements

ID	Description	Type
ACAS	Airborne Collision Avoidance System	MF
AD	Airspace Design	Data
AP/FD	Autopilot/Flight Director	MF
AMAN	Arrival Manager (tools)	MF
EXEC	Executive (Tactical) Controller	HR
FCRW	Flight Crew	HR
FDP	Flight Data Processing	MF
FMS	Flight Management System	MF
MSAW	Minimum Safe Altitude Warning	MF
PLNR	Planner Controller	HR
P-RNAV	P-RNAV Procedure	Data
STCA	Short-term Conflict Alert	MF
TAWS	Terrain Awareness Warning System	MF

Examples of how FSRs then map on to the relevant Logical Elements is shown in Table 7.

Table 7 ~ Example Mapping of FSRs to Logical Model

ID	Safety Requirement	Maps to:
FSR#3	Point Merge structures shall be segregated from restricted airspace	AD
FSR#7	Sequencing and spacing of traffic shall be established initially in adjacent En-route/ Terminal airspace sectors according to the metering requirements, and to an initial estimation of the order of aircraft in the final landing sequence, that would achieve the optimum runway throughput commensurate with the need to maintain separation minima/wake turbulence criteria and maintain the required departure flow	AMAN, PLNR
FSR#10	Vertical separation, of at least 1,000 ft, between adjacent Sequencing Legs shall be provided, by appropriate published altitude restrictions along the entire length of the Sequencing Legs	P-RNAV

ID	Safety Requirement	Maps to:
FSR#11	Aircraft on the same Sequencing Leg shall be separated longitudinally, by ATC, by a 3nautical mile radar -separation minimum, or the appropriate wake-turbulence separation minimum, whichever is the greater	EXEC
FSR#16	Except where instructed otherwise by ATC, the aircraft shall assume responsibility for maintaining safe altitude from the start of descent on the "Direct-to" leg until acquiring the ILS glidepath	FCRW, TAWS

The mapping process would then be completed by deriving appropriate (lower-level, Logical) FSRs, for each Logical Model element, in response to the higher-level FSRs assigned to it.[40]

Given then a complete Logical Model, a technique that can be used very effectively in modelling the *behaviour* of transactional system such as ATM is some form of Use Case analysis. A suitable notation for this purpose would be a sequence diagram (SD), straightforward guidance on which can be found at Sparx Systems (2022).

For many ATM applications, SDs have proved to be a very useful design-analysis technique in that they:

- provide a means of cross-checking the completeness, correctness and consistency of the lower-level FSRs which are mapped on to the SD;
- tell us more about the intended operation of the ATM system than could the FSRs individually;
- are an effective way of highlighting transitions between, inter alia, separation modes at various points in the flight;
- provide very useful, scenario-based information for real-time operational simulations and the development of operator training material; and
- provide, for the subsequent failure analysis, a valuable insight into sources of potential system failures.

Furthermore, since it also defines the required behaviour of the ATC system), it is designated as a functional safety requirement in its own right.

In a full safety assessment, other normal scenarios might also need to be similarly analysed, including scenarios N1 and N2.

3.6.4 *Adequacy of the Functional Safety Requirements*

In the barrier-model approach outlined in Sub-section 3.4 above, it was noted that it is the functional properties of a barrier that determines the probability of successful mitigation of the input hazard, in the absence of failure internal to the barrier. It was also noted that, in case of the SESAR AIMs, the required probability of success, and the maximum rates of occurrence of failure and corrupt operation, of each barrier is, as far possible, based on actual historic data.

In practice, establishing a *direct* relationship between the required functional properties (FSRs) of a barrier, and the required probability of its successful mitigation of input

---
[40] Not done herein in order to avoid unnecessary detail…

hazards, can be far from straightforward, depending on the circumstances. This is illustrated by considering two general cases, as follows:

- when ATM operations, albeit conducted in a different way from previous operations in the subject environment, remain fully compliant with established ICAO Standards and Recommended Practices (SARPs);
- when ATM operations deviate from those SARPs in some way.

The first case applies to Point Merge for which, in the various normal and abnormal scenarios, the FSRs are specified so as to ensure compliance with, for example, ICAO separation minima throughout each step/portion of arrival flight in Approach airspace.

The (qualitative) safety argument would then be relative — i.e. that, given previous (ICAO complaint) arrival operations in the airspace were deemed to be tolerably safe, Point Merge operations would themselves be safe in the absence of failure. Such an argument should be reinforced by demonstrating the viability of the FSRs, as a whole, through real-time simulations, from an ATC and/or aircraft perspective, as appropriate.

The second case would apply, for example, whenever separation was applied below the associated ICAO minima and would require a more direct approach. In the specific case of reduced vertical separation minima (RVSM) in European En-route airspace, data from real-time monitoring of aircraft height-keeping accuracy was used to compute (in effect) the probability of successful vertical separation between two aircraft separated nominally by 1,000 ft, in the absence of failure. Equivalent approaches have been applied in the safety assessment of reduced wake-turbulence separation, using real-time, LIDAR measurement of wave-vortex phenomena.

3.6.5 *Point Merge Operations under Abnormal Environmental Conditions*

The following are examples of what were identified as abnormal conditions relevant to Point Merge operations:

- Aircraft Emergency — medical, technical, etc.
- Aircraft experiences ACAS Resolution Advisory (RA)
- Unplanned runway change, e.g. unplanned change of direction
- Unforeseen runway closure, e.g. blocked runway
- Missed Approach
- Very strong winds, e.g. > 30 knots

Table 8 contains two examples and shows, for each abnormal condition concerned, the immediate operational effect, the possible mitigations of the safety consequence of that effect and the related FSR(s).

Table 8 ~ Example Mitigation for Abnormal Operations

Ref.	Abnormal Event	Operational Effect	Mitigation of Effects	FSR
1	Aircraft Emergency	Aircraft in the landing sequence needs priority over preceding aircraft	Move the affected aircraft up the sequence order, if necessary, creating a gap by vectoring a preceding aircraft out of the sequence	FSR#20

Ref.	Abnormal Event	Operational Effect	Mitigation of Effects	FSR
2	Aircraft experiences an ACAS RA	Aircraft in the landing sequence needs to follow the RA	If necessary to maintain separation, and once the RA has been resolved, remove the aircraft from the landing sequence	FSR#21

It is also possible to quantify the residual risk associated with each of the abnormal events; however, this is beyond the scope of this article. What is more important at this stage is that the above analysis identified the abnormal conditions that might be encountered in the Point Merge Operational Environment and specified potential mitigations of the consequences thereof.

3.6.6 Point Merge Operations under Internal-failure Conditions

Finally, for Phases 9 and 10, is the analysis of potential failures internal to the overall Point Merge ATM system.

IEC 61508 suggests a Risk Classification Scheme (RCS) as a possible method for deriving SIRs at this level but, having already cast doubt on the validity of RCSs used traditionally in ATM, we will now outline a scheme based on that used on the SESAR Programme, which resolves most, if not all, of those doubts. The approach has one RCS dedicated to each type of accident and a hazard-severity scheme based on the success or failure of the individual stages of the Barrier Model outlined above.

The illustration shown in Table 9 is for the MAC accident type, in Terminal airspace, for which the tolerable level of risk of an accident is 1E-9 per flight hour.

Table 9 ~ Illustrative Risk Classification Scheme

Severity Class	Hazardous Situation	Operational Effect	MTFoO[41]
MAC-SC1	An aircraft comes into physical contact with another aircraft	Accident — Mid-air collision	1E-9
MAC-SC2a	An imminent collision was not mitigated by an airborne collision avoidance but for which geometry has prevented physical contact	Near Mid-air Collision	1E-6
MAC-SC2b	Airborne collision avoidance prevents near collision	Imminent Collision	1E-5
MAC-SC3	An imminent collision was prevented by ATC Collision prevention	Imminent Infringement	1E-4
MAC-SC4a	An imminent separation infringement coming from a crew/aircraft-induced conflict was prevented by tactical conflict management	Tactical Conflict (crew/aircraft induced)	1E-3

---

[41] MTFoO is the Maximum Tolerable Frequency of Occurrence per flight hour.

Severity Class	Hazardous Situation	Operational Effect	MTFoO[41]
MAC-SC4b	An imminent separation infringement coming from a planned conflict was prevented by tactical conflict management	Tactical Conflict (planned)	1E-2

The tolerable level of risk for each for each hazardous situation (except for the ultimate occurrence, of an accident) is expressed in terms of the Maximum Tolerable Frequency of occurrence of the Operational Effect (MTFoO), the values for which were obtained from the corresponding AIM model. In allocating the risk budget to each hazard in a given severity class, a pre-defined number of operational hazards was assumed for each severity class, e.g. a factor of 10 for each operational effect.

The use of the scheme then follows standard ATM safety practices, in deriving SIRs for lower-level elements of the ATM system — in this case, at the *logical* level of system design as introduced in Sub-section 3.6.2 above.

In assessing such outcomes of system failures, account must be taken of:

- any mitigations of effect that might be available and FSRs specified for any new mitigating measures. For example, "*FSR#22, Aircraft shall report loss of P-RNAV capability to ATC immediately*" could be a mitigation against an onboard failure affecting P-RNAV performance;
- the existence of possible common-cause failures that could undermine the (thus far) assumed independence of barriers, OSFs, SRSs or safety functions.

Finally, in assessing the effect of Point Merge operations on overall risk, from a system-failure perspective, this could be done one of two ways:

- *absolutely*, by considering *every* failure and calculating its risk contribution from the consequences and expected failure rate; or
- *relatively*, by comparing the risk between Point Merge and existing operations but only for any new system failures or existing failures for which the consequences had changed.

The latter approach would usually be preferred whenever the risk of *existing* operations had already been shown to be tolerable but, in either case, the overriding need is to comply with, *inter alia*, the following requirement of IEC 61508, Sub-section 7.5.2.5:

> "*If, in assessing the EUC Risk, the average frequency of dangerous failures of a single EUC control system function is claimed as being lower than 1e-5 dangerous failures per hour then the EUC Control System shall [itself also] be considered to be a safety-related control system [and] subject to the requirements of this Standard*".

4 Conclusions

This paper is the second in a series of three parts, which sets out to show what functional safety assessments for transport applications might look like if they followed the safety principles and lifecycle steps set out in IEC 61508-1 and IEC 61508-4. The first part (Fowler 2022) gave an overview of those principles and lifecycle steps, together with some transport-orientated guidance, illuminated by applying them to a simple, hypothetical example of the assessment of a proposed means of enabling pedestrians to cross a busy road safely.

The scope of that exercise was limited to the seven IEC 61508 lifecycle phases relating to the specification of safety requirements. This was because most of the key principles underpinning IEC 61508 — i.e. the universal principles set out in Parts 1 and 4 of the Standard, which govern the determination of the required risk-reducing properties of safety-related systems — take effect during these earlier phases, whereas the subsequent realisation and operating phases are less specific to the Standard.

The application, herein, of those principles to the ATM example of Point Merge operations has found that applying the subject IEC 61508 lifecycle phases directly to a typical project in the ATM sector was reasonably straightforward, and the results fitted well with the forward-looking IACO Global ATM Concept and SESAR approach to ATM safety assessment. In particular:

- treating the flow of traffic through the airspace as being the "EUC" worked very well and rightly focussed the initial stages of the safety assessment where it should always be, i.e. on the hazards that exist in the airspace, which are inherent in aviation and which the ATM system has to be shown to be able to mitigate sufficiently, in order to achieve a tolerable level of risk;
- treating the overall ATM system as the "EUC Control System" followed naturally from our interpretation of the EUC and also worked well; it provided clarity on what was, and what was not, new in relation to Point Merge, and also between safety and non-safety issues;
- above all, the early IEC 61508 lifecycle steps, followed herein, demanded that the safety functionality and performance of the ATM system in the Point Merge context be specified so as to reduce EUC risk to better than a tolerable level, when operating correctly, *before* considering what happens to EUC risk in the event of system failure.

Hence, following the principles of the specific phases of IEC 61508 provides a considerable overall benefit of ensuring a better balance in the approach to functional-safety assessment than might otherwise be the case — for which see Fowler (2015).

Acknowledgments

The authors wish to acknowledge the considerable help, support and understanding of many colleagues from EUROCONTROL and beyond, over many years, without which this paper would not have come to fruition.

The copyright holder of the quotations from published standards used for illustration in this paper is the International Electrotechnical Commission, Geneva.

References

EUROCONTROL. (2018). *Safety Assessment Methodology — Safety Case Development Manual*. EUROCONTROL, The European Organisation for the Safety of Air Navigation. Available at https://www.eurocontrol.int/tool/safety-assessment-methodology, Accessed 8th September 2022.

EUROCONTROL. (2021). *Point Merge — Improving and harmonising arrival operations*. EUROCONTROL, The European Organisation for the Safety of Air Navigation. Available at https://www.eurocontrol.int/concept/point-merge, Accessed 19th November 2022.

Fowler D, Perrin E and Pierce R. (2009). *2020 Foresight — A systems-engineering approach to assessing the safety of the SESAR Operational Concept*. Paper 446 in Proceedings of the Eighth USA/Europe Air Traffic Management Research and Development Seminar (ATM 2009), Napa, California, USA. Available at https://drive.google.com/file/d/1Tq7Qs7Reuuk9Y_4dtoV-DJNkUVPzB51t/view, Accessed 19th November 2022.

Fowler D. (2015). *Functional Safety by Design — Magic or Logic?* In Proceedings of the 23rd Safety-Critical Systems Symposium, Bristol, UK. Available at https://scsc.uk/r129/7:1. Accessed 19th June 2022.

Fowler D. (2022). *IEC 61508 Viewpoint on System Safety in the Transport Sector: Part 1 — An Overview of IEC 61508*, in Safety-Critical Systems eJournal, Vol. 1, Iss. 2. Available at https://scsc.uk/r176.3:1, Accessed 29th December 2022.

ICAO. (2005). *Global ATM Operational Concept*. The International Civil Aviation Organisation. ICAO Doc 9854, 1st edition, 2005. Available at https://www.icao.int/Meetings/anconf12/Document%20Archive/9854_cons_en[1].pdf, Accessed 19th November 2022.

ICAO. (2011). *Aviation Occurrence Categories — Definitions and Usage Notes*. ICAO, The International Civil Aviation Organization. Version 4.2, Oct 2011. Available at https://www.icao.int/APAC/Meetings/2012_APRAST/OccurrenceCategoryDefinitions.pdf, Accessed 29th December 2022.

ICAO. (2014). *Procedures for Air Navigation (Operations) — Vol II, Construction of Visual and Instrument Flight Procedures*. ICAO, The International Civil Aviation Organization. Doc 8168-2, Edition 6, 2014. Available from https://skybrary.aero/sites/default/files/bookshelf/5801.pdf, Accessed 7th September 2022.

IEC. (2010). *Functional Safety of Electrical/electronic/programmable electronic Safety-related Systems*. IEC 61508, Ed.2. International Electrotechnical Commission. Geneva.

Reason J. (2000). *Human Error: Models and Management*, British Medical Journal, BMJ 2000;320:768. Available at http://www.bmj.com/cgi/content/full/320/7237/768, Accessed 21st September 2022.

SESAR. (2018a). *Safety Reference Material*. SESAR Joint Undertaking. Edition 00.04.01, 14 Dec 2018. Available at https://www.sesarju.eu/sites/default/files/documents/transversal/SESAR2020%20Safety%20Reference%20Material%20Ed%2000_04_01_1%20(1_0).pdf, Accessed 19th November 2022.

SESAR. (2018b). *Guidance to Apply SESAR Safety Reference Material*. SESAR Joint Undertaking. Edition 00.03.01, 14 Dec 2018. Available at https://www.sesarju.eu/sites/default/files/documents/transversal/SESAR%202020%20-%20Guidance%20to%20Apply%20the%20SESAR2020%20Safety%20Reference%20Material.pdf, Accessed 19th November 2022.

SESAR. (2021). *Delivering the Digital European Sky*. SESAR Joint Undertaking. Available at https://www.sesarju.eu/sites/default/files/documents/reports/SESAR%203%20launch%20brochure.pdf, Accessed 19th November 2022.

Sparx Systems. (2022). *UML 2 Tutorial – Sequence Diagram*. Sparx Systems Pty Ltd. Available at https://sparxsystems.com/resources/tutorials/uml2/sequence-diagram.html, Accessed 29th December 2022.

Appendix A. Point Merge Functional Safety Requirements

The following table lists all Point Merge FSRs that have been derived from the analysis at 3.6 above and shows traceability back to the SRSs in Table 5.

Table 10~ Consolidated List of FSRs for SRSs

ID	Safety Requirement	Traceability
FSR#1	Vertical separation at intersections of Point Merge routes with SIDs shall be provided by aircraft conformance to appropriate published altitude restrictions	SCM-AOM
FSR#2	Vertical separation at intersections of Point Merge routes with pre-defined routes for transit flights, overflights and other arrivals shall be provided strategically by aircraft conformance to appropriate published altitude restrictions	SCM-AOM
FSR#3	Point Merge structures shall be segregated from restricted airspace	SCM-AOM
FSR#4	All P-RNAV routes (i.e. from IAF to FAF) shall be designed in accordance with ICAO PANS-OPS, (Doc 8168) Vol II	SCM-AOM
FSR#5	The required aircraft-arrival rate shall be derived in Approach airspace and fed upstream to adjacent En-route / Terminal airspace sectors as "metering" requirements based on runway capacity (arrivals and departures) and the limited ability of Approach airspace to absorb momentary traffic overloads	SCM-DCB
FSR#6	Holding points for arrivals shall be provide in an area between the IAF and Sequencing Leg entry point for use in the event that Approach airspace becomes overloaded or that the arrival flow becomes otherwise disrupted	SCM-AOM
FSR#7	Sequencing and spacing of traffic shall be established initially in En-route/ Terminal airspace sectors according to the metering requirements, and to an initial estimation of the order of aircraft in the final landing sequence, that would achieve the optimum runway throughput commensurate with the need to maintain separation minima/wake turbulence criteria and maintain the required departure flow	SCM-ASS
FSR#8	The required aircraft-departure flow rate shall be derived by airport ATC and fed upstream to adjacent En-route / Terminal sectors for synchronisation with the arrival flow requirements	SCM-DS
FSR#9	ATC shall monitor aircraft conformance with all clearances and instructions, throughout each flight, including when aircraft are following predefined P-RNAV routes and associated altitude constraints	ATC-TCM AA, ATC-TCM AG

ID	Safety Requirement	Traceability
FSR#10	Entry into Approach airspace is coordinated with the adjacent upstream sector(s) according to the agreed entry conditions, including the aircraft being stable at the defined altitude well before Sequencing Leg entry	ATC-PTCM-AA
FSR#11	Vertical separation, of at least 1,000 ft, between adjacent Sequencing Legs shall be provided, by aircraft conformance to appropriate published altitude restrictions along the entire length of the Sequencing Legs	ATC-PTCM-AA
FSR#12	Aircraft on the same Sequencing Leg shall be separated longitudinally, by ATC, by a 3 nautical mile radar-separation minimum, or the appropriate wake-turbulence separation minimum, whichever is the greater	ATC-TCM AA
FSR#13	The minimum altitude of each Sequencing Leg shall be sufficient to provide vertical clearance from terrain/obstacles along its entire length	ATC-PTCM-AG
FSR#14	An aircraft shall not be turned off the Sequencing Leg towards the Merge Point until it is spaced behind the previous aircraft, i.e. the aircraft immediately preceding it in the final sequence, sufficiently to ensure that at least minimum longitudinal separation / wake-vortex criteria will be established well before vertical / lateral separation minima are infringed as a consequence of flow convergence	ATC-TCM AA
FSR#15	As each aircraft turns off the Sequencing Leg towards the Merge Point, vertical separation shall be maintained between it and all aircraft on the adjacent sequencing leg until horizontal separation is established (and can be maintained) between them	ATC-TCM AA
FSR#16	The minimum altitude of the Merge Point shall be set such that there is no terrain/obstacle that is higher than the Merge Point anywhere in the sector of the circle defined by the Merge Point and its outermost Sequencing Leg	ATC-PTCM-AG
FSR#17	Except where instructed otherwise by ATC, the aircraft (flight crew) shall assume responsibility for maintaining safe altitude from the start of descent on the "Direct-to" leg until acquiring the ILS glidepath	AB-TCM AG
FSR#18	All non-P-RNAV aircraft shall be vectored along the Point Merge routes to emulate P-RNAV aircraft, while being provided with sufficient obstacle / terrain clearance by ATC	ATC-TCM
FSR#19	Each Point Merge route shall include a Run-off procedure so that aircraft will automatically continue to the Merge Point, on a predefined vertical profile, if no Direct-to instruction is received before reaching the end of the Sequencing Leg	ATC-PTCM-AG
FSR#20	In the event of an aircraft emergency, ATC shall move the subject aircraft forward in the sequence order, (by an early Direct-to or by radar vectoring, as appropriate) sufficiently to minimise the delay to its landing	ATC-TCM AA

ID	Safety Requirement	Traceability
FSR#21	Where it is necessary to resolve a conflict (or other urgent situation, e.g. an aircraft ACAS RA), ATC shall remove the affected aircraft from the landing sequence and reinsert upstream, i.e. later in the sequence, by radar vectoring.	ATC-TCM AA
FSR#22	Aircraft shall report loss of P-RNAV capability to ATC immediately	ATC-PTCM AA, ATC-PTCM AG

The Terminological Analysis Method SemAn and its Implementation

Peter Bernard Ladkin[1], Lou Xinxin[2], Dieter Schnäpp[3]

3. Causalis Ingenieurgesellschaft mbH, Bielefeld, Germany.
4. Causalis Ing.-GmbH. Currently at TÜV Süd, München, Germany.
5. Technische Universität Braunschweig, Institut ITL. Currently at DKE, Offenbach.

Abstract

We present the method "SemAn" for the semantic analysis of electrotechnological definitions appearing in IEC standards. SemAn is accompanied by a software tool, the SemAn Analyser, which outputs partial SemAn results in a pretty-printed and annotated format retaining the symbol-for-symbol syntax of the original definiens text. We discuss the purpose and use of this method and tool.

1 Introduction

1.1 Intellectual Background

Gottlob Frege published his *Begriffschrift* (literally, "concept-writing") in 1879 (Frege 1879); see also Wikipedia (Begriffschrift 2023). It was by no means the first attempt to render natural language into a form in which logical reasoning could be formulated and used (Aristostle's Syllogistic is perhaps the first such writing), but it has become the most successful, resulting almost immediately in what we know today as Predicate Logic, or First-Order Logic (Goldrei 2005). The use of such formal languages and logic is widespread in digital-computer science, not only in building circuits which exemplify calculations based on the "logical constants" AND, OR and NOT, but in formal languages for specifying and describing computations, as well as systems which check whether such descriptions (including high-level-language "source code") fulfil their expectations.

The ability to render natural language into formal language is taught to most university freshman philosophy students in introductory logic courses. However, rendering the semantics of most of any natural language (such as English) in a modern-logical system is far more problematic, quite apart from the doubts concerning whether such an enterprise can be at all successful (Wittgenstein 1953/1967); see also (Kripke 1982). A series of sophisticated attempts at a formal semantics for English were made by Richard Montague from 1955 to around 1970 (Montague 1974), using Higher-Order Modal Logic. Montague Semantics has subsequently been quite successfully pursued in linguistics (Janssen 2011). There are other formal semantics such as Situation Semantics (Kratzer 2007). Almost all these formal (logical) renderings refer to objects, their properties and relations between them. There is a discipline which looks at what objects the use of a natural language presumes; known as natural language ontology (Moltmann 2022). The study of ontology (rather, ontologies) is now pursued in terminological definition in computer science, and increasingly in related engineering disciplines, e.g. the SCSC Ontology Working Group (Safety-Critical Systems Club 2023).

Ontologies speak to what objects there are. Besides objects, Fregean *Begriffschrift* and its formal-logical successors speak to properties of those objects and their relations; at time of writing, properties and relations are not as well-developed interests in computer science as objects are, although they are essential for a rendering of natural language into such formal languages.

Functional requirements specifications for digital-computer-based systems may often be rendered in formal languages specially developed for the purpose, as may, rather more easily, specifications for algorithms; see, for example Lamport (2003). The purposes of this move to formality include avoiding ambiguity, as well as enabling mathematically-rigorous checking that, say, a computer program actually fulfils its functional requirements. However, in broader engineering disciplines, it is often required that functional specifications are written in natural language — indeed, that the natural-language specification is the legally-valid specification of requirements. There are thus two main reasons why it is desirable that engineering concepts in natural language be rendered more formally:

1. It ensures that engineers are using a term to refer to one and the same concept in various working environments, in particular when they are discussing technical matters; and
2. It allows legal requirements to be formulated in such a way that enables mathematically-rigorous checking that, say, a computer program written by a supplier fulfils those requirements.

Both of these are major undertakings. The first is good practice, but only the second is (recently) recognised as an engineering discipline in its own right. The importance of the former is, however, understated. Concepts such as "risk" are formally defined in electrotechnical standards — and there are many of them, some of them very different from others. Risk is a central concept for safety engineering, and there is at time of writing an Advisory Group of the International Electrotechnical Commission (IEC) attempting to arrive at a "harmonised" definition of the concept, because of the engineering problems caused by the plethora of existing definitions (IEC 2023).

More importantly, people have been jailed in England based on arguments about the meaning of electrotechnical terminology and what this implies for software-based system behaviour. The transcript of the trial of Ms. Seema Misra for fraud in the use of the Post Office Horizon system is available (Mason 2015). There is a commentary on the use of technical terminology in this and related cases (Ladkin 2020). We are happy to report that Ms. Misra was acquitted on appeal in April 2021.

We conclude it is important to get electrotechnical terminology "right". Whatever "right" may be, considering what happened to Ms. Misra, it should reflect the reality of systems and their behaviour; other desirable properties may be clarity, and non-ambiguity (absence of homonyms).

It is not our purpose here to discuss general properties of terminology further, but rather to present a technique and a software implementation of that technique that has had some encouraging application to the analysis of electrotechnical terminology defined in standards of the International Electrotechnical Commission to enhance clarity and highlight ambiguity and point, in some cases, towards resolution.

The technique is called "SemAn", and the software tool the "SemAn Analyser". SemAn is conceptually a translation of (actual) terminology definitions into a language of Sorted

First-Order Quantifier-Free Logic. Illustrations are given below of how this helps to analyse the concepts involved. The SemAn Analyser annotates the natural-language definitions through the devices of pretty-printing and annotation with the logical constants AND and OR (quite literally, "annotates" — all symbols of the original definition are retained in the exact order in which they occur); again, examples are given below.

In contrast to philosophical or (most) linguistic purposes, the point of SemAn and the SemAn Analyser is not to render the exact meaning of a natural language phrase, but to exhibit a (*not* "the") logical structure, which will show engineers more clearly what is or seems to be meant, and highlight various possibilities for improvement. Terminology work is ongoing at the IEC and the SemAn Analyser annotations have been (cautiously, in preliminary viewing) welcomed.

SemAn and the SemAn Analyser were developed on the terminology introduced in the IEC standards and standards-like documents on functional safety and cybersecurity[42]. We can confidently state that for this specific terminology corpus, which includes over 450 terms with between 60 and 70 of them multiply/variantly defined, SemAn and the SemAn Analyser render a service known to be needed and indeed "required" by the ISO/IEC Directives but (we would suggest) often absent.

1.2 Conventions Used

In this paper, we give and discuss SemAn in two ways: as a principled method, and as the output to a tool partially implementing the method, known as the SemAn Analyser. We write manual SemAn, in Sub-sections 4.3 and 4.3, in a language of sorted predicate logic. The output of the SemAn Analyser is given pretty-printed in `Courier` font. We need to distinguish the two analyses, for example a manual SemAn introduces Meaning Postulates (MPs), and the SemAn Analyser has no facility to do this. We find that distinguishing the analyses typographically is the easiest way to do so.

2 Semantic Analysis by Means of SemAn: Preliminaries

2.1 The Scope of SemAn

The term "semantic analysis" is used here as a technical term which refers to a specific way in which definitions in technical terminology may be analysed. The SemAn method has been developed specifically for electrotechnical terminology occurring in Clause 3, "Terms and Definitions", of IEC standards. Manual examples of SemAn are given first, below, to show the method. Output of the SemAn Analyser is formatted ("pretty-printed") text with annotations illustrating logical structure.

SemAn is particularly geared towards comparative analysis, in which one has syntactically-varying definitions of the same term (homonyms), or syntactically-similar definitions of different terms (quasi-synonyms). SemAn allows the similarities and divergences between the terms to be illustrated in a canonical and intuitive way. SemAn

---

[42] The original list of definitions was compiled in Project Harbsafe by Sven Müller, at the time with VDE and at time of writing with DB Systel GmbH, from IEC-61508-4 2010, IEC-62443-2-1 2010, IEC-62443-2-4 2015, IEC-62443-3-1 2009, IEC-62443-3-2 2020, IEC-62443-3-3 2013, IEC-63069 2019, ISO/IEC-51 2014, and IEC-120 2018 (IEC various dates) (ISO/IEC2014).

exhibits the logico-semantic structure of individual natural-language definitions, so it also enables individual definitions to be improved to enhance understanding.

There is no one unique resulting analysis of a definition in SemAn. One may choose different primitives (unanalysed words or phrases): in one analysis, a syntactic unit may be taken to be primitive; in another analysis, a slight divergence of that syntactic unit from another item in a related definition may require the unit be further analysed (as a compound of further primitives) so that the divergence can be exactly specified[43].

The software tool SemAn Analyser gives one output per conformant definition, illustrating the logical form of the definition while taking the individual syntactic units to be primitive. It annotates the *definiens*[44] with logical constants and punctuation and pretty-prints it, as for example in Sub-section 2.4. Further examples of SemAn Analyser output are given in Section 3.

2.2 The Formal Language of SemAn

Formal semantic analysis in the linguistics of natural language, as it is practiced today, uses formal annotation into which a target definition is parsed. So does SemAn. The language used is isomorphic to the language of first-order logic (FOL). An introduction to the language of propositional logic and FOL is to be found in Goldrei (2005). Nearly a century and a half of experience with FOL has established its pre-eminence as a system in which assertions may be made with precision, and formal inferences may be precisely codified (there are other logics, often known as higher-order or non-classical logics, depending on their type, which are useful for similar purposes in domains in which FOL is limited). The language of FOL (LFOL) consists of

- predicate symbols;
- object symbols (divided into constants, which SemAn uses, and variables, which SemAn does not use);
- functional symbols (largely not used in SemAn);
- the logical constants AND, OR (used widely in SemAn and SemAn Analyser);
- the logical constant NOT (largely not used in SemAn and SemAn Analyser, because negations are often incorporated into the terms themselves); and
- quantifiers, largely incorporated into the syntactic items themselves (as negation often is).

The meaningful syntactic units of LFOL are sentences. There are no meaningful parts of sentences, such as phrases, which are not themselves sentences. This entails that translating natural language expressions into LFOL requires expanding the expressions to conform with the phraseology of LFOL.

2.3 Translating Natural Language Phrases into the Language of SemAn

As far as is yet known, there is no generally-accepted algorithm for translating natural language sentences into LFOL in a way that preserves their meaning. However, there are some more or less standard translation rules, partly illustrated below.

---

[43] An example is given in the manual SemAn of "harm" in Sub-section 4.2 below, in which "physical injury" and "damage to the health of a person" are discussed.

[44] In linguistics and analytical philosophy, a term being defined is known as the "*definiendum*" and the definition the "*definiens*". IEC uses the words "term" and "definition", but these have wider general use than just in Clause 3 of standards. We thus prefer to use technical terms for the linguistic items appearing in such Clauses 3.

(English) *John or Joan opened the front door*

First, the phrase in subject position, *John or Joan*, has no equivalent in LFOL. In LFOL, OR may only be used to conjoin sentences. Second, there are no syntactic elements corresponding to phrases in LFOL, only sentences and their component symbols. Third, the sentence intuitively speaks to one of two situations; one in which John opened the front door, and another in which Joan opened the front door (as well as a third in which they both did, but presumably not simultaneously). These observations may be used to convert the English sentence into one conforming to LFOL with the same intuitive meaning, namely:

(LFOL) *John opened the front door OR Joan opened the front door*

In English, phrases in subject position or object position can also be lists, with one constant (usually separating the last two list words) and separated by commas, as in

(English) *John, Joan or Jeremiah opened the front door*

Similar principles apply here as above, and we obtain the translation

(LFOL) *John opened the front door OR Joan opened the front door OR Jeremiah opened the front door*

A further step is that of constructing synonyms for predicates. In this example, three different people seem to have engaged in the same action, *"opened the front door"*. In LFOL, the following action can be performed. A simpler symbol may be used to stand for the verb phrase *"opened the front door"*. Second, whereas in English the subject (the person who opened the door) is typically written first and the predicate (the action) follows, with no punctuation, as in *John opened the front door*, in LFOL the assertion is expressed in a symbolic form akin to that of the elementary mathematics of functions: the argument (whoever did the opening) is expressed in parentheses after the predicate, as in *opened-the-front-door(John)* (here, hyphens are used to indicate that the predicate is denoted by a string of words rather than a single word). When symbol P is chosen to represent *opened the front door*, then this becomes syntactically easier to read.

(LFOL) Let the symbol *P* stand for the predicate *"opened the front door"*. Then the assertion becomes:

P(John) OR P(Joan) OR P(Jeremiah)

SemAn uses such a natural-language version of LFOL as has been illustrated above. By experience, the illustrated translations seem to cover the routine majority of the task of translation. This language will become clearer when examples are discussed below.

3 The SemAn Analyser

3.1 *Modus Operandi*

The SemAn Analyser, in contrast to (manual) SemAn, does not use LFOL at all. It parses, annotates and pretty-prints the words and punctuation in the definition itself, in the order in which they occur. A manual translation from SemAn Analyser output into LFOL is intended to be straightforward. If a translation is not straightforward, this serves as an indication that the original definition proposed may be deficient; unclear, say. The recommended remedy is to modify the source definition so that the translation of SemAn Analyser output into LFOL becomes straightforward.

The SemAn Analyser:

- Takes all English words as primitive formal symbols
- Exhibits the logical structure of phrases by means of annotations using the logical constants (AND, OR, more rarely NOT) and marked indents

3.2 Implementation

The SemAn Analyser uses Dependency Parsing (Jurafsky and Martin 2020). It is programmed using the Dependency-Parsing suite spaCy (ExplosionAI n.d.). The programming is largely due to the second author, with help from the third author. All authors were continually involved in the evolution of the output specification.

3.3 A Simple Example

Consider the two following definitions of "signal". These are not original IEC terminology, but are "cleaned up" from existing definitions. The *definiendum* is given in bold-face font on a line by itself. The *definiens* follows on the next line, optionally prefixed by an "area of application" given in angle brackets. Here, the areas of application are "electrical", respectively "information".

signal
<electrical> electrical impulse controlled or observed by a test resource

signal
<information> visual, audible, or other indication used to convey information

The annotated versions would ideally be[45]:

```
signal:
<electrical> electrical impulse controlled or observed by a test
resource
\\
electrical impulse
                    > [OR] controlled
                    > [OR] or observed
                              > by a test resource
signal:
<information> visual, audible, or other indication used to convey
information
\\
     > [OR] visual
     > [OR] , audible
     > [OR] , or other indication
                    > used to convey information
```

SemAn Analyser thus exhibits the first as a sort, *electrical impulse*, with one of two relations to a *test resource*, that of being *controlled* or that of being *observed*. The second definition is a disjunction: the qualifier of all three disjuncts is that they are *used to convey information*, and the information conveyer may be *visual* or *audible* or an *other indication*.

---

[45] It has been suggested that there might be an alternative reading. This may well be. One of the purposes of SemAn Analyser output is to make clear such possibilities. SemAn Analyser output is dependent upon a non-deterministic parser, so such possibilities can be expected to arise simply from the parsing operation itself.

In this case, with simple and short definitions which have no key terms in common, a comparison of the two *definiens* shows that they are clearly distinct concepts.

Note: the above SemAn renderings are manual. The current implementation of the SemAn Analyser does not in fact output these annotations, although we wish it did — it renders both definitions without the annotations shown here. However, the examples of *application*, *harm* and *asset*, following, are indeed output by the current implementation of SemAn Analyser.

3.4 "Application"

An example which intuitively illustrates the benefits of logical annotation in more complex definitions is that of *application*, defined as

```
software program that performs specific functions initiated
by a user command or a process event and that can be
executed without access to system control, monitoring, or
administrative privileges
```

Parsed, this becomes:
```
\\
     software program
           > [AND] that performs specific functions
                       > initiated by a | [OR] user command
                                        | [OR] or a process event
           > [AND] and that can be executed without access
                       > to | [OR] system control
                            | [OR] , monitoring
                            | [OR] , or administrative privileges
```

This shows the clear logical structure that:

- this is a software program (defines the *sort*, the type of object which is being talked about);
- that this program has two properties:
  o of performing specific functions …
  o of executing without access to …
- and that these properties have further logical details.

3.5 "Harm"

The annotated/pretty-printed output of the SemAn Analyser invoked on the term *harm* is as follows::
```
67.
harm:
physical injury or damage to the health of people or damage to
property or the environment
\\
     [OR] physical injury
     [OR] or damage
              > [OR] to the health
                          > of people
              > [OR] to property
              > [OR] or the environment
[Source: IEC 61508-4:2010]
```

It can be seen that the SemAn Analyser takes the definiens as syntactically given and marks it up. It treats *physical injury* as a primitive. Below (Sub-section 4.2), a manual SemAn does not take this phrase as primitive, but invokes *Meaning Postulates*, which allow *physical injury* to be compared with *damage to the health of people* in order to determine if the definition can be expressed more succinctly and clearly (answer: yes).

It follows that the output of the SemAn Analyser is not a full SemAn, but a preliminary processing of the definition that exhibits certain formal features of the definition, enabling improvements to be made where they are appropriate, and which enables a human analyst to continue the SemAn if desired; for example by considering the meaning of *physical injury* and relating it to *damage to the health of people*. It is also clear from the example of *signal* that the current implementation of the SemAn Analyser does not quite yet do all we wish to expect of it.

4 Examples of SemAn Analyser Output and of SemAn

4.1 Output of SemAn Analyser on *asset*

There are two non-identical definitions of *asset* in the IEC 62443 series of standards. Both are considered below, in order to illustrate the harmonisation task, and to show how much easier it is made by using the SemAn Analyser.

SemAn Analyser output on the two definitions of asset is:
```
10.
asset:
physical or logical object owned by or under the custodial duties
of an organization, having either a perceived or actual value to
the organization
\\
        physical or logical object
            > [AND] owned by or under the custodial duties
                    > of an organization
            > [AND] , having either a perceived or actual value
                    > to the organization
[Source: IEC 62443-2-1:2010]
[Source: IEC TS 62443-1-1:2009]

11.
asset:
physical or logical object having either a perceived or actual
value to the IACS
\\
        physical or logical object
            > having either a perceived or actual value
                > to the IACS
[Source: IEC 62443-3-3:2013]
```

This annotated parsing/pretty-printing immediately shows a number of similarities and differences in the two definitions. First, an *asset* is a *physical or logical object*[46]. Second, it *[has] a perceived or actual value*. To whom the value accrues is different in the two cases (some implicit *organisation* in the first, presumably a human organisation such as a company; in the second, a system, namely the *IACS* (Industrial Automation and Control System)). Similarly, the first definition mentions custodial duties associated with the asset; the second mentions no such duties.

This comparison gives clear indications of difference, and therefore the scope of discussion, to domain experts attempted to harmonise the two definitions. The harmonisation task here is twofold:

- To whom/what does the *value* of the *asset* accrue?
- Is the ownership/custody of the asset a key property? Is it implicit, or does it need to be explicit?

4.2 Example: A Manual SemAn of *harm*

1. harm IEC 61508-4 subclause 3.2.1 and IEC Guide 120 subclause 3.7 :

physical injury or damage to the health of people or damage to property or the environment

SemAn goes further than the SemAn Analyser, using domain knowledge about the concepts (words and phrases) occurring in the definition (recall that the SemAn Analyser takes these as primitive). Invoking domain knowledge results in a meaning postulate. Because the result analysis has used the meaning postulates, they are restated along with the result of the SemAn.

First is to fill this definition out by "expanding conflations", as follows.

- Expand syntactic conflation: "OR" is used to conjoin two noun phrases. The SemAn Analyser has identified two "levels" of conjoined phrase:
  o associated with *physical injury*
  o associated with *damage*

  A first step is thus to expand. The *damage* is associated with the same qualifying phrase, namely

  to the health of people OR to property OR to the environment

  There are two ways this qualifying phrase can be treated:
  o Parentheses can be used to make a unit out of this phrase:
    (to the health of people OR to property OR to the environment)
  o An auxiliary definition can be used:
    Let *P* stand for *to the health of people OR to property OR to the environment*

- The resulting phrase is:

  physical injury (to the health of people OR to property OR to the environment)
  OR
  damage (to the health of people OR to property OR to the environment)

---

[46] An "or" occurring in an input phrase, as here, is simply a syntactic token. The "OR" outputted as annotation by the SemAn Analyser is intended to be the logical constant OR. The SemAn Analyser at present has no mechanism for recognising syntactic tokens representing logical constants in the input and manipulating its output accordingly.

Alternatively

P(physical injury) OR P(damage)

The second alternative is obviously of no help whatever in further analysis. The first alternative is used to proceed.

- Consider next the first conjunct:

physical injury (to the health of people OR to property OR to the environment)

The ORs can be expanded further:

physical injury to the health of people
OR
physical injury to property
OR
physical injury to the environment

Semantic domain knowledge is invoked: (Meaning Postulate MP1) only people or sentient beings can be physically injured, not property or the environment. According to (MP1), then, this may be further reduced:

physical injury to the health of people

Using further domain knowledge, we note that physical injury to the health is redundant:

physical injury to people

- Consider the second conjunct:

damage (to the health of people OR to property OR to the environment)

Again, this expands to:

damage to the health of people
OR
damage to property
OR
damage to the environment

- Conjoining the two expanded/reduced phrases gives

physical injury to people
OR
(damage to the health of people
OR
damage to property
OR
damage to the environment)

Note that logical OR is associative: *A OR (B OR C)* is the same as *(A OR B) OR C*, and thus either may be written unambiguously without parentheses: *A OR B OR C* (Goldrei 2005). So this can be written:

physical injury to people
OR
damage to the health of people
OR
damage to property

OR
damage to the environment

- *Physical injury* is a term which contains *injury*, and (Meaning Postulate MP2, obviously related to MP1) injury can only occur to sentient beings. The term *people* is used; (domain knowledge) *people* is a plural of *person*, as is *persons*. The question arises if *harm* can be caused to one *person*, or must it always be more than one (plural)? Singular or plural? (Meaning Postulate from domain knowledge MP3) Harm to one person is still harm. The issue could be clarified by rewriting *people* as *one or more persons*

  physical injury to one or more persons
  OR
  damage to the health of one or more persons
  OR
  damage to property
  OR
  damage to the environment

- The first two conjoined clauses have as part *one or more persons*. Furthermore, they are semantically related: (MP4) *Physical injury* is *damage to the health* of (a person or persons). But is all *damage to the health* also *physical injury*? No, there can be damage to health that is predominantly psychiatric: post-traumatic stress syndrome for example. So (MP5) *damage to the health* includes *physical injury* but not vice versa. Put in terms of logic,

  physical injury to one or more persons
  IMPLIES
  damage to the health of one or more persons

  but not vice versa. It follows that the first clause can be omitted without semantic loss. However, an analyst might wish to retain it as a means of emphasis[47].

- Result:

  damage to the health of one or more persons
  OR
  damage to property
  OR
  damage to the environment

  Alternatively,

  physical injury to one or more persons
  OR
  other damage to the health of one or more persons
  OR
  damage to property
  OR
  damage to the environment

---

[47] There are circumstances in which additional words are logically unnecessary, but help to ensure understanding, and that it is ideally part of an analyst's skillset to recognise such cases.

- Finally, these could be consolidated, by regrouping according to English conventions, for example:

  physical injury or other damage to the health of one or more persons
  OR
  damage to property or to the environment

  Alternatively,

  damage to the health of one or more persons, or to property, or to the environment

- The second definition can now be considered.

  2. harm IEC Guide 51 subclause 3.1:

  injury or damage to the health of people, or damage to property or the environment

- Comparing with the analysis of IEC 61508-4 subclause 3.2.1 above, it is clear that
  - the analysis can proceed largely as before;
  - (MP6) *damage to the health* can be considered equivalent to *injury*

- Result:

  damage to the health of people, or damage to property or the environment

  Equivalently

  injury to people, or damage to property or the environment

Given that people and one or more persons are synonyms, as are injury to and damage to the health of, it follows that, under MP1 … MP6, the two definitions are synonymous. The results may be expressed as follows:

- Under meaning postulates[48]

  (MP1) only people or sentient beings can be *physically injured*, not property or the environment;

  (MP2) *injury* can only occur to sentient beings;

  (MP3) *harm* to one *person* is still *harm*;

  (MP4) *Physical injury* is *damage to the health* of (a person or persons);

  (MP5) *damage to the health* includes *physical injury* but not vice versa; and

  (MP6) *damage to the health* can be considered equivalent to *injury*,

  the two definitions are synonymous and equivalent to:
  physical injury or other damage to the health of one or more persons, or damage to property or to the environment
  damage to the health of one or more persons, or to property, or to the environment
  injury to people, or damage to property or the environment

- It follows that there is a harmonisation task, but one which is in this case purely syntactic: an analyst must choose between the three example definitions above (or ones

---

[48] Note these MPs are specific to the SemAn of "*harm*". This article does not address the appropriate formulation of MPs across multiple definitions and resolution of possible conflicts. We are not so far along.

in which synonymic phrases are used, such as *people* instead of *one or more persons* or vice versa).

This analysis is laborious, and the result relatively easily foreseeable from the start, but the purpose is to illustrate the principles and steps involved in a manual SemAn, including the formulation of MPs and this is shown more easily on such straightforward examples[49].

4.3 SemAn Example: *asset*

1. asset, IEC 62443-1-1 subclause 3.2.6 and IEC 62443-2-1 subclause 3.1.3

physical or logical object owned by or under the custodial duties of an organization, having either a perceived or actual value to the organization

The SemAn proceeds with similar steps to that of *harm* in Sub-section 4.2. The steps are not elaborated here in as much detail. However, the SemAn itself is more complex.

- Expand: An *asset* is a *physical object OR a logical object <with additional properties>*. The adjectives here are (Meaning Postulate MP1) applicative, so an *asset* is an object. It is left unexplained exactly what a logical object is. (One might speculate that a *metaphysical object* is meant, but most engineers do not use that term.) Introduce the primitive *Ob* to denote the thing of sort Obj which is being talked about. The mathematics-type notation typical of formal logic is used: *P(Ob)* says *Ob is physical*, whereas *L(Ob)* says *Ob is logical*. For objecthood, then, the term *Ob* of sort Obj has been introduced and yields the assertion *P(Ob) OR L(Ob)*.
- Fill out *<additional properties>*: another OR syntactic conflation is expanded.

owned by an organisation OR under the custodial duties of an organisation.

There is another sort here, *organisation*. Whereas for *Ob*, a specific *asset* is meant, the organisation is unspecified: (MP2) *some organisation* is meant. The term *some* is a quantifier and in logic, one would be tempted to quantify: *"there is an organisation Org such that ..."*. But, for a given *asset*, it can be assumed that (Meaning Postulate MP3) there is just one organisation that owns it or just one organisation that has custody of it. Note that this meaning postulate is not like the ones involved in the analysis of *harm*; it involves rather an assumption about the way of the world; that if there are multiple owners or custodians, just one can be singled out to be *Org* for the purposes of the definition. So, for *Ob*, there is a single *Org* of sort *Organisation* (let us say *Orgn*) which either *Owns* it or *HasCustody* of it:

Owns(Ob,Org) OR HasCustody(Ob,Org).

- Fill out ",": there is a list of properties here, starting with *owned by ... OR under the custodial duties of ...* and then *having ...* . It is clear that *AND* is meant by the comma.
- Fill out further. Result: *(Ob has a perceived value to Org) OR (Ob has an actual value to Org)*. Choose primitives *PV* and *AV* for the predicates *has a perceived value to* and *has an actual value to*. The result is *PV(Ob,Org) OR AV (Ob,Org)*.
- Result: it seems the analysis has arrived at the following, in formal form:

P(Ob) OR L(Ob) AND Owns(Ob,Org) OR HasCustody(Ob,Org) AND PV(Ob,Org) OR AV (Ob,Org)

---

[49] There might be disputes concerning the MPs, and such disputes could be problematic in, say, courts of law. The result given here follows from the MPs given. We construe the SemAn task here as identifying the need for, and formulating, MPs. The validity of MPs so formulated may indeed be doubted, but resolution of such doubts we see as a task more appropriate for the accompanying, more philosophic-analytic, technique ConcAn (Ladkin 2022).

However, there is an AND..OR ambiguity which needs to be disambiguated. AND..OR ambiguities arise because *A AND (B OR C)* does not have the same meaning *as (A AND B) OR C* and when there are no parentheses, as in *A AND B OR C*, one cannot tell which is meant. To disambiguate, parentheses are used:

(P(Ob) OR L(Ob)) AND (Owns(Ob,Org) OR HasCustody(Ob,Org)) AND (PV(Ob,Org) OR AV (Ob,Org))

- Rewriting the result: This formula looks "formal" and is typical for the indication of the logical structure of phrases and sentences/assertions. But it is hard to read. There are some ways to make such formulas easier to read, for example the vertical stacking of clauses, as in TLA$^+$ (Lamport 2003)[50]. In the TLA$^+$ "pretty-printing" style, all clauses in a conjunction are preceded by the conjunction sign and stacked vertically, *mutatis mutandis* for disjunction. Indentation allows the elimination of the parentheses used for disambiguation:

&& P(Ob) OR L(Ob)
&& Owns(Ob,Org) OR HasCustody(Ob,Org)
&& PV(Ob,Org) OR AV (Ob,Org)

The OR clauses within the conjuncts can be similarly formatted if so wished (the symbol ∨ is used to denote OR), to yield:

&& ∨ P(Ob)
   ∨ L(Ob)
&& ∨ Owns(Ob,Org)
   ∨ HasCustody(Ob,Org)
&& ∨ PV(Ob,Org)
   ∨ AV (Ob,Org)

but there seems to be little point to doing so here. It is up to the analyst to decide which is most helpful. The sorts of *Ob* and *Org* have been so far left implicit, but there might be circumstances in which one needs to reason with them taken into account (see below). When introduced, the formal sentence in the language of sorted logic looks like:

&& Obj(Ob)
&& Orgn(Org)
&& P(Ob) OR L(Ob)
&& Owns(Ob,Org) OR HasCustody(Ob,Org)
&& PV(Ob,Org) OR AV(Ob,Org)

Consider now the second definition of asset.

2. asset IEC 62443-3-3 subclause 3.1.1
physical or logical object having either a perceived or actual value to the IACS

- Fill it out: The first observation is that too much was done with the first definition. The predicate *physical* need not have been separated from the predicate *logical*: instead of *P(Ob) OR L(Ob)* we could have used one predicate *PorL(Ob)*. But no matter; it was done, and will be left so.
- Fill it out: again, *perceived value OR actual value*, but the subject of the valuation has changed. Now, it is not an *organisation* (a group of people) but is an engineering object, a system, namely the Industrial Automation and Control System — IACS — to

---

[50] TLA = Temporal Logic of Actions

which the IEC 62443 series is specifically targeted. Here, (Meaning Postulate MP3) there is no possible ambiguity as to which IACS is meant: it is the one to which this standard is currently being applied. A sort *IACS* is introduced along with a primitive *theIACS* for an object of this sort.

- Result:

&& Obj(Ob)
&& IACS(theIACS)
&& P(Ob) OR L(Ob)
&& PV(Ob,theIACS) OR AV(Ob,theIACS)

There are now two analysed definitions of *asset*, which are not identical. The term *asset* is thus a homonym. The task of harmonisation is to select one of these as the primary definition. There are most often two ways in which this may be done. First, definitions may be specialised to domains of application, as illustrated in Sub-section 3.3. So, for example, *signal* means one thing in railway control, and another thing in wire-transmitted telecommunications, leading to two definitions, one for *signal (railways)* and a different one for *signal (telecommunications)*. The specialisations in electrotechnical terminology usually follow the designations of the IEC Technical Committees (TC 9 is Electrical equipment and systems for railways); there are many Technical Committees which could (and do) use a telecommunications notion (in fact, signal has many definitions; see Sub-section 3.3). The second way is by reconciling the two different definitions into one. Considerations towards the second path are illustrated here.

- Much of both definitions is the same, but some of it is definitively different. The IACS in question is uniquely determined: it is whichever system the IEC 62443 series of standard is applied to in the instance of its application. The organisation involved (according to the first definition) might also be unique, but it could be that many organisations are involved in the joint ownership or custodianship of an asset. Is an IACS, as a nonsentient physical object, an object of which it might make any sense at all to speak of as having values? Or is the valuer an implicit organisation which is considering *Ob* and *theIACS* together, to determine whether there is a perceived or actual "value" (causal influence?) of the one on the other? Say, *PV(Ob,theIACS,Org) OR AV(Ob,theIACS,Org)*. The SemAn analyst cannot decide such matters; the domain specialists writing the standard must do so.

4.4 Output of SemAn Analyser on *asset*

There are two non-identical definitions of asset in the IEC 62443 series of standards. Here is the output of the SemAn Analyser on both:

```
10.
asset:

physical or logical object owned by or under the custodial duties of
an organization, having either a perceived or actual value to the
organization

\\
      physical or logical object
           > [AND] owned by or under the custodial duties
                   > of an organization
           > [AND] , having either a perceived or actual value
                   > to the organization
```

```
[Source: IEC 62443-2-1:2010]
[Source: IEC TS 62443-1-1:2009]

11.
asset:

physical or logical object having either a perceived or actual value
to the IACS

\\
    physical or logical object
        > having either a perceived or actual value
            > to the IACS
[Source: IEC 62443-3-3:2013]
```

This annotated parsing/pretty-printing shows immediately and clearly the similarities and differences immediately which we have recognised in the more laborious manual SemAn. Namely, first, an *asset* is a *physical or logical object*; and, second, this object *[has] a perceived or actual value*. To whom the value accrues is clearly different in the two cases. Further, one definition mentions custodial duties associated with the asset; the other does not. This comparison gives clear indications of the differences seen during the manual SemAn, and leads to the same scope of discussion for domain experts attempting to harmonise the two definitions as did the manual analysis.

5 Conclusions

We have argued, briefly, that getting electrotechnical terminology "right" is an important task, for many reasons (not least, that using it properly may help keep some innocent people out of jail!). Logical annotation seems to us to be a helpful method of doing so, and we have explicated here a method of logical analysis, SemAn, and an annotator, the SemAn Analyser, which annotates according to SemAn but without (as yet) using Meaning Postulates.

We have endeavoured to show by example that such analyses are useful in identifying similarities and distinctions in definitions which are ripe for clarification. Meaning Postulates can help, but skill is involved in the formulation of the Meaning Postulates and we don't see at present how this process may be automated.

Experience has shown that use of the SemAn Analyser eases the task of performing a SemAn, as it clearly did in the case of *asset* in Sub-sections 4.3 and 4.4. In the case of *harm*, Sub-section 4.2 showed that there were many Meaning Postulates that played a role in eliminating/reducing some of the terms occurring in the definition, which the SemAn Analyser treats as primitive. So here the manual SemAn achieved results which the SemAn Analyser could not obtain. (Also, we observed in Sub-section 3.3 that the current implementation of the SemAn Analyser does not quite do all we wish it to do.) Third parties involved in terminology work have indicated to us that they find it helpful.

Correspondence Address

The Corresponding Author is Peter Bernard Ladkin, Causalis Ing.-GmbH, Bielefeld, Germany; e-mail: Ladkin@causalis.com.

Acknowledgments

The SemAn method was developed by the first author in the project Harbsafe, financed by (as it then was) the German Federal Ministry for Economic Affairs and Energy, No. 03TNG006A-B in the Wipano programme, awarded to the Technical University of Braunschweig (TU-BS), Institut IVA, and DKE (the Deutsche Kommission Elektrotechnik Elektronik Informationstechnik im DIN und VDE), which is a German electrotechnical standardisation organisation, in 2017—2019.

The SemAn Analyser was developed by Causalis Ingenieurgesellschaft mbH as subcontractor to TU-BS, Institut IVA (then to become Institut IITL) in the project Harbsafe II, Nos. 03TN0018A-C, granted to TU-BS, DKE and INOSOFT AG, financed by the German Federal Ministry for Economic Affairs and Climate Action, in 2020—2022, also in the Wipano programme.

References

Begriffschrift. (2023). In *Wikipedia*. https://en.wikipedia.org/wiki/Begriffsschrift. Accessed 13th January 2023.

ExplosionAI. (n.d.). spaCy DependencyParser. https://spacy.io/api/dependencyparser. Accessed 13th January 2023.

Frege G. (1879). *Begriffsschrift: eine der arithmetischen nachgebildete Formelsprache des reinen Denkens*. Halle an der Saale: Verlag von Louis Nebert.

Goldrei D. (2005). *Proposition and Predicate Calculus: A Model of Argument*. Springer-Verlag, London.

IEC. (2023). *Standards Management Board – Joint Task Force on the Concept of Risk and Associated Terms*. International Electrotechnical Commission. Overview available from https://www.iec.ch/dyn/www/f?p=103:85:702664603091386::::FSP_ORG_ID,FSP_LANG_ID:28611,25. Accessed 13th January 2023.

IEC 61508-4:2010. *Functional Safety of Electrical/electronic/programmable electronic Safety-related Systems– Part 4: Definitions and abbreviations*. IEC 61508-4, Edition 2. International Electrotechnical Commission. Geneva. 2010.

IEC TS 62443-1-1:2009. *Industrial communication networks – Network and system security – Part 1-1: Terminology, concepts and models*. IEC TS 62443-1-1, Edition 1. International Electrotechnical Commission. Geneva. 2009.

IEC 62443-2-1:2010. *Industrial communication networks – Network and system security – Part 2-1: Establishing an industrial automation and control system security program*. IEC 62443-2-1, Edition 1. International Electrotechnical Commission. Geneva. 2010

IEC 62443-2-4:2015+AMD1:2017. *Security for industrial automation and control systems - Part 2-4: Security program requirements for IACS service providers*. IEC 62443-2-4, Edition 1.1. International Electrotechnical Commission. Geneva. 2017.

IEC 62443-3-1:2009. *Industrial communication networks - Network and system security - Part 3-1: Security technologies for industrial automation and control systems*. IEC 62443-3-1, Edition 1. International Electrotechnical Commission. Geneva. 2009.

IEC 62443-3-2:2020. *Security for industrial automation and control systems - Part 3-2: Security risk assessment for system design*. IEC 62443-3-2, Edition 1. International Electrotechnical Commission. Geneva. 2020.

IEC 62443-3-3:2013. *Industrial communication networks – Network and system security – Part 3-3: System security requirements and security levels*. IEC 62443-3-3, Edition 1.0. International Electrotechnical Commission. Geneva. 2013.

IEC TR 63069:2019. *Industrial-process measurement, control and automation - Framework for functional safety and security*. IEC TR 63069, Edition 1. International Electrotechnical Commission. Geneva. 2019.

IEC Guide 120. *Security aspects - Guidelines for their inclusion in publications*. IEC Guide 120, Edition 1. International Electrotechnical Commission. Geneva. 2018

ISO/IEC Guide 51. *Safety aspects – Guidelines for their inclusion in standards*. ISO/IEC Guide 51, Edition 3. International Organization for Standardization and International Electrotechnical Commission. Geneva. 2014.

Janssen T. M. V. (2011). *Montague Semantics*. In Stanford Encyclopedia of Philosophy. 2011, revised 2021. Available from https://plato.stanford.edu/entries/montague-semantics/. Accessed 13th January 2023.

Jurafsky D, and Martin J. H. (2023). *Speech and Natural Language Processing, Chapter 14: Dependency Parsing*. Preprint draft of January 7, 2023. Available from https://web.stanford.edu/~jurafsky/slp3/14.pdf. Accessed 13th January 2023.

Ladkin P. B. (2020). *Robustness of Software*. In Digital Evidence and Electronic Signature Law Review, Vol. 17. Available from https://journals.sas.ac.uk/deeslr/article/view/5171. Accessed 13th January 2023.

Ladkin P. B. (2022). *Some Principles of Conceptual Analysis for Electrotechnical Terminology (ConcAn)*. Submitted for publication, 2022. {**Editor's Note:** It is hoped that this paper can be published in Volume 2, Issue 2, of this Journal}

Lamport L. (2003). *Specifying Systems: The TLA$^+$ Language and Tools for Hardware and Software Engineers*. Addison-Wesley

Kratzer A. (2007). *Situations in Natural Language Semantics*. In Stanford Encyclopedia of Philosophy. 2007, revised 2021. Available from https://plato.stanford.edu/entries/situations-semantics/. Accessed 13th January 2023.

Kripke S. A. (1982). *Wittgenstein on Rules and Private Language: An Elementary Exposition*. Wiley Blackwell

Mason S. (2015). *Case Transcript: England & Wales - Regina v Seema Misra, T20090070 - Commentary and Index to the transcript by Stephen Mason*. In Digital Evidence and Electronic Signature Law Review, Vol. 12. Available from https://journals.sas.ac.uk/deeslr/issue/view/328. . Accessed 13th January 2023.

Moltmann F. (2022). *Natural Language Ontology*. In Stanford Encyclopedia of Philosophy. Available from https://plato.stanford.edu/entries/natural-language-ontology/. Accessed 13th January 2023.

Montague R. (1974). *Formal Philosophy: Selected Papers of Richard Montague* (Ed. H. Richmond H. Thomason). Yale University Press 1974.

Safety-Critical Systems Club. (2023). *SCSC — Group: Ontology Working Group*. https://scsc.uk/go. Accessed 13th January 2023.

Wittgenstein L. (1967). *Philosophical Investigations* (G. E. M. Anscombe, Trans.). Basil Blackwell, Third Edition. (Original work written 1953).

Appendix A.   Multiply-Defined Concepts: Diff. Notes

A.1   Introduction

This document presents a list of concepts in the IEC functional safety and cybersecurity standards listed in the main body of the paper. Amongst the 450+ concepts defined in those documents; these are the concepts which have multiple definitions.

The list of multiply-defined concepts was developed in 2018 in Project Harbsafe (see the Acknowledgments section above), and has been reformatted for this paper.

A.2   Summary

Identical definitions	22
Minor difference (including syntactic)	11
Moderate difference	7
Substantial difference	21
Unknown (one is reference)	2
Total	63

Notes to Summary

- where there are different classes of difference within the definitions of one term, the highest difference category is assigned to the term
- "*availability*" occurs in two syntactic variants, counted here as one
- "*authenticate/authentication*" occurs as verb and noun, counted as one
- "*configuration baseline*" only occurs once — an error in the MultDefConcepts list
- there are five different versions of "*integrity*", counted as one
- "*non-repudiation*" is spelled multiple ways, counted as one
- "*risk tolerance*" and "*risk tolerance level*" are counted as one…

A.3   List of Multiply-defined Concepts

Table 11 ~ List of Multiply-defined Concepts

Concept	Sources	Remarks
access control	IEC 62443-1-1 IEC 62443-3-1	minor difference labelled enumeration (-3-1), or not

Concept	Sources	Remarks
accountability	IEC Guide 120 IEC 62443-1-1 IEC 62443-3-1	identical
application	IEC 61508-4 IEC 62443-1-1	substantial difference IEC 61508-4: referring to system: EUC IEC 62443-1-1: specialist meaning for SW
asset	IEC 62443-1-1 IEC 62443-2-1 IEC 62443-3-3	Identical includes ownership/custody and subject (organisation) moderate difference no ownership; subject IACS
asset owner	IEC 62443-2-4+AMD IEC 62443-3-3	moderate difference IEC 62443-2-4+AMD: subject: organization IEC 62443-3-3: subject: company
attack	IEC 62443-1-1 IEC Guide 120 IEC 62443-3-3	identical definition + paraphrase (in "i.e." clause) minor difference definition only, no paraphrase
authenticate	IEC 62443-1-1	difference from noun verb: concrete action: verify
authentication	IEC Guide 120 IEC 62443-1-1 IEC 62443-3-1 IEC 62443-3-3	identical noun: measure designed to verify (different objects) substantial difference noun: abstractly formulated action: assurance
authorization	IEC Guide 120 IEC 62443-1-1 IEC 62443-3-1	identical
availability	IEC Guide 120 IEC62443-3-3 IEC 62443-3-1	moderate difference no subject of property substantial difference probability, circumscribed in time, qualified
availability (performance)	IEC 62443-1-1	substantial difference that of which the probability (above) is assessed

Concept	Sources	Remarks
channel	IEC 61508-4 IEC 62443-1-1	substantial difference IEC 61508-4: independent implementation of safety function IEC 62443-1-1: link in a conduit
ciphertext	IEC 62443-1-1 IEC 62443-3-1	minor (syntactic) difference
client	IEC 62443-1-1 IEC 62443-3-1	identical
conduit	IEC 62443-1-1 IEC 62443-3-3	moderate difference IEC 62443-1-1: for channels, common secreqs IEC 62443-3-3: for assets, protection
confidentiality	IEC 62443-1-1 IEC 62443-3-1 IEC Guide 120 IEC 62443-3-3	identical moderate difference essentially semantically equivalent, negative formulation substantial difference positive formulation as restrictions
configuration baseline	IEC 61508-4	only defined once
consequence	IEC 62443-2-1 IEC 62443-3-3	substantial difference IEC 62443-2-1: abstract, subject "incident" IEC 62443-3-3: condition or state, subject "event"
control system	IEC 62443-2-4+AMD IEC 62443-3-3	substantial difference IEC 62443-2-4+AMD: also that "used in design" IEC 62443-3-3: HW & SW of an IACS
countermeasure	IEC 62443-1-1 IEC 62443-3-3	identical
decryption	IEC 62443-1-1 IEC 62443-3-1	identical
defence in depth	IEC 62443-1-1 IEC 62443-3-1	substantial difference IEC 62443-1-1: usual: layers IEC 62443-3-1: architecture, abstract

Concept	Sources	Remarks
demilitarized zone	IEC 62443-1-1 IEC 62443-3-3	substantial difference IEC 62443-1-1: usual internal vs. external IEC 62433-3-3: generalised: between zones (ambiguity "zone")
denial of service	IEC 62443-1-1 IEC 62443-3-1	identical
digital signature	IEC 62443-1-1 IEC 62443-3-1	identical
encryption	IEC 62443-1-1 IEC 62443-3-1	identical
environment	IEC 61508-4 IEC 62443-3-3	substantial difference IEC 61508-4: abstract: parameters IEC 62443-3-3: surrounding entities & circumstances
equipment under control	IEC 61508-4 IEC 62443-1-1	identical
harm	IEC Guide 120 ISO/IEC Guide 51 IEC 61508-4	identical minor difference
hazard	IEC 61508-4 ISO/IEC Guide 51	identical
hazardous event	IEC 61508-4 ISO/IEC Guide 51	minor difference semantically equivalent
hazardous situation	IEC 61508-4 ISO/IEC Guide 51	identical
incident	IEC 62443-2-1 IEC 62443-3-3	minor difference punctuation
industrial automation and control system	IEC 62443-1-1 IEC 62443-2-4+AMD IEC 62443-3-3	moderate differences all collections … that … IEC62443-1-1: of personnel, HW, SW IEC 62443-3-3: of personnel, HW, SW, policies IEC 62443-2-4+AMD: of personnel, HW, SW, policies, procedures

Concept	Sources	Remarks
integrity	IEC 62443-1-1 IEC 62443-3-1	identical
	IEC 62443-3-3 IEC Guide 120	moderate differences (changed to substantial) various concepts of "integrity" dealt with elsewhere
– software safety integrity	IEC 61508-4	substantial differences
– software safety integrity level	IEC 61508-4	substantial differences
– safety integrity	IEC 61508-4	substantial differences
– safety integrity level	IEC 61508-4 IEC 62443-1-1	moderate differences, also different from above
interception	IEC 62443-1-1 IEC 62443-3-1	minor difference IEC 62443-1-1: synonym also given — otherwise identical
interface	IEC 62443-1-1 IEC 62443-3-1	identical
local area network	IEC 62443-1-1 IEC 62443-3-1	identical
non-repudiation	IEC 62443-3-3 IEC Guide 120	identical
	IEC 62443-1-1 IEC 62443-3-1	identical, but substantially different from above heterographs IEC 62443-3-3/Guide 120: positive formulation: prove IEC 62443-1-1/3-1: service providing protection against...
plaintext	IEC 62443-1-1 IEC 62443-3-1	identical
product supplier	IEC 62443-2-4+AMD IEC 62443-3-3	identical
reasonably foreseeable misuse	IEC 61508-4 ISO/IEC Guide 51	identical

Concept	Sources	Remarks
remote access	IEC 62443-1-1 IEC 62443-2-1 IEC 62443-2-4+AMD IEC 62443-3-3	substantial differences IEC 62443-1-1: zone + "different geog. location" + rights IEC 62443-2-1: "perimeter" rather than "zone" IEC 62443-2-4+AMD: access through external interface (usual) IEC 62443-3-3: zone + "perimeter"
repudiation	IEC 62443-1-1 IEC 62443-3-1	identical
residual risk	IEC 61508-4 ISO/IEC /Guide 51 IEC 62443-1-1	minor differences IEC 61508-4: "protective measures" Guide 51: "risk reduction measures (protective measures)" IEC 62443-1-1: "security controls or countermeasures: specific to sec. risk
risk	IEC 61508-4 ISO/IEC Guide 51 IEC Guide 120 IEC 62443-1-1/3-1	identical identical, but substantial difference from above IEC 61508-4, etc.: combination of probability with severity IEC 62443-1-1, etc: expectation of loss, restricted to "vulnerability"
risk assessment	ISO/IEC Guide 51 IEC 62443-1-1 IEC 62443-2-1	substantial differences IEC Guide 51: risk analysis + risk evaluation IEC 62443-1-1: description of process, restricted to "vulnerabilities" IEC 62443-2-1: description of process, no restriction
risk tolerance /level	IEC 62443-1-1 IEC 62443-2-1	substantial difference (change 2018-12-27: minor difference) IEC 62443-1-1: term "level", else semantically equivalent

Concept	Sources	Remarks
safety	IEC 61508-4 IEC 62443-1-1 ISO/IEC Guide 51 IEC Guide 120	identical identical but minor difference from above semantically equivalent if "unacceptable" = "not tolerable
safety instrumented system	IEC 62443-2-4+AMD IEC 62443-3-3	substantial difference IEC 62443-2-4+AMD: system used to implement FS IEC 62443-3-3: system used to implement SFs
security	IEC Guide 120 IEC 62443-1-1	substantial difference IEC Guide 120: protection ensuring inviolability IEC 62443-1-1: enumerated listing of features
security incident	IEC 62443-1-1 IEC 62443-2-4+AMD	substantial difference IEC 62443-1-1: "adverse" event or a threat of occurrence IEC 62443-2-4+AMD: compromise or attempt of significance to asset owner
security level	IEC 62443-1-1 IEC 62443-3-3	substantial difference IEC 62443-1-1: required effectiveness of countermeasures and properties IEC 62443-3-3: measure of confidence of vulnerability-freeness
security program	IEC 62443-1-1 IEC 62443-2-4+AMD	substantial difference IEC 62443-1-1: combination of all aspects of secmanagement IEC 62443-2-4+AMD: portfolio of secservices applicable to IACS
security services	IEC 62443-1-1 IEC 62443-3-1 IEC Guide 120	identical
server	IEC 62443-1-1 IEC 62443-3-1	identical
service provider	IEC 62443-2-4+AMD IEC 62443-3-3	moderate difference IEC 62443-2-4+AMD: organisation that has agreed to provide service IEC 62443-3-3: individual or organisation providing support

Concept	Sources	Remarks
sniffing	IEC 62443-1-1 IEC 62443-3-1	minor difference IEC 62443-1-1: a reference to another entry
spoof	IEC 62443-1-1 IEC 62443-3-1	identical
system	IEC 62443-1-1 IEC 62443-2-4+AMD	identical
system software	IEC 62443-1-1 IEC 62443-3-1 IEC 61508-4	Identical SW to facilitate ops and maintenance moderate difference from above SW relates to functioning of device itself or its services
threat	IEC 62443-1-1 IEC Guide 120 IEC 62443-3-1 IEC 62443-3-3	identical potential for violation of security moderate difference, also to above IEC 62443-3-1: potentially damaging action or capability IEC 62443-3-3: potentially circumstance/event adversely affecting operations
tolerable risk	IEC 61508-4 ISO/IEC Guide 51	minor difference IEC Guide 51: "level of ..."
vulnerability	IEC 62443-1-1 IEC 62443-2-4+AMD IEC 62443-3-1 IEC Guide 120	identical
wide area network	IEC 62443-1-1 IEC 62443-3-1	minor differences IEC 62443-1-1: "to connect computers, networks or other devices..." IEC 62443-3-1: "to connect computers..."
zone	IEC 62443-1-1 IEC 62443-3-3	minor difference? IEC 62443-1-1: a reference to another subclause

Appendix B. SemAn Analyser Output on Multiply-Defined Concepts

B.1 Introduction

The SemAn Analyser results below were developed in 2021-2 by TU-BS and Causalis Ing.-GmbH in Project Harbsafe II (see the Acknowledgments section above).

B.2 SemAn Analyser Results

```
1. (no definition)

2.
access control(a):

a) protection of system resources against unauthorized access

\\
    a) protection
        > of system resources
            > against unauthorized access
[Source: IEC TR 62443-3-1:2009]

3.
access control(b):

b) process by which use of system resources is regulated according to a security
policy and is permitted only by authorized entities according to that policy

\\
    b) process
        > by which use
            > of system resources
            > [AND] is regulated according to a security policy
            > [AND] and is permitted only by authorized entities
                > according to that policy
[Source: IEC TR 62443-3-1:2009]

4.
access control:

protection of system resources against unauthorized access;

a process by which use of system resources is regulated according to a security
policy and is permitted by only authorized entities according to that policy

\\
    protection
        > of system resources
            > against unauthorized access
    ;

    a process
        > by which use
            > of system resources
```

```
                            > [AND] is regulated according to a security policy
                            > [AND] and is permitted only by authorized entities
                                          > according to that policy
[Source: IEC TS 62443-1-1:2009]

5.
accountability:

property of a system that ensures that the actions of a system entity may be
traced uniquely to that entity, which can be held responsible for its actions

\\
      property
            > [AND] of a system
            > [AND] that ensures that the actions
                          > [AND] of a system entity
                          > [AND] may be traced uniquely to that entity
                                        > , which can be held responsible for its
actions
[Source: IEC Draft Guide 120]
[Source: IEC TR 62443-3-1:2009]
[Source: IEC TS 62443-1-1:2009]

8.
application:

task related to the EUC rather than to the E/E/PE system

\\
      task
            > [AND] related to the EUC
            > [AND] rather than to the E/E/PE system
[Source: IEC 61508-4:2010]

9.
application:

software program that performs specific functions initiated by a user command or
a process event and that can be executed without access to system control,
monitoring, or administrative privileges

\\
      software program
            > [AND] that performs specific functions
                          > initiated by a |[OR] user command
                                           |[OR] or a process event

            > [AND] and that can be executed without access
                          > to | [OR] system control
                               | [OR] , monitoring
                               | [OR] , or administrative privileges
[Source: IEC TS 62443-1-1:2009]

10.
asset:

physical or logical object owned by or under the custodial duties of an
organization, having either a perceived or actual value to the organization

\\
      physical or logical object
            > [AND] owned by or under the custodial duties
                          > of an organization
            > [AND] , having either a perceived or actual value
                          > to the organization
[Source: IEC 62443-2-1:2010]
[Source: IEC TS 62443-1-1:2009]
```

11.
asset:

physical or logical object having either a perceived or actual value to the IACS

\\
    physical or logical object
        > having either a perceived or actual value
            > to the IACS
[Source: IEC 62443-3-3:2013]

13.
asset owner:

individual or company responsible for one or more IACS

\\
    [OR] individual
    [OR] or company
            > responsible for
                    > one or more IACS
[Source: IEC 62443-3-3:2013]

14.
asset owner:

individual or organization responsible for one or more IACSs

\\
    [OR] individual
    [OR] or organization
            > responsible for
                    > one or more IACS
[Source: IEC 62443-2-4:2015+AMD1:2017]

15.
attack:

assault on a system that derives from an intelligent threat

\\
    assault
        > [AND] on a system
        > [AND] that derives from an intelligent threat
[Source: IEC 62443-3-3:2013]

16.
attack:

assault on a system that derives from an intelligent threat - i.e., an intelligent act that is a deliberate attempt (especially in the sense of a method or technique) to evade security services and violate the security policy of a system

\\
    assault
        > [AND] on a system
        > [AND] that derives from an intelligent threat
    - i.e.
    , an intelligent act
        > that is a deliberate attempt
            > [AND] to evade security services
            > [AND] and violate the security policy
                    > of a system
[Source: IEC Draft Guide 120]
[Source: IEC TS 62443-1-1:2009]

```
18.
Authenticate

verify the identity of a user, user device, or other entity, or the integrity of
data stored, transmitted, or otherwise exposed to unauthorized modification in an
information system, or to establish the validity of a transmission

\\
     [OR] verify the identity
               > of | [OR] a user
                    | [OR] , user device
                    | [OR] , or other entity
     [OR] , or the integrity
               > of data
                    > stored, transmitted, or otherwise exposed to unauthorized
modification
                              > in an information system
     [OR] , or to establish the validity
               > of a transmission
[Source: IEC TS 62443-1-1:2009]

19.
authentication:

security measure designed to establish the validity of a transmission, message or
originator or a means of verifying an individual's authorization to receive
specific categories of information

\\
     security measure
         > designed to establish the | [OR] validity
                                     |       > of a | [OR] transmission
                                     |              | [OR] , message
                                     |              | [OR] , or originator
                                     | [OR] or a means
                                     |       > of verifying an individual's
authorization
                                     |              > to receive specific
categories
                                     |                     > of information
[Source: IEC 62443-2-1:2010]

20.
authentication:

provision of assurance that a claimed characteristic of an identity is correct

\\
     provision
         > of assurance
             > that a claimed characteristic
                 > [AND] of an identity
                 > [AND] is correct

[Source: IEC 62443-3-3:2013]

21.
authentication:

security measure designed to establish the validity of a transmission, message,
or originator, or a means of verifying an individual's authorization to receive
specific categories of information

\\
     security measure
         > designed to establish the | [OR] validity
                                     |       > of a | [OR] transmission
                                     |              | [OR] , message
```

```
                                          |                 | [OR] , or originator
                                          | [OR] , or a means
                                          |         > of verifying an individuals
authorization
                                          |              > to receive specific
categories
                                          |                     > of information
[Source: IEC Draft Guide 120]
[Source: IEC TR 62443-3-1:2009]
[Source: IEC TS 62443-1-1:2009]

24.
authorization:

right or permission that is granted to a system entity to access a system
resource

\\
      [OR] right
      [OR] or permission
            > [AND] that is granted to a system entity
            > [AND] to access a system resource
[Source: IEC Draft Guide 120]
[Source: IEC TS 62443-1-1:2009]

25.
authorization:

right or a permission that is granted to a system entity to access a system
resource

\\
      [OR] right
      [OR] or a permission
            > [AND] that is granted to a system entity
            > [AND] to access a system resource
[Source: IEC TR 62443-3-1:2009]

27.
availability:

property of ensuring timely and reliable access to and use of control system
information and functionality

\\
      property
            > of ensuring timely and reliable | [AND] access to
                                              | [AND] and use
                                              |         > of control system  |
[AND] information
                                              |                              |
[AND] and functionality
[Source: IEC 62443-3-3:2013]

28.
availability:

property of being accessible and usable upon demand by an authorized entity

\\
      property
            > of being accessible and usable upon demand
                  > by an authorized entity
[Source: IEC Draft Guide 120]


29.
```

availability:

probability that an asset, under the combined influence of its reliability, maintainability and security will be able to fulfil its required function over a stated period of time or at a given point in time

```
\\
    probability
        > that an asset
            > [AND] , under the combined influence
                    > of its | [AND] reliability
                             | [AND] , maintainability
                             | [AND] and security
            > [AND] will be able to fulfil its required function
                    > [OR] over a stated period
                                > of time
                    > [OR] or at a given point
                                > in time
```
[Source: IEC TR 62443-3-1:2009]

30.
availability:

ability of an item to be in a state to perform a required function under given conditions at a given instant or over a given time interval, assuming that the required external resources are provided

```
\\
    ability
        > [AND] of an item
                > to be in a state
        > [AND] to perform a required function
                > under given conditions
                        > [OR] at a given instant
                        > [OR] or over a given time interval
                > [AND] , assuming that the required external resources
                            > are provided
```
[Source: IEC TS 62443-1-1:2009]

31.
channel:

element or group of elements that independently implement an element safety function

```
\\
    [OR] element
    [OR] or group
            > [AND] of elements
            > [AND] that independently implement
                    > an element safety function
```
[Source: IEC 61508-4:2010]

32.
channel:

specific communication link established within a communication conduit

```
\\
    specific communication link
        > established within a communication conduit
```
[Source: IEC TS 62443-1-1:2009]

33.

```
ciphertext:

data that have been transformed by encryption so that the semantic information
content is no longer intelligible or directly available
\\
    data
        > that have been transformed by encryption
            > so that the semantic information content
                > [OR] is no longer intelligible
                > [OR] or directly available
[Source: IEC TR 62443-3-1:2009]

34.

ciphertext:

data that has been transformed by encryption so that its semantic information
content (i.e., its meaning) is no longer intelligible or directly available

\\
    data
        > that has been transformed by encryption
            > so that the semantic information content
                > [OR] is no longer intelligible
                > [OR] or directly available

[Source: IEC TS 62443-1-1:2009]

35.
client:

device or application receiving or requesting services or information from a
server application

\\
    [OR] device
    [OR] or application
            > [OR] receiving or requesting services
            > [OR] or information
                    > from a server application
[Source: IEC TR 62443-3-1:2009]
[Source: IEC TS 62443-1-1:2009]

37.
conduit:

logical grouping of communication channels, connecting two or more zones, that
share common security requirements

\\
    logical grouping
        > of communication channels
            > , connecting  | [OR] two
                            | [OR] or more zones
                            |       > , that share common security
requirements
[Source: IEC 62443-3-3:2013]

38.
conduit:

logical grouping of communication assets that protects the security of the
channels it contains

\\
    logical grouping
        > [AND] of communication assets
        > [AND] that protects the security
```

```
                            > of the channels
                                    > it contains
[Source: IEC TS 62443-1-1:2009]
```

39.
confidentiality:

preserving authorized restrictions on information access and disclosure,
including means for protecting personal privacy and proprietary information

```
\\
    preserving authorized restrictions
          > on     | [AND] information access
                   | [AND] and disclosure
                   |        > , including means
                   |                  > for protecting | [AND] personal privacy
                   |                                   | [AND] and proprietary
information
[Source: IEC 62443-3-3:2013]
```

40.
confidentiality:

property that information is not made available or disclosed to unauthorized
individuals, entities, or processes

```
\\
    property
          > [AND] that information
          > [AND] is not | [OR] made available
                         | [OR] or disclosed to unauthorized | [OR] individuals
                         |                                   | [OR] , entities
                         |                                   | [OR] , or
processes
[Source: IEC Draft Guide 120]
```

41.
confidentiality:

assurance that information is not disclosed to unauthorized individuals,
processes or devices
```
\\
    assurance
          > that information
                  > is not disclosed to unauthorized | [OR] individuals
                                                     | [OR] , processes
                                                     | [OR] or devices
[Source: IEC TR 62443-3-1:2009]
```

42.
confidentiality:

assurance that information is not disclosed to unauthorized individuals,
processes or devices
```
\\
    assurance
          > that information
                  > is not disclosed to unauthorized | [OR] individuals
                                                     | [OR] , processes
                                                     | [OR] ,or devices
[Source: IEC TS 62443-1-1:2009]
```

43.

configuration baseline:

information that allows the software release to be recreated in an auditable and systematic way, including: all source code, data, run time files, documentation, configuration files, and installation scripts that comprise a software release;

information about compilers, operating systems, and development tools used to create the software release

```
\\
    information
        > that allows the software release
            > [AND] to be recreated in an auditable and systematic way
            > [AND] , including: all | [AND] source code
                                     | [AND] data
                                     | [AND] run time files
                                     | [AND] , documentation
                                     | [AND] , configuration files
                                     | [AND] , and installation scripts
                                     |       > that comprise a software
release
; information about compilers
    > [AND], operating systems
    > [AND], and development tools
            > used to create the software release
```
[Source: IEC 61508-4:2010]

44.
consequence:

result that occurs from a particular incident

```
\\
    result
        > that occurs from a particular incident
```
[Source: IEC 62443-2-1:2010]

45.
consequence:

condition or state that logically or naturally follows from an event

```
\\
    [OR] condition
    [OR] or state
            > that logically or naturally follows from an event
```
[Source: IEC 62443-3-3:2013]

46.
control system:

hardware and software components of an IACS

```
\\
    hardware and software components
        > of an IACS
```
[Source: IEC 62443-3-3:2013]

47.
control system:

hardware and software components used in the design and implementation of an IACS

```
\\
    hardware and software components
        > used in the | [AND] design
                      | [AND] and implementation
```

```
                             |            > of an IACS
[Source: IEC 62443-2-4:2015 + AMD1:2017]

48.
countermeasure:

action, device, procedure, or technique that reduces a threat, a vulnerability,
or an attack by eliminating or preventing it, by minimizing the harm it can
cause, or by discovering and reporting it so that corrective action can be taken

\\
     [OR] action
     [OR] , device
     [OR] , procedure
     [OR] , or technique
              > [AND] that reduces | [OR] a threat
                                   | [OR] , a vulnerability
                                   | [OR] , or an attack
                     > [OR] by eliminating
                     > [OR] or preventing it
                     > [OR] , by minimizing the harm
                                   > it can cause,
                     > [OR] or by | [AND] discovering
                                  | [AND] and reporting it
              > [AND] so that corrective action
                           > can be taken
[Source: IEC 62443-3-3:2013]
[Source: IEC TS 62443-1-1:2009]
[Source: IEC TS 62443-1-1:2009]


51.
decryption:

process of changing ciphertext into plaintext using a cryptographic algorithm and
key (see 3.1.24 "encryption")

\\
     process
          > of changing ciphertext
                > [AND] into plaintext
                > [AND] using a | [AND] cryptographic algorithm
                                | [AND] and key
[Source: IEC TR 62443-3-1:2009]


52.
decryption:

process of changing cipher text into plaintext using a cryptographic algorithm
and key

\\
     process
          > of changing cipher text
                > [AND] into plaintext
                > [AND] using a | [AND] cryptographic algorithm
                                | [AND] and key
[Source: IEC TS 62443-1-1:2009]


53.
defense in depth:

security architecture based on the idea that any one point of protection may, and
probably will, be defeated

\\
```

```
            security architecture
                > based on the idea
                      > that any one point
                             > of protection
                                    > may, and probably will, be defeated
[Source: IEC TR 62443-3-1:2009]
```

54.
defense in depth:

provision of multiple security protections, especially in layers, with the intent to delay if not prevent an attack

```
\\
      provision
            > [AND] of multiple security protections
                     > ,especially in layers
            > [AND] , with the intent
                                 > to delay if not prevent an attack
[Source: IEC TS 62443-1-1:2009]
```

55.
demilitarized zone:

common, limited network of servers joining two or more zones for the purpose of controlling data flow between zones

```
\\
      common, limited network
            > [AND] of servers
            > [AND] joining two or more zones
                      > for the purpose
                             > of controlling data flow
                                    > between zones
[Source: IEC 62443-3-3:2013]
```

56.
demilitarized zone:

perimeter network segment that is logically inserted between internal and external networks

```
\\
      perimeter network segment
            > that is logically inserted
                  > between | [AND] internal
                            | [AND] and external networks
[Source: IEC TS 62443-1-1:2009]
```

57.
denial of service:

prevention or interruption of authorized access to a system resource or the delaying of system operations and functions

```
\\
      [OR] prevention
      [OR] or interruption
            > of authorized access
                  > to a system resource
      [OR] or the delaying
            > of system | [AND] operations
                        | [AND] and functions
[Source: IEC TS 62443-1-1:2009]
[Source: IEC TR 62443-3-1:2009]
```

59.
digital signature:

result of a cryptographic transformation of data which, when properly
implemented, provides the services of origin authentication, data integrity, and
signer non-repudiation

\\
```
    result
        > of a cryptographic transformation
            > [AND] of data
            > [AND] which, when properly implemented, provides the services
                        > of | [AND] origin authentication
                             | [AND] , data integrity
                             | [AND] and signer non-repudiation
```
[Source: IEC TR 62443-3-1:2009]
[Source: IEC TS 62443-1-1:2009]

61.
encryption:

cryptographic transformation of plaintext into ciphertext that conceals the
data's original meaning to prevent it from being known or used

\\
```
    cryptographic transformation
        > [AND] of plaintext
        > [AND] into ciphertext
        > [AND] that conceals the data's original meaning
                    > to prevent it
                        > from being known or used
```
[Source: IEC TR 62443-3-1:2009]
[Source: IEC TS 62443-1-1:2009]

63.
environment:

all relevant parameters that can affect the achievement of functional safety in
the specific application under consideration and in any safety lifecycle phase

\\
```
    all relevant parameters
        > that can affect the achievement
            > of functional safety
                > in the specific | [AND] application
                                  |        > under consideration
                                  | [AND] and in any safety lifecycle
phase
```
[Source: IEC 61508-4:2010]

64.
environment:

surrounding objects, region or circumstances which may influence the behavior of
the IACS and/or may be influenced by the IACS

\\
```
    surrounding | [OR] objects
                | [OR] , region
                | [OR] or circumstances
        > [OR] which may influence the behavior
                    > of the IACS
        > [OR] and/or may be influenced by the IACS
```
[Source: IEC 62443-3-3:2013]

65.

```
equipment under control:

equipment, machinery, apparatus or plant used for manufacturing, process,
transportation, medical or other activities

\\
     [OR] equipment
     [OR] , machinery
     [OR] , apparatus
     [OR] or plant
              > used for | [OR] manufacturing
                         | [OR] , process
                         | [OR] , transportation
                         | [OR] , medical or other activities
[Source: IEC TS 62443-1-1:2009]
[Source: IEC 61508-4:2010]

67.
harm:

physical injury or damage to the health of people or damage to property or the
environment

\\
     [OR] physical injury
     [OR] or damage
              > [OR] to the health
                       > of people
     [OR] or damage
              > [OR] to property
              > [OR] or the environment
[Source: IEC 61508-4:2010]

68.
harm:

injury or damage to the health of people, or damage to property or the
environment

\\
     [OR] injury
     [OR] or damage
              > to the health
                    > of people
     [OR] , or damage
              > to | [OR] property
                   | [OR] or the environment
[Source: IEC Draft Guide 120]
[Source: IEC Guide 51:2014]


70.
hazard:

potential source of harm

\\
     potential source
          > of harm
[Source: IEC 61508-4:2010]
[Source: IEC Guide 51:2014]

72.
hazardous event:

event that may result in harm

\\
```

```
            event
                > that may result in harm
[Source: IEC 61508-4:2010]
```

73.
hazardous event

event that can cause harm

```
\\
     event
            > that can cause harm

[Source: IEC Guide 51:2014]
```

74.
hazardous situation:

circumstance in which people, property or the environment are exposed to one or more hazards

```
\\
     circumstance
            > in which | [OR] people
                       | [OR] , property
                       | [OR] or the environment
                       |      > are exposed to one or more hazards
[Source: IEC 61508-4:2010]
[Source: IEC Guide 51:2014]
```

76.
incident: correct except for the splitting

event that is not part of the expected operation of a system or service that causes or may cause, an interruption to, or a reduction in, the quality of the service provided by the system

```
\\
     event
            > [AND] that is not part
                       > of the expected operation
                              > of a | [OR] system
                                     | [OR] or service
            > [AND] that causes or may cause,
                       > [OR] an interruption to,
                       > [OR] or a reduction in,
                              > the quality
                                     > of the service
                                            > provided by the system
[Source: IEC 62443-2-1:2010]
```

77.
incident:

event that is not part of the expected operation of a system or service that causes, or may cause, an interruption to, or a reduction in, the quality of the service provided by the control system

```
\\
     event
            > [AND] that is not part
                       > of the expected operation
                              > of a | [OR] system
                                     | [OR] or service
            > [AND] that causes, or may cause,
                       > [OR] an interruption to,
                       > [OR] or a reduction in,
                              > the quality
```

```
                                        > of the service
                                            > provided by the control system
[Source: IEC 62443-3-3:2013]

78.
industrial automation and control system:

collection of personnel, hardware, software and policies involved in the
operation of the industrial process and that can affect or influence its safe,
secure and reliable operation

\\
    collection
        > [AND] of | [AND] personnel
                   | [AND] , hardware
                   | [AND] , software
                   | [AND] and policies
        > [AND] involved in the operation
                   > of the industrial process
        > [AND] and that can | [OR] affect
                             | [OR] or influence its | [AND] safe,
                             |                       | [AND] secure
                             |                       | [AND] and reliable
operation
[Source: IEC 62443-3-3:2013]

79.
industrial automation and control system:

collection of personnel, hardware, software, procedures and policies involved in
the operation of the industrial process and that can affect or influence its
safe, secure and reliable operation

\\
    collection
        > [AND] of | [AND] personnel
                   | [AND] , hardware
                   | [AND] , software
                   | [AND] , procedures
                   | [AND] and policies
        > [AND] involved in the operation
                   > of the industrial process
        > [AND] and that can | [OR] affect
                             | [OR] or influence its | [AND] safe,
                             |                       | [AND] secure
                             |                       | [AND] and reliable
operation
[Source: IEC 62443-2-4:2015 + AMD1:2017]

80.
industrial automation and control system:

collection of personnel, hardware, and software that can affect or influence the
safe, secure, and reliable operation of an industrial process

\\
    collection
        > [AND] of | [AND] personnel
                   | [AND] , hardware
                   | [AND] , and software
        > [AND] that can | [OR] affect
                         | [OR] or influence the | [AND] safe,
                         |                       | [AND] secure,
                         |                       | [AND] and reliable operation
                         |                                > of an
industrial process
[Source: IEC TS 62443-1-1:2009]
```

81.
integrity:

property of protecting the accuracy and completeness of assets

\\
```
     property
           > of protecting the  | [AND] accuracy
                                | [AND] and completeness
                                |         > of assets
```
[Source: IEC 62443-3-3:2013]

82.
integrity:

property of accuracy and completeness

\\
```
     property
           > of | [AND] accuracy
                | [AND] and completeness
```
[Source: IEC Draft Guide 120]

83.
integrity:

quality of a system reflecting the logical correctness and reliability of the operating system, the logical completeness of the hardware and software implementing the protection mechanisms, and the consistency of the data structures and occurrence of the stored data

\\
```
     quality
           > [AND] of a system
           > [AND] reflecting the  | [AND] logical correctness
                                   | [AND] and reliability
                                   |         > of the operating system
                                   | [AND] , the logical completeness
                                   |         > of the | [AND] hardware
                                   |                  | [AND] and software
                                   |                  |        >
implementing the protection mechanisms
                                   | [AND] , and the consistency
                                   |         > of the | [AND] data structures
                                   |                  | [AND] and occurrence
                                   |                  |        > of the
stored data
```
[Source: IEC TR 62443-3-1:2009]
[Source: IEC TS 62443-1-1:2009]

85.
interception:

capture and disclosure of message contents or use of traffic analysis to compromise the confidentiality of a communication system based on message destination or origin, frequency or length of transmission and other communication attributes

\\
```
     [OR] [AND] capture
          [AND] and disclosure
                    > of message contents
     [OR] or use
              > of traffic analysis
                    > [AND] to compromise the confidentiality
                              > of a communication system
                    > [AND] based on | [OR] message destination
                                     | [OR] or origin
```

```
                                        | [OR] , frequency
                                        | [OR] or length
                                        |      > of transmission
                                        | [OR] and other communication attributes
[Source: IEC TR 62443-3-1:2009]

86.
interception:

sniffing, capture and disclosure of message contents or use of traffic analysis
to compromise the confidentiality of a communication system based on message
destination or origin, frequency or length of transmission, and other
communication attributes

\\
     [AND] sniffing
     [AND] capture
     [AND] and disclosure
              > of message contents
     [OR] or use
              > of traffic analysis
                      > [AND] to compromise the confidentiality
                                   > of a communication system
                      > [AND] based on | [OR] message destination
                                       | [OR] or origin
                                       | [OR] , frequency
                                       | [OR] , and other communication
attributes
                                       | [OR] or length
                                       |      > of transmission
[Source: IEC TS 62443-1-1:2009]


87.
interface:

logical entry or exit point that provides access to the module for logical
information flows

\\
     [OR] logical entry
     [OR] or exit point
              > that provides access
                      > [AND] to the module
                      > [AND] for logical information flows
[Source: IEC TR 62443-3-1:2009]
[Source: IEC TS 62443-1-1:2009]

89.
local area network:

communications network designed to connect computers and other intelligent
devices in a limited geographic area

\\
     communications network
           > designed to connect | [AND] computers
                                 | [AND] and other intelligent devices
                  > in a limited geographic area
[Source: IEC TS 62443-1-1:2009]
[Source: IEC TR 62443-3-1:2009]

91.
non repudiation:

ability to prove the occurrence of a claimed event or action and its originating
entities
\\
```

```
            ability
                > to prove the | [AND] occurrence
                               |         > of a claimed | [OR] event
                               |                        | [OR] or action
                               | [AND] and its originating entities
[Source: IEC Draft Guide 120]
[Source: IEC 62443-3-3:2013]
```

93.
non repudiation:

security service that provides protection against false denial of involvement in a communication

```
\\
    security service
        > that provides protection
              > against false denial
                    > of involvement
                          > in a communication
[Source: IEC TR 62443-3-1:2009]
[Source: IEC TS 62443-1-1:2009]
```

95.
plaintext:

unencoded data that is input to and transformed by an encryption process or that is output by a decryption process

```
\\
    unencoded data
        > [OR] that is input to and transformed
                    > by an encryption process
        > [OR] or that is output
                    > by a decryption process
[Source: IEC TR 62443-3-1:2009]
[Source: IEC TS 62443-1-1:2009]
```

97.
product supplier:

manufacturer of hardware and/or software product

```
\\
    manufacturer
        > of | [OR] hardware
             | [OR] and/or software product

[Source: IEC 62443-3-3:2013]
[Source: IEC 62443-2-4:2015 + AMD1:2017]
```

99.
reasonably foreseeable misuse:

use of a product, process or service in a way not intended by the supplier, but which may result from readily predictable human behaviour

```
\\
    use
        > [AND] of a | [OR] product
                     | [OR] , process
                     | [OR] or service
        > [AND] in a way
                    > [AND] not intended by the supplier
                    > [AND] , but which may result from readily predictable
human behaviour
[Source: IEC 61508-4:2010]
```

100.
reasonably foreseeable misuse:

use of a product or system in a way not intended by the supplier, but which can result from readily predictable human behaviour

```
\\
    use
        > [AND] of a | [OR] product
                     | [OR] or service
        > [AND] in a way
                > [AND] not intended by the supplier
                > [AND] , but which may result from readily predictable
human behaviour
```
[Source: IEC Guide 51:2014]

101.
remote access:

communication with, or use of, assets or systems within a defined perimeter from any location outside that perimeter

```
\\
    [OR] communication with,
    [OR] or use of, | [OR] assets
                    | [OR] or systems
                    |           > [AND] within a defined perimeter
                    |           > [AND] from any location
                    |                       > outside that perimeter
```
[Source: IEC 62443-2-1:2010]

102.
remote access:

access to a control system by any user communicating from outside the perimeter of the zone being addressed

```
\\
    access
        > to a control system
            > by any user
                > communicating from
                    > outside the perimeter
                        > of the zone
                            > being addressed
```
[Source: IEC 62443-3-3:2013]

103.
remote access:

access to a control system through an external interface of the control system

```
\\
    access
        > to a control system
            > through an external interface
                > of the control system
```
[Source: IEC 62443-2-4:2015 + AMD1:2017]

104.
remote access:

use of systems that are inside the perimeter of the security zone being addressed from a different geographical location with the same rights as when physically present at the location

\\

```
                use
                    > of systems
                        > [AND] that are inside the perimeter
                                > of the security zone
                        > [AND] being addressed from a different geographical location
                                > with the same rights
                                        > as when physically present at the location
[Source: IEC TS 62443-1-1:2009]
```

105.
repudiation:

denial by one of the entities involved in a communication of having participated
in all or part of the communication

```
\\
        denial
            > [AND] by one of the entities
                        > involved in a communication
            > [AND] of having participated in | [OR] all
                                             | [OR] or part
                                             |           > of the communication
[Source: IEC TR 62443-3-1:2009]
[Source: IEC TS 62443-1-1:2009]
```

107.
residual risk:

risk remaining after protective measures have been taken

```
\\
    risk
        > remaining after protective measures
                > have been taken
[Source: IEC 61508-4:2010]
```

108.
residual risk:

risk remaining after risk reduction measures have been implemented

```
\\
    risk
        > remaining after risk reduction measures
                > have been implemented
[Source: IEC Guide 51:2014]
```

109.
residual risk

remaining risk after the security controls or countermeasures have been applied

```
\\
    remaining risk
        > after the | [OR] security controls
                    | [OR] or countermeasures
                    |           > have been applied
[Source: IEC TS 62443-1-1:2009]
```

110.
risk:

combination of the probability of occurrence of harm and the severity of that
harm

\\

```
            combination
                > of the  | [AND] probability
                          |             > of occurrence
                          |                     > of harm
                          | [AND] and the severity
                          |             > of that harm
[Source: IEC 61508-4:2010]
[Source: IEC Draft Guide 120]
[Source: IEC Guide 51:2014]
```

113.
risk:

expectation of loss expressed as the probability that a particular threat will exploit a particular vulnerability with a particular consequence

```
\\
    expectation
        > of loss
                > expressed as the probability
                        > that a particular threat
                                > will exploit a particular vulnerability
                                        > with a particular consequence
[Source: IEC TR 62443-3-1:2009]
[Source: IEC TS 62443-1-1:2009]
```

115.
risk assessment:

process of identifying and evaluating risks to the organization's operations, the organization's assets or individuals by determining the likelihood of occurrence, the resulting impact, and additional countermeasures that would mitigate this impact

```
\\
    process
        > of identifying and evaluating risks
                > [AND] to the | [OR] organization's operations
                               | [OR] , the organization's assets
                               | [OR] or individuals
                > [AND] by determining | [AND] the likelihood
                                       |             > of occurrence
                                       | [AND] , the resulting impact
                                       | [AND] , and additional countermeasures
                                       |             > that would mitigate this
impact
[Source: IEC 62443-2-1:2010]
```

116.
risk assessment:

overall process comprising a risk analysis and a risk evaluation

```
\\
    overall process
        > comprising a | [AND] risk analysis
                       | [AND] and a risk evaluation
[Source: IEC Guide 51:2014]
```

117.
risk assessment:

process that systematically identifies potential vulnerabilities to valuable system resources and threats to those resources, quantifies loss exposures and consequences based on probability of occurrence, and recommends how to allocate resources to countermeasures to minimize total exposure

```
\\
    process
        > that systematically identifies potential  | [AND] vulnerabilities
                                                    |         > to valuable
system resources
                                                    | [AND] and threats
                                                    |         > to those
resources
                                                    | [AND] , quantifies loss
exposures
                                                    | [AND] and consequences
                                                    |         > based on
probability
                                                    |               > of
occurrence
                                                    | [AND] , and recommends how
to allocate resources
                                                    |         > to
countermeasures
                                                    |         > to minimize
total exposure
[Source: IEC TS 62443-1-1:2009]
```

118.
risk tolerance:

risk the organization is willing to accept

```
\\
    risk
        > the organization
            > is willing to accept
[Source: IEC 62443-2-1:2010]
```

119.
risk tolerance level:

level of residual risk that is acceptable to an organization

```
\\
    level
        > of residual risk
            > that is acceptable to an organization
[Source: IEC TS 62443-1-1:2009]
```

120.
safety:

freedom from unacceptable risk

```
\\
    freedom
        > from unacceptable risk
[Source: IEC 61508-4:2010]
[Source: IEC TS 62443-1-1:2009]
```

121.
safety:

freedom from risk which is not tolerable

```
\\
    freedom
        > from risk
            > which is not tolerable
```

[Source: IEC Draft Guide 120]
[Source: IEC Guide 51:2014]

124.
safety instrumented system:

system used to implement one or more safety-related functions

\\
    system
        > used to implement one or more safety-related functions
[Source: IEC 62443-3-3:2013]

125.
safety instrumented system:

system used to implement functional safety

\\
    system
        > used to implement functional safety
[Source: IEC 62443-2-4:2015 + AMD1:2017]

126.
safety integrity:

probability of an E/E/PE safety-related system satisfactorily performing the specified safety functions under all the stated conditions within a stated period of time

\\
    probability of
        > an E/E/PE safety-related system
            > satisfactorily performing the specified safety functions
                > [AND] under all the stated conditions
                > [AND] within a stated period
                    > of time
[Source: IEC 61508-4:2010]

127.
safety integrity level:

discrete level for specifying the safety integrity requirements of the safety-instrumented functions to be allocated to the safety-instrumented systems

\\
    discrete level
        > for specifying the safety integrity requirements
            > of the safety-instrumented functions
                > to be allocated to the safety-instrumented systems
[Source: IEC TS 62443-1-1:2009]

128.
safety integrity level:

discrete level, corresponding to a range of safety integrity values, where safety integrity level 4 has the highest level of safety integrity and safety integrity level 1 has the lowest

\\
    discrete level
        > corresponding to a range
            > of safety integrity values

```
                                  > , where | [AND] safety integrity level 4
                                            |       > has the highest level
                                            |               > of safety integrity
                                            | [AND] and safety integrity level 1
                                            |       > has the lowest
[Source: IEC 61508-4:2010]


129.
security:

a condition that results from the establishment and maintenance of protective
measures that ensure a state of inviolability from hostile acts or influences

\\
    a condition
        > that results from the | [AND] establishment
                                | [AND] and maintenance
                                |       > of protective measures
                                |               > that ensure a state
                                |                       > of inviolability
                                |                               > from | [OR]
hostile acts
                                |                                      | [OR]
or influences
[Source: IEC Draft Guide 120]

130.
security:

a) measures taken to protect a system

\\
    a) measures
        > taken to protect a system
[Source: IEC TS 62443-1-1:2009]

131.
security:

b) condition of a system that results from the establishment and maintenance of
measures to protect the system

\\
    b) condition
        > [AND] of a system
        > [AND] that results from the | [AND] establishment
                                      | [AND] and maintenance
                                      |       > of measures
                                      |               > to protect the
system
[Source: IEC TS 62443-1-1:2009]

132.
security:

c) condition of system resources being free from unauthorized access and from
unauthorized or accidental change, destruction, or loss


\\
    c) condition
        > of system resources
            > being free from | [AND] unauthorized access
                              | [AND] and from | [OR] unauthorized
                              |                | [OR] or accidental change
                              |                | [OR] , destruction
                              |                | [OR] , or loss
```

[Source: IEC TS 62443-1-1:2009]

133.
security:

d) capability of a computer-based system to provide adequate confidence that
unauthorized persons and systems can neither modify the software and its data nor
gain access to the system functions, and yet to ensure that this is not denied to
authorized persons and systems

\\
    d) capability
        > of a computer-based system
            > [AND] to provide adequate confidence
                    > that unauthorized | [AND] persons
                                        | [AND] and systems
                                        | > can neither |
[OR] modify the software
                                        | |
[OR] nor gain access
                                        | |
> to the | [AND] system functions
                                        | |
| [AND] and its data
            > [AND] , and yet to ensure that this is not denied to
authorized persons
[Source: IEC TS 62443-1-1:2009]

134.
security:

prevention of illegal or unwanted penetration of, or interference with the proper
and intended operation of an industrial automation and control system

\\
    prevention
        > [OR] of illegal or unwanted penetration of
        > [OR] , or interference
                > with the | [AND] proper
                           | [AND] and intended operation
                           | > of an industrial automation and
control system
[Source: IEC TS 62443-1-1:2009]

135.
security incident:

security compromise that is of some significance to the asset owner or failed
attempt to compromise the system whose result could have been of some
significance to the asset owner

\\
    [OR] security compromise
            > that is of some significance
                > to the asset owner
    [OR] or failed attempt
            > [AND] to compromise the system
            > [AND] whose result
                        > could have been of some significance
                            > to the asset owner
[Source: IEC 62443-2-4:2015 + AMD1:2017]

136.

security incident:

adverse event in a system or network, or the threat of the occurrence of such an event

\\
```
     [OR] adverse event
              > in a | [OR] system
                     | [OR] or network
     [OR] , or the threat
              > of the occurrence
                     > of such an event
```
[Source: IEC TS 62443-1-1:2009]

137.
security level:

measure of confidence that the IACS is free from vulnerabilities and functions in the intended manner

\\
```
     measure
         > of confidence
              > that the IACS
                     > [AND] is free from vulnerabilities
                     > [AND] and functions in the intended manner
```
[Source: IEC 62443-3-3:2013]

138.
security level:

level corresponding to the required effectiveness of countermeasures and inherent security properties of devices and systems for a zone or conduit based on assessment of risk for the zone or conduit

\\
```
     level
         > [AND] corresponding to the | [AND] required effectiveness
                                      |         > of countermeasures
                                      | [AND] and inherent security properties
                                      |         > [AND] of devices
                                      |         > [AND] and systems
                                      |                 > for a | [OR] zone
                                      |                         | [OR] or conduit
         > [AND] based on assessment
                 > of risk
                     > for the zone
```
[Source: IEC TS 62443-1-1:2009]

139.
security program:

portfolio of security services, including integration services and maintenance services, and their associated policies, procedures, and products that are applicable to the IACS

\\
```
     portfolio
         > [AND] of security services
         > [AND], including | [AND] integration services
                            | [AND] and maintenance services
                            | [AND] , and their associated | [AND] policies
                            |                              | [AND] , procedures
                            |                              | [AND] , and
```

```
                                                                                  > that
are applicable to the IACS
[Source: IEC 62443-2-4:2015 + AMD1:2017]



140.
security program:

combination of all aspects of managing security, ranging from the definition and
communication of policies through implementation of best industry practices,
ongoing operation and auditing

\\
    combination
        > of all aspects
            > [AND] of managing security
            > [AND], ranging from the  | [AND] definition
                                       | [AND] and communication
                                       |         > of policies
            > [AND] through | [AND] implementation
                            |         > of best industry practices
                            | [AND] , ongoing operation
                            | [AND] and auditing
[Source: IEC TS 62443-1-1:2009]

141.
security services:

mechanisms used to provide confidentiality, data integrity, authentication, or no
repudiation of information

\\
    mechanisms
        > used to provide | [OR] confidentiality
                          | [OR] , data integrity
                          | [OR] , authentication
                          | [OR] , or no repudiation
                          |         > of information
[Source: IEC Draft Guide 120]



142.
security services:

mechanisms used to provide confidentiality, data integrity, authentication or no
repudiation of information

\\
    mechanisms
        > used to provide | [OR] confidentiality
                          | [OR] , data integrity
                          | [OR] , authentication
                          | [OR] or no repudiation
                          |         > of information
[Source: IEC TR 62443-3-1:2009]

143.
security services:

mechanisms used to provide confidentiality, data integrity, authentication or no
repudiation of information

\\
    mechanisms
        > used to provide | [OR] confidentiality
                          | [OR] , data integrity
                          | [OR] , authentication
```

```
                             | [OR] , or no repudiation
                             |          > of information
[Source: IEC TS 62443-1-1:2009]
```

144.
server:

device or application that provides information or services to client
applications and devices

```
\\
    [OR] device
    [OR] or application
            > that provides | [OR] information
                            | [OR] or services
                            |         > to | [OR] client applications
                            |              | [OR] and devices
[Source: IEC TR 62443-3-1:2009]
[Source: IEC TS 62443-1-1:2009]
```

146.
service provider:

organization that has agreed to undertake responsibility for providing a given
support service and obtaining, when specified, supplies in accordance with an
agreement

```
\\
    organization
        > that has agreed to undertake responsibility
            | [AND] for providing a given support service
            | [AND] and obtaining, when specified, supplies
            |         > in accordance
            |              > with an agreement
[Source: IEC 62443-3-3:2013]
```

147.
service provider:

individual or organization that provides a specific support service and
associated supplies in accordance with an agreement with the asset owner

```
\\
    [OR] individual
    [OR] or organization
            > that provides a | [AND] specific support service
                              | [AND] and associated supplies
                              |         > in accordance
                              |              > with an agreement
                              |                   > with the asset
owner
[Source: IEC 62443-2-4:2015 + AMD1:2017]
```

148. (omitted since it has only one word)

149. (omitted since it has only one word)

150.
software safety integrity:

part of the safety integrity of a safety-related system relating to systematic
failures in a dangerous mode of failure that are attributable to software

```
\\
```

```
        part
            > of the safety integrity
                    > [AND] of a safety-related system
                    > [AND] relating to systematic failures
                                > [AND] in a dangerous mode
                                            > of failure
                                > [AND] that are attributable to software
[Source: IEC 61508-4:2010]
```

151.
software safety integrity level:

systematic capability of a software element that forms part of a subsystem of a safety-related system

```
\\
      systematic capability
            > of a software element
                    > that forms part
                            > of a subsystem
                                    > of a safety-related system
[Source: IEC 61508-4:2010]
```

152.
spoof:

pretending to be an authorized user and performing an unauthorized action

```
\\
      [AND] pretending to be authorized user
      [AND] and performing an unauthorized action
[Source: IEC TR 62443-3-1:2009]
[Source: IEC TS 62443-1-1:2009]
```

154.
system:

interacting, interrelated, or interdependent elements forming a complex whole

```
\\
      [OR] interacting,
      [OR] interrelated,
      [OR] or interdependent elements
                > forming a complex whole
[Source: IEC 62443-2-4:2015 + AMD1:2017]
[Source: IEC TS 62443-1-1:2009]
```

156.
system software:

part of the software of a PE system that relates to the functioning of, and services provided by, the programmable device itself, as opposed to the application software that specifies the functions that perform a task related to the safety of the EUC

```
\\
      part
            > [AND] of the software
                        > of a PE system
            > [AND] that relates to the  | [AND] functioning of, and services
                                         |         > provided by, the
programmable device itself
                                         | [AND] , as opposed to the application
software
                                         |           > that specifies the functions
                                         |                 > that perform a task
                                         |                       > related to the
```

safety
                                            | > of the
EUC
[Source: IEC 61508-4:2010]

157.
system software:

special software designed for a specific computer system or family of computer
systems to facilitate the operation and maintenance of the computer system and
associated programs and data

\\
    special software
        | [AND] designed for a specific | [OR] computer system
        | | [OR] or family
        | | > of computer systems
        | [AND] to facilitate the operation
        | [AND] and maintenance
        | > of the | [AND] computer system
        | | [AND] and associated | [AND] programs
        | | | [AND] and data
[Source: IEC TR 62443-3-1:2009]
[Source: IEC TS 62443-1-1:2009]

159.
threat:

circumstance or event with the potential to adversely affect operations, assets,
control systems or individuals via unauthorized access, destruction, disclosure,
modification of data and/or denial of service

\\
    [OR] circumstance
    [OR] or event
            > with the potential
                > to adversely affect | [OR] operations
                                      | [OR] , assets
                                      | [OR] , control systems
                                      | [OR] or individuals
                        > via | [OR] unauthorized access
                              | [OR] , destruction
                              | [OR] , disclosure
                              | [OR] , modification
                              | > of data
                              | [OR] and/or denial
                              | > of service
[Source: IEC 62443-3-3:2013]

160.
threat:

potential for violation of security, which exists when there is a circumstance,
capability, action, or event that could breach security and cause harm

\\
    potential
        > [AND] for violation
                > of security
        > [AND], which exists when there is a | [OR] circumstance
                                              | [OR] , capability
                                              | [OR] , action
                                              | [OR] , or event
                                              | > that could | [AND]
breach security

```
                                                            |               | [AND]
and cause harm
[Source: IEC Draft Guide 120]




161.
threat:

potentially damaging action or capability to adversely impact through a
vulnerability

\\
      potentially | [OR] damaging action
                  | [OR] or capability
                  |        > to adversely impact
                  |              > through a vulnerability
[Source: IEC TR 62443-3-1:2009]

162.
threat:
potential for violation of security, which exists when there is a circumstance,
capability, action, or event that could breach security and cause harm

\\
      potential
            > [AND] for violation
                        > of security
            > [AND] , which exists when there is a | [OR] circumstance
                                                  | [OR] , capability
                                                  | [OR] , action
                                                  | [OR] , or event
                                                  |        > that could | [AND]
breach security
                                                  |               | [AND]
and cause harm
[Source: IEC TS 62443-1-1:2009]

163.
tolerable risk:

risk which is accepted in a given context based on the current values of society

\\
      risk
          > which is accepted in a given context
                > based on the current values
                      > of society
[Source: IEC 61508-4:2010]

164.
tolerable risk:

level of risk which is accepted in a given context based on the current values of
society


\\
      level
          > of risk
                > which is accepted in a given context
                      > based on the current values
                            > of society
[Source: IEC Guide 51:2014]



165.
```

vulnerability:

flaw or weakness in the design, implementation, or operation and management of a
component that can be exploited to cause a security compromise

\\
    [OR] flaw
    [OR] or weakness
            > [AND] in the | [OR] design
                           | [OR] , implementation
                           | [OR] , or operation
                           | [OR] and management
                           | > of a component
            > [AND] that can be exploited to cause a security compromise
[Source: IEC 62443-2-4:2015 + AMD1:2017]

166.
vulnerability:

flaw or weakness in a system's design, implementation, or operation and
management that could be exploited to violate the system's security policy

\\
    [OR] flaw
    [OR] or weakness
            > [AND] in a system's | [OR] design
                                  | [OR] , implementation
                                  | [OR] , or operation
                                  | [OR] and management
            > [AND] that could be exploited to violate the system's security
policy
[Source: IEC Draft Guide 120]

167.
vulnerability:

flaw or weakness in a system's design, implementation, or operation and
management that could be exploited to violate the system's integrity or security
policy

\\
    [OR] flaw
    [OR] or weakness
            > [AND] in a system's | [OR] design
                                  | [OR] , implementation
                                  | [OR] , or operation
                                  | [OR] and management
            > [AND] that could be exploited to violate the system's | [OR]
integrity
                                                                     | [OR] or
security policy

[Source: IEC TR 62443-3-1:2009]
[Source: IEC TS 62443-1-1:2009]

169.
wide area network:

communications network designed to connect computers, networks and other devices
over a large distance, such as across a country or the world

\\
    communications network
        > designed to connect | [AND] computers
                              | [AND] , networks
                              | [AND] and other devices

```
                            |           > over a large distance
                            |                   > , such as across a | [OR]
country
                            |                                        | [OR]
or the world
[Source: IEC TS 62443-1-1:2009]
```

170.
wide area network:

communications network designed to connect computers over a large distance, such as across a country or the world

```
\\
    communications network
        > designed to connect computers
            > over a large distance
                >, such as across a | [OR] country
                                    | [OR] or the world
[Source: IEC TR 62443-3-1:2009]
```

171.
zone:

grouping of logical or physical assets that share common security requirements

```
\\
    grouping
        > of logical or physical assets
            > that share common security requirements
```

[Source: IEC 62443-3-3:201

This collation page left blank intentionally.

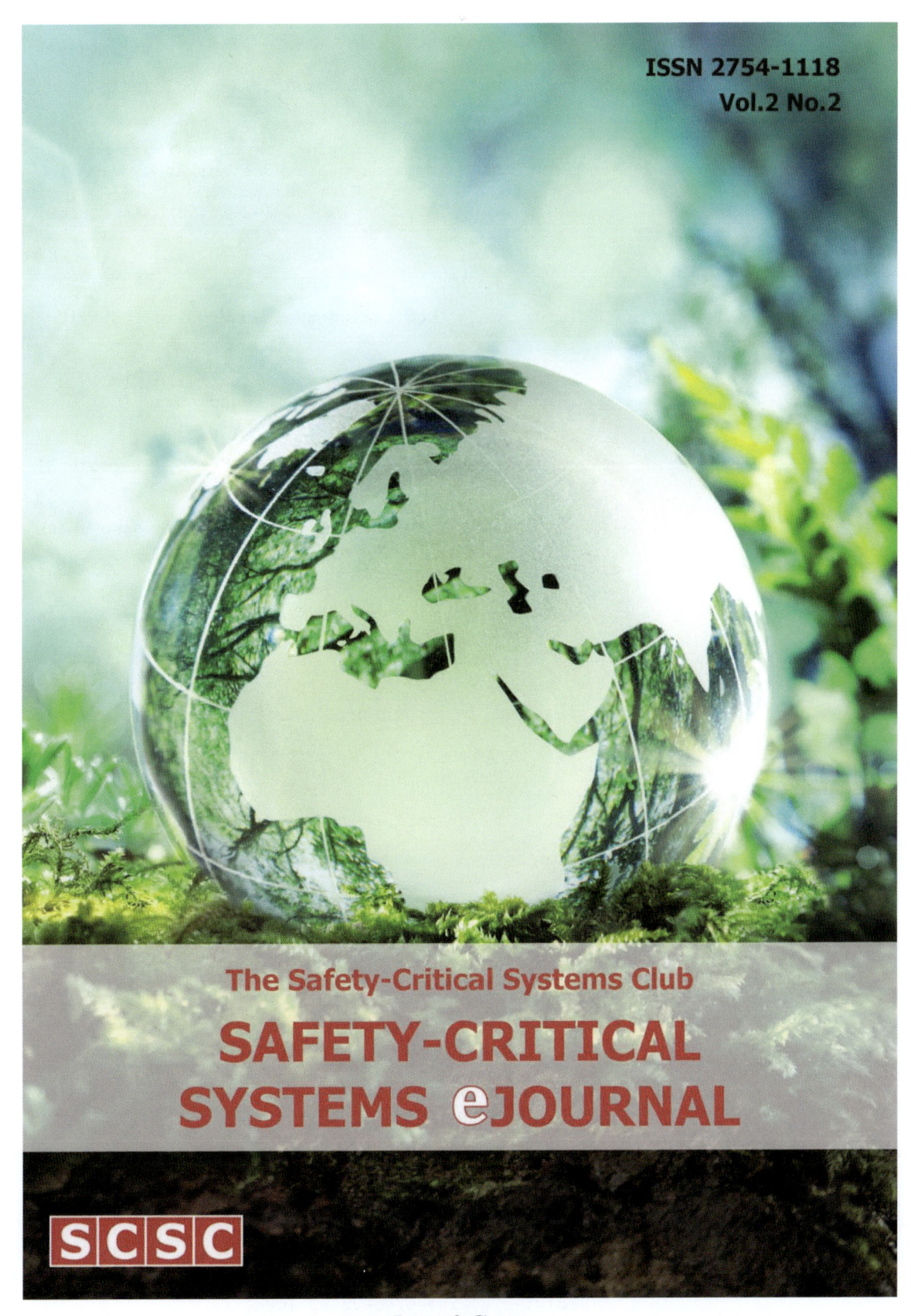

Issue 2 Cover

This collation page left blank intentionally.

Editorial to the 2023 Summer Issue

Welcome to the second issue of the second volume of the Safety-Critical Systems eJournal, which is published by the Safety-Critical Systems Club (SCSC). This issue contains three papers:

- Rob Ashmore, Mark Hadley and James Sharp (UK), address *"Reducing the Risk of a Software Common Mode Failure"*. They provide examples showing that this is not just a theoretical risk and review some previous research, extant standards, and how the problem has been addressed in real-world systems. They conclude that there is no preferred way of protecting against common mode failure in software-based systems and therefore propose a set of criteria that can be used to assess the protections that have been implemented within a system design.
- Derek Fowler and Alasdair Graebner (UK) build upon Derek's paper in the last issue of Volume 1, on using IEC61508 in the Transport Sector, by providing another worked example, *"An IEC 61508 Viewpoint on the Safety Assessment of Railway Control Systems"*. The example considers moving-block Automatic Train Control for a hypothetical underground railway system.
- Malcolm Jones (UK) is "*Chasing the Black Swan*". There may be an 'as yet' undiscovered flaw or lack of understanding in the design of a product, process or facility that could lead to a catastrophic event. How should one continue to search for such a possible flaw with a view to subsequent removal or mitigation — when is 'enough-enough'?

My thanks go to the authors for contributing their papers, and also to the anonymous peer-reviewers (at least three per paper) for suggesting improvements. Apologies also to those reviewers who made some recommendations that were not taken up.

No letters have been received for publication in this issue, but there has been correspondence. An author (not in this issue) and a couple of reviewers independently said that they thought that the referencing of standards, in particular IEC61508, would be clearer were we to follow the recommendations of the standardisation body, rather than the Harvard method we have been using. This issue contains two papers that reference IEC61508, and they do it differently. Derek's paper is the third in a series and so has been kept consistent with its predecessors. I will do a review of referencing and update the Author Guidelines (to be found in the paper template) accordingly.

Previous editorials have said that the next volume of the Safety-Critical Systems eJournal will start with a themed issue. This has been put back a month so that the themed issue will be the second of the year, published to coincide with the Safety-Critical Systems Symposium, SSS'24. The theme is the technologies underpinning autonomous vehicles and how we assure them. Note that this theme is broad — for example "technologies", as well as vision processing, machine learning, etc., can include things like concepts of operation, regulation, standards, ownership of liability, and so on.

Finally a reminder that this year's cover image is to highlight the Systems Approach to Safety of the Environment Working Group, which aims to produce clear guidance on how engineered systems should be developed and managed throughout their entire lifecycle so as to preserve, protect and enhance the environment. If you would like to join, or find out more about this group, please go to their page on the SCSC website: https://scsc.uk/ge

John Spriggs, SCSC Journal Editor
August 2023

This collation page left blank intentionally.

Reducing the Risk of a Software Common Mode Failure

Rob Ashmore, Mark Hadley and James Sharp

Dstl, Portsdown West, UK

Abstract

We describe the nature of a common mode failure, illustrating why software-based components can be particularly susceptible. A number of historical accidents and incidents are used to demonstrate this is not just a theoretical risk. Previous academic research, existing standards and historical civil air programmes are surveyed. This shows the importance of software common mode failure is recognised, but there is no preferred way of protecting against it. A set of criteria are proposed, which provide a means of assessing protections that have been implemented within a system design. These are used to highlight approaches to protection that are suggested for future air systems (and other safety-related applications).

1 Introduction

In an attempt to increase reliability, system architectures often include replicated items. The desired increase in reliability is based on an assumption, typically implicit, that each item will fail independently. A Common Mode Failure (CMF) is an event that undermines this desired independence.

If the replicated items are running software, then this has the potential to cause a CMF. This potential is heightened by the nature of software: using identical copies of the same software, and providing them with identical inputs, offers no protection against software CMF. This is very different to the situation for mechanical or discrete electronics components where identical items, which fail independently, can provide protection.

We are primarily concerned with protecting against software CMF in future air systems, but note that many of the same considerations apply to other safety-related applications.

Initially, in Section 2, a selection of historical examples illustrate the real-world importance of software CMF. An informal review of key academic literature is provided in Section 3. Treatment of software CMF in a selection of standards (and standards-like) documents is discussed in Section 4. Previous approaches adopted within the civil air domain are briefly described in Section 5. Criteria to assist in evaluating protections against software CMF are listed in Section 6, and are related to potential protection approaches that could be adopted in system designs in Section 5. Closing remarks are provided in Section 8.

© Crown copyright (2023), Dstl. This material is licensed under the terms of the Open Government Licence except where otherwise stated. To view this licence, visit https://www.nationalarchives.gov.uk/doc/open-government-licence/version/3 or write to the Information Policy Team, The National Archives, Kew, London TW9 4DU, or email: psi@nationalarchives.gov.uk

2 Historical Examples

Software CMF is not just a theoretical concern. It has been the cause of a number of accidents and incidents, a selection of which are briefly summarised below:

Ariane 5 (Lions 1996): Two SRIs (Inertial Reference Systems[51]) were operating in parallel, with identical hardware and software. A numeric overflow was detected and, by design, the active SRI shut down. The backup SRI had shut down in the preceding time period for exactly the same reason. The lack of a functioning SRI led the loss of the launcher.

NATS System Failure (Walmsley et al. 2015): NATS run a primary System Flight Server (SFS), with a secondary SFS always ready in order to preserve availability. Prior to this incident, recent changes had exposed a latent fault in the SFS software. When an action caused this fault to become a failure, by design the primary SFS shut down. Since it ran identical software, the secondary SFS also shut down. Up to 1900 flights and 230,000 passengers were affected by the resulting outage.

Subsonic / Supersonic Boundary (JSSSC 2010): A front-line aircraft had been rigorously developed, thoroughly tested and dozens were in operational use. As part of an upgrade, a weapons test required extensive telemetry. Analysis showed that all aircraft computers failed and then restarted as the aircraft passed through Mach 1. The aircraft had sufficient momentum and mechanical control that it coasted through this anomaly without the pilot noticing.

Airbus A330-302 (TTSB 2021): On June 14, 2020, China Airlines flight CI202, an Airbus A330-302 aircraft, took off from Shanghai bound for Taipei. At touchdown, the aircraft experienced the quasi-simultaneous failure of the 3 Flight Control Primary Computers (FCPCs), which meant that ground spoilers, thrust reversers and autobrake became unavailable. The flight crew rapidly applied full manual brake to stop the aircraft safely about 30 feet before the end of the runway. The software at the core of this incident had supported more than 8.7 million flight cycles, with no other observations of this type of issue.

These examples show that software CMF can be a significant issue, even in systems that have been rigorously developed and that have a significant amount of service history.

3 Academic Research

3.1 Fault Avoidance

Avoiding the introduction of faults, as far as possible, is the first way of protecting against software CMF. For example, Powell et al. (2011) note that: "*The first defense against design faults is of course to attempt to avoid their occurrence in the first place by applying the techniques of fault prevention (i.e., 'careful design') and fault removal (i.e. 'verification and testing')*".

---

[51] SRI is Système de Référence Inertiel, i.e. Inertial Reference System

(Note that, generally speaking, the academic literature uses the term "design fault" to include faults from a number of software development phases, including, requirements, design, implementation, and maintenance.)

Fault avoidance typically involves the application of appropriately rigorous software development and assurance standards; for example, RTCA/DO-178C (RTCA 2011).

3.2 Fault Tolerance

Powell et al. (2011) also discuss protection against software CMF under the general heading of tolerance to design faults. The first-level response to tolerating design faults comes in two forms, data diversity and design diversity. Both of these forms aim to prevent identical software being presented with identical inputs, thus introducing some (typically, limited) independence.

Data diversity is focused on inputs to the software, whereas design diversity is concerned with the software itself. Broadly speaking there are three basic approaches (see, for example, Powell et al. (2011), Siewiorek et al. (2004) and Laprie et al. (1990)) to introducing design diversity, these being recovery blocks, n-version programming, and n-self checking.

The following subsections provide further information on approaches to fault tolerance.

3.3 Data Diversity

This type of diversity can be achieved by providing identical software with different inputs, for example from sensors located at different points on the airframe. The key premise behind data diversity is that software problems arising during operational use are subtle and hence only triggered for small parts of the input space (see, for example, Ammann and Knight (1988)). Hecht (1993) collected evidence from a number of sources, including spacecraft avionics and telephone switches, which also supports this view.

However, only a limited amount of diversity can be introduced by providing identical software with different input data. In particular, this data typically comes from different sensors that are sampling the same (or at least a very similar) real-world situation. It is unlikely, for example, that two properly-functioning air data sensors will provide radically different data.

One situation in which wildly different data could be provided is following a sensor failure. The software would be expected to handle this failure, but data diversity, in the form of different sensors providing inputs to different copies of the software, would provide an additional layer of protection. An alternative way of providing protection against this specific type of problem would be checking inputs before they are used and, if necessary, replacing out-of-range values with a known-safe alternative.

In theory, it is possible to create artificial data diversity, for example, by adding noise to input signals. In practice it can be difficult to determine an appropriate way to alter inputs, so that their essential meaning is preserved but they are sufficiently different to provide some protection against software CMF.

3.4 Design Diversity — General

The intent of design diversity is to create versions of software that fail in non-identical ways. This typically involves changes to earlier parts of the software development lifecycle (e.g. design and implementation).

Design diversity typically provides greater protection than data diversity as, for example, it is unlikely that two separate programming teams will have made identical errors. That said, as discussed below, common mode failures can still occur even with non-identical software. Furthermore, design diversity incurs greater costs, as additional software development is required.

3.5 Design Diversity — Recovery Blocks

Randell introduced the concept of recovery blocks in 1975 (Randell 1975). These were motivated by the observation that it is standard practice to structure a program of any significant complexity into a series of blocks (e.g. modules, procedures, subroutines, methods).

Before a "significant" block is executed, a recovery point is stored. The first alternate block is run and its output is subjected to an acceptance test. If the output is not acceptable then the program is rewound to the recovery point, the second alternate block is executed and its output is tested for acceptance. The process is repeated until either an acceptable output is found or all alternates have been exercised.

Theoretical issues with the recovery block approach include inaccuracies in the acceptance test, and the possibility of interacting tasks causing a domino effect of cascading recoveries. Tomek et al. (1993) also note that it can be difficult to achieve diversity in the alternate implementations of the recovery blocks; this is partly due to their relatively small size, and partly due to the fact that they are forced to operate on identical inputs.

An experimental evaluation of the recovery block approach was conducted by Anderson et al. (1985). This was based on what was then considered to be a medium-scale development (approximately 8000 lines of CORAL[52] 66), specifically, a naval command and control system. The software was developed by professional programmers to "normal commercial" standards. Of 222 potential failures identified during the evaluation, 165 (approx. 74%) were adequately addressed using the recovery block mechanism. The authors believe that the prototype recovery algorithms (i.e. those for storing and rewinding to the recovery point) were a limiting factor in their results. The use of recovery blocks did, however, lead to larger code size, extra memory demands and longer run time.

3.6 Design Diversity — N-Version Programming

In this approach, several alternate versions are run in parallel and their output is passed to an adjudicator. The adjudicator provides a consolidated output for use by the rest of the system. For example, this consolidation could check that outputs are within pre-defined bounds and then return an average; another alternative would be the use of a simple majority voter.

One of the earliest evaluations of n-version programming was performed in 1996 by Knight and Leveson. In this study (Knight and Leveson 1996), 27 different students each wrote a program to satisfy the same set of requirements. Each program had to pass a series of acceptance tests. Once each program was "acceptable", the collection of programs was subjected to a large barrage of tests. Several common faults were detected between the programs and, more significantly, the number of common faults was higher than would be predicted if the programs exhibited independent faults.

---

[52] CORAL is the Computer On-line Real-time Applications Language

A more recent study (from 2006) was conducted by van der Meulen and Revilla. This considered over 36,000 programs that were submitted as potential solutions to problems posed on a programming website. They concluded (van der Meulen and Revilla 2006) that using different languages led to more diverse programs (e.g. authors were more likely to code a for loop incorrectly when using C than when using Pascal) and, furthermore, that the benefit of multi-version programming reduces as the individual program versions themselves get more reliable.

One problem that n-version programming cannot solve is that of an incorrect requirement. There are also other aspects of programs where apparent diversity could be undermined. For example, Voas et al. (1997) cite a case where common mode failures were injected in program initialisation, despite other aspects of the programs being quite diverse.

A weakness of the three studies referenced above is that they are based on programs written either by students or by "hobby programmers". None of them is based on the type of software that would emerge from a rigorous development process like that associated with aircraft systems. It is not clear, for example, how limits on allowable cyclomatic complexity may constrain implementation options. Likewise, the extent to which software education implicitly reduces diversity is not clear, nor is it clear whether international development programmes offer an opportunity to increase this type of design diversity, for example, due to different educational approaches and cultural norms (Olson and Olson 2003).

The main conclusion to draw from the above examples is that whilst n-version programming can offer some benefits it does not protect against all software common mode faults. Furthermore, the level of benefit that it provides is less than would follow from a naive assumption of complete independence between the versions.

3.7 Design Diversity — N-Self Checking

The n-self checking approach can be considered as a hybrid of the other two approaches. It involves the use of at least two self-checking software components. A component could be made by combining a version of the software and an acceptance test. Alternatively, it could be made by combining several versions of the software with an adjudicator.

The approach of n-self checking software has been studied less extensively in academia than either recovery blocks or n-version programming. Despite that, as indicated later (in Section 5), it forms the basis of at least one system in the civil sector.

3.8 Design Diversity — Different Functionality

In some applications it may be possible to achieve design diversity by implementing software that achieves the same system-level outcome but using different functionality. The use of a different control law in an aircraft flight control system is a potential example. Likewise, implementing software deliberately intended to manage degraded modes of operation, is another.

In some cases, an easy way of achieving some design diversity may be to use an older version of software alongside the most recent one. This might be appropriate if the change between the two software versions was solely related to performance issues. It is not appropriate, however, if the new version fixed a safety-related issue.

3.9 Watchdog Timers

The previous discussions have focussed on fault tolerant approaches that are embodied in software. Another approach involves the use of a watchdog timer: see, for example, Namjoo and McCluskey (1995).

In general, the system is designed so that it signals the watchdog once during each pre-scheduled interval. If the timer is not reset (and, in some cases, if it is reset more than once) during an interval then the watchdog raises an error. This error can be trapped and used, for example, to restart a processor.

Hence, watchdog timers, which are often implemented in hardware, can be used to provide protection against particular types of software error, including those that cause applications to crash and those that result in infinite loops.

3.10 Summary

The academic literature includes a variety of mechanisms for protecting against software design faults that would otherwise cause CMF. Avoiding, as far as possible, the introduction of faults by the application of suitably rigorous software development processes, is important but it does not fully resolve the problem. Additional mechanisms for protecting against software CMF have different strengths and weaknesses. In particular, there is no reliable way of entirely removing the possibility of software CMF: when multiple copies of software are used, it will always represent a risk. Likewise, whilst the value of diversity is noted, there is no preferred way of mitigating this risk. Furthermore, there does not appear to be a standard way of assessing the level of protection (or risk mitigation) provided by a particular approach, or combination of approaches; as indeed is highlighted in the introduction to Annex C, Part 3 of IEC 61508:2010:

> *"Given the large number of factors that affect software systematic capability it is not possible to give an algorithm for combining the techniques and measures that will be correct for any given application."*

4 Standards

The following paragraphs summarise how software CMF is covered in a number of standards, including ones specific to the air domain as well as ones applicable to other domains that use safety-related software.

DEF STAN 00-970: This UK Defence Standard, *"Certification Specifications for Airworthiness"* (UKMOD 2020), does not directly highlight CMF as an issue, whether specific to software or in any other context.

However, software CMF is indirectly included via references that describe an Acceptable Means of Compliance (AMC). For example, Requirement UK25.1309e is concerned with safety-related Programmable Elements (PE). The associated AMC references ARP 4761 (SAE 1996) and RTCA/DO-178C (RTCA 2011). As discussed below, both of these include specific comments on software CMF.

MIL-HDBK-516C: This U.S. Department of Defense Military Handbook, *"Airworthiness Certification Criteria"* (USDoD 2014), includes several mentions of common mode failure.

For example, within Section 6, "Flight Technology", to satisfy one of the criteria requires *"the probability of a common mode failure is extremely remote (1×10^{-9} or as specified by the procuring activity) and is verified by fault tree and hazard analysis"*. Likewise, in Section 7, "Propulsion and Propulsion Installations", satisfying one of the criteria requires *"controls and subsystems are systemically and operationally isolated to avoid possible cascading failures due to any single or common cause"*.

These extracts emerge from subsystem considerations, specifically vehicle control and propulsion. Within MIL-HDBK-516C, software-specific considerations are in Section 15, "Computer Systems and Safety". That section notes typical certification source data include *"various technical analyses and studies (e.g. common mode analysis, ...)"*.

These extracts show that CMF is highlighted in MIL-HDBK-516C, both in general and specifically in relation to software. However, there is no detailed information on how best to protect against this possibility.

ARP 4761: This Aerospace Recommended Practice, *"Guidelines and Methods for Conducting the Safety Assessment Process on Civil Airborne Systems and Equipment"* (SAE 1996), records the potential for CMF, both in general and from the specific perspective of software. It provides a range of techniques for identifying elements that are potentially susceptible to CMF. However, it does not provide a description of ways of protecting against software CMF.

RTCA/DO-178C: This *de facto* assurance standard, *"Software Considerations in Airborne Systems and Equipment Certification"* (RTCA 2011), discusses architectural considerations, with further subsections considering partitioning, multiple-version dissimilar software and safety monitoring.

It notes that partitioning may be achieved by using different hardware for each software component. It also notes that, alternatively, partitioning provisions may be made to allow multiple software components to run on the same hardware platform. Regardless of the adopted approach, partitioned software components should not affect each other's code, inputs, outputs, or data storage.

With respect to multiple-version dissimilar software, RTCA/DO-178C notes that processes completed before dissimilarity is introduced remain a potential source of common errors (e.g. n-version software being developed from the same set of requirements). It also notes that the degree of dissimilarity, and hence the degree of protection, is not usually measurable. As such, dissimilarity is usually used to offer additional protection, beyond that achieved by other DO-178C activities.

IEC 61508: Typically, aviation-specific standards would be preferred to IEC 61508, which adopts a more generic outlook. However, IEC 61508 can still provide useful guidance. For example, in relation to software requirements, Part 3 thereof (IEC 61508-3:2010) notes that:

> *"In order to address independence, a suitable common cause failure analysis shall be carried out. Where credible failure mechanisms are identified, effective defensive measures shall be taken."*

Thus, the importance of protecting against common mode (or, using the terminology of IEC 61058, common cause) failure is also highlighted in relation to both software architecture and software design.

In addition, Annex C thereto includes guidance on a number of techniques and measures that may offer some defence against common mode failure. Examples include fault detection, diverse monitor techniques, re-try fault recovery mechanisms, and graceful degradation.

Nuclear: Whilst it would not be appropriate to apply nuclear standards to aviation directly, they can nevertheless provide informative guidance. One example of this is the US Nuclear Regulatory Commission (NRC) Regulatory Guide (RG) 1.152, "*Criteria for Use of Computers in Safety Systems of Nuclear Power Plants*" (USNRC 2011), which states:

> *"With the introduction of digital systems into plant safety system designs, concerns have emerged about the possibility that a design error in the software in redundant safety system channels could lead to a common-cause failure or common-mode failure of the safety system function. Conditions may exist under which some form of diversity may be necessary to provide additional assurance beyond that provided by the design and quality assurance programs that incorporate software quality assurance and verification and validation."*

> *"With respect to software diversity, experience indicates that the independence of failure modes may not be achieved in cases in which multiple versions of software are developed from the same software requirements."*

Again, this guidance highlights the possibility of software CMF, whilst also noting that some factors (e.g. an incorrect requirement) can defeat assumed levels of software independence.

More-detailed, software-specific guidance for the nuclear industry is provided by a "common position of international nuclear regulators and authorised technical support organisations" on "licensing of safety critical software for nuclear reactors" (TF SCS 2022). Released in 2021 and revised the following year, this recent document notes, for example:

> *"The potential for common cause software failures across all defence barriers utilising computer based systems should be analysed."*

> *"Options must be taken as to what are the most effective methods and techniques to ensure diversity of failure behaviour across diverse software programs. ... Current practice is founded on engineering judgment, which identifies what are considered to be the best means to force diversity with some limited support from research. The possibility of providing further scientific support to these judgments is an open research issue."*

These extracts (and other content) highlight the importance of software CMF, whilst recognising there is no preferred way of introducing diversity to protect against it.

Summary: Software CMF is highlighted in a number of standards and guidance documents. In some cases, possible ways of protecting against this are mentioned (including partitioning and n-version programming). There is, however, no consensus on a preferred approach to protecting against software CMF.

5 Civil Air Sector

5.1 Airbus A320

The following description is based on that provided by Brière and Traverse (1993).

The Airbus A320 was the first civil aircraft equipped with a digital electrical flight control system. This system is designed to tolerate both hardware and software design faults. The aircraft was certified and entered service in the first quarter of 1988.

Two dissimilar types of computer are used in the flight control system:

- Elevator and Aileron Computers (ELACs). These are manufactured by Thomson CSF and are based around the 68010 microprocessor.
- Spoiler and Elevator Computers (SECs). These are based on the 80186 microprocessor and are manufactured in conjunction with SFENA/Aerospatiale.

Each computer features a control channel and a monitoring channel. That is, each computer is self-checking (in the sense of being part of an n-self checking implementation). In total, four different pieces of software exist, covering all combinations of type of computer (i.e. ELAC or SEC) and type of channel (i.e. control or monitor).

The software was developed to RTCA/DO-178A Level 1, which was at that time the most stringent civil aviation software standard. The basic rule adopted by Airbus was that the software is built in the best possible way. Dissimilarity between the four pieces of software is an additional precaution; it is not used to reduce the required software quality effort. (This matches the approach espoused in the more recent RTCA/DO-178C. (RTCA 2011))

For any given function, one computer is designated as being active, with the others being available as "hot spares". Failure detection is achieved by comparing the control output with the monitor. For a failure to be declared this difference needs to be greater than a threshold, and to persist for a given period. If a failure occurs, the computer is isolated from external systems.

Even though the architecture includes four control and monitoring computers, only one of these is required to control the aircraft. Three such computers would be sufficient to meet the safety requirements (derived from system safety assessments); the fourth is included for operational reasons, as it allows a take-off to tolerate a single failed computer.

In addition to the digital electrical flight control system, there is also a mechanical back up. This is connected to the trimmable horizontal stabilizer (giving control of pitch) and the rudder (giving control of yaw). Note, however, that the safety objectives of the fly-by-wire system are defined without taking credit for the mechanical backup.

As of December 1992, the A320 had accrued 1.5 million flight hours. These included one case where, due to the combination of an air conditioning failure and a batch of ELACs being fitted with a component that did not fully meet the required temperature operating range, both ELACs were lost. Failure detection and reconfiguration was successful, with control being handled by the SECs.

5.2 Boeing 777

The following description is based on Yeh (2001).

The Primary Flight Computers (PFCs) in the Boeing 777 form a triple-triple redundant system. Safety requirements apply to PFC failures that could preclude continued safe flight and landing. The associated numerical probabilities are 10^{-10} per flight hour for both functional reliability and functional availability.

The 777 has three channels, each of which has an identical PFC. Within each channel there are three dissimilar computing lanes. This dissimilarity is based on the use of different hardware, specifically: an Intel 80486; a Motorola 68040; and an AMD 29050. This dissimilar hardware leads to a requirement for different Ada compilers.

Although the software in each computing lane was developed by different teams, all of them used the same language, namely Ada. In addition, as noted in a separate article by Yeh, Boeing's experience during the 7J7 development (which led to the 777 flight control system) was that the separate development teams had to ask so many questions to clarify the requirements that their independence was irreparably compromised (Yeh 1988).

A median value select algorithm is used on the output from the PFCs. This is supplemented by cross-lane monitoring within each PFC. There is also cross-channel consolidation between the PFCs (to maintain convergence) and cross-channel equalisation (to keep PFC channel tracking within statistically analysable bounds).

The 777 implementation is best viewed as being "replicated n-version programming". The "replicated" reflects the use of three identical PFCs. The "n-version programming" reflects that three computing lanes are used in each PFC; note, however, that the majority of dissimilarity between these lanes comes from the hardware (and associated compiler) rather than the software's design and implementation.

5.3 Summary

These examples provide valuable experience from real-world attempts to implement software design diversity. Neither of these involved any specific claim, quantified or otherwise, or the efficacy of this approach. In one case, it was simply an additional precaution; in the other only limited design diversity was actually achieved. Overall, this experience suggests design diversity cannot be relied upon as a protection measure against software CMF.

6 Evaluation Criteria

6.1 Structure

The preceding subsections have shown that, whilst it is an important issue, there is no preferred way of protecting against software CMF. Likewise, there is no commonly-agreed way of establishing the level of protection offered by a particular combination of approaches.

To overcome this issue, a set of criteria have been developed that, in combination, allow a qualitative assessment to be conducted. The selected criteria can be organised into three categories: the first addresses fault *prevention*; the second covers fault tolerance approaches against different types of potential failure-causing *inputs*; the third considers fault tolerance approaches based on the nature of the software's *outputs*.

6.2 Prevention

A single criterion relates to fault *prevention*. It considers the *software development processes* that have been used. Ideally, these would follow a widely-recognised industry standard (e.g. RTCA/DO-178C (RTCA 2011)).

6.3 Inputs

The following paragraphs summarise *input*-related criteria.

A failure related to an *unexpected external influence* from another piece of software. Such a situation may arise when one piece of (co-hosted) software runs for longer than expected, thus reducing the amount of processing time available for other software functions. Another way this situation could arise would be one application unintentionally corrupting the memory of another application. The standard way of protecting against such failures is an appropriately robust partitioning scheme.

A failure related to *a specific input bit pattern (or patterns)*. Relevant bit patterns include those corresponding to Not a Number (NaN) or Infinity (INF) (e.g. following division by zero), as well as (for example) patterns that evaluate to very small floating-point numbers. Data diversity offers a degree of protection against this potential failure mechanism. Checking inputs before they are used (i.e. defensive programming) offers a lesser, but still useful, degree of protection.

A failure related to an unlikely, *transitory environment or aircraft attitude*. Examples of such environments include crossing the Equator, flying over the North Pole, crossing the International Date Line and breaking Mach 1.0. Since the output from different (non-failing) sensors would be expected to be correlated, data diversity would not be expected to offer protection against this mechanism. Design diversity may offer some protection and, furthermore, the transitory nature of the inputs means recovery via restart (e.g. enabled via a watchdog) may also provide some protection.

A failure related to an *unlikely, but sustained environment or aircraft attitude*. Potential examples could include the aircraft having a negative forward velocity or the aircraft being inverted. As with the previous criterion, data diversity would not be expected to offer protection. In addition, the sustained nature of this criterion means that recovery via restarts would also offer little protection. Conversely, data diversity and design diversity may offer some protection. A testing regime that investigated a wide range of such situations would also help.

A failure related to *a particular sequence of events* (i.e. a failure that is caused by a specific internal state rather than a particular input). A potential example here could be a sequence of inputs that led to a navigation filter becoming unstable. The importance of the sequence means that both data diversity and design diversity would offer some protection. It also means that such issues are harder to discover via testing.

6.4 Outputs

The following paragraphs summarise *output*-related criteria.

A case where *no output* is provided. This could occur, for example, if a processor gets stuck in an infinite loop, or if the Operating System (OS) crashes. Hardware watch dogs are a standard protection approach for this criterion, because they readily facilitate failure detection and failure recovery.

A case where *a known incorrect output is provided from one computational branch (of several)*. This situation could arise, for example, due to a failing sensor giving an invalid input to a single computational branch, with the invalid nature of the input being recognised and the branch setting an output error flag. Note that the main reason why different computational branches provide different types of output is because of the presence of some diversity (either in data or design): this diversity provides some protection against this criterion. An adjudicator, or voter, that discounts the incorrect output is also required.

A case where *a known incorrect output is provided from all computational branches*. This situation could arise in a situation where a "bad" input is provided and there is no diversity in the implementation. Being able to provide pre-defined "safe" outputs (as part of input checking) offers some protection against this situation. Restarting all the computational branches is another viable protection method (provided the aircraft can sustain controlled flight whilst the restart occurs).

A case where *an unknown incorrect output is provided from one computational branch (of several)*. Note that, as indicated above, this situation can only occur if there is some diversity in the implementation. An undetected failed sensor, which only feeds a single computational branch, could cause this situation. An adjudicator, or voter, that compares the outputs from the different branches offers some protection in this case.

A case where *an unknown incorrect output is provided from all computational branches*. This situation could arise if the platform (and hence, by extension, the embedded software) is used outside its design envelope. Diversity, and particularly design diversity, may offer some limited protection. A suitably wide, and imaginative, testing regime could also help: this is likely to benefit from a combination of software engineers and domain experts.

7 Suggested Protection Approaches

The preceding subsections have established that software CMF is an important issue, having been the cause of previous incidents and accidents, the subject of academic research, a topic in relevant standards documents and a consideration in civil aviation platforms. Nevertheless, there is no preferred way of protecting against software CMF.

It is suggested that subsystems where software CMF may pose a hazard adopt several protective approaches. These are likely to include multiple examples drawn from the following list; where appropriate additional approaches (not listed here) may also be used.

Fault Prevention, which aims to minimise the number of faults present in the software. This is generally achieved through the use of processes that apply an appropriate level of control to software development activities. RTCA/DO-178C (RTCA 2011) is an example of such processes.

Partitioning, which isolates failures in the region where they occur, rather than allowing them to cascade across the entire system. This is related to, but also supplemental to, partitioning that protects one application's memory area from the actions of another application.

Data Diversity, which involves providing different copies of software (which may or may not be identical) with different inputs. This is easiest to adopt when data diversity is naturally generated, e.g. from different sensors. Artificial data diversity can be introduced, but it can be difficult to determine the appropriate level of diversity to be used.

Input Checking, which (not surprisingly) involves checking inputs before they are used. This is a natural part of defensive programming and supports partitioning, e.g. by preventing bad data polluting subsequent computations.

Design Diversity, which typically involves using software developed by separate programming teams to perform the same function.

Failure Detection, which is concerned with identifying software failures so that they can be adequately managed and, ultimately, recovered from.

Failure Recovery, which typically involves returning the software to a "known safe" state and resuming processing.

Extensive Testing, which might involve imaginative test construction on the part of test engineers and domain experts, combined with automated test approaches, e.g. fuzzing.

For ease of reference, Table 12 indicates the relationship between evaluation criteria and the approaches suggested above. Within this table, a "++" symbol indicates a case where the approach may be expected to provide significant benefit; a "+" symbol indicates a case where moderate benefit may be expected.

Table 12 ~ Indicative Relationship between Evaluation Criteria and Suggested Approaches for Providing Protection Against Software CMF

	Fault Prevention	Partitioning	Data Diversity	Input Checking	Design Diversity	Failure Detection	Failure Recovery	Extensive Testing
Prevention: Software development processes	++							
Inputs: Unexpected external influences		++						
Inputs: Specific input bit pattern (or patterns)			++	+				+
Inputs: Unlikely, transitory environment or aircraft attitude					+	++	++	
Inputs: Unlikely, but sustained environment or aircraft attitude			+		+			++
Inputs: Particular sequence of events			++		++			
Outputs: No output						++	++	
Outputs: Known incorrect output from one computational branch			++		++	+	+	
Outputs: Known incorrect output from all computational branches					+	++	++	
Outputs: Unknown incorrect output from one computational branch			++		++	+	+	+

	Fault Prevention	Partitioning	Data Diversity	Input Checking	Design Diversity	Failure Detection	Failure Recovery	Extensive Testing
Outputs: Unknown incorrect output from all computational branches			+		+			++

It should be noted that Table 12 is intended to illustrate one way to substantiate an argument that protection against software CMF had been appropriately considered. In particular, the table's contents are subjective in nature and not intended to provide strict direction, nor form the basis of any algorithm to support the combination of identified techniques. Consequently, it is not appropriate to dissect Table 12 in forensic detail. Nevertheless, there is merit in highlighting some key points.

When considering the criteria (i.e. looking across each of the rows), it is apparent that each criterion has at least one "++", with most criteria having at least one additional "+". There are two exceptions, which are criteria that only have a single "++", specifically, "Prevention: Software development processes" and "Inputs: Unexpected external influences". This is a consequence of the focus adopted for this paper. It would be possible to add significantly more detail on both of these aspects (e.g. use of formal static analysis tools, analysis of potential interference paths in multi-core processors) with a corresponding increase in symbols in the table. In addition, it is expected that these activities would be undertaken as part of any safety-related software development. Consequently, the two single "++" criteria are not judged to represent significant limitations in the approaches that are available to protect against software CMF.

When considering the approaches (i.e. looking down the columns), it is apparent that most approaches have multiple entries, both "++" and "+". There are three exceptions to this. Two of these exceptions are "Fault Prevention" and "Partitioning", which directly relate to the two criteria discussed above. The other exception is "Input Checking". As with the previous items, the apparently limited value of input checking is a direct consequence of this paper's intentionally narrow focus on software CMF. In particular, input checking is of significant wider value in safety-related software implementations.

Overall, constructions like Table 12 should help systems engineers understand, in a qualitative sense, levels of protection against software CMF. It also highlights that protection will likely have to be built from a number of approaches, and that common safety-related software approaches, e.g. fault prevention, partitioning, and input checking, are by themselves unlikely to be sufficient.

8 Closing Remarks

Software CMF is a significant issue, having been the cause of a number of accidents and incidents. It (and protection against it) has been the subject of significant academic research. Its importance is highlighted in standards and it has influenced development approaches on key civil air programmes. However, there is currently no preferred way of protecting against software CMF, nor is there an established mechanism for assessing any protection that has been implemented. To address this limitation, a set of evaluation criteria have been developed (and used on a previous platform-specific piece of work). These allow suggested protection approaches to be advanced for future air domain programmes (and other safety-related systems).

Disclaimers

This article is an overview of UK MOD sponsored research and is released for informational purposes only. The contents of this document should not be interpreted as representing the views of the UK MOD, nor should it be assumed that they reflect any current or future UK MOD policy. The information contained in this document cannot supersede any statutory or contractual requirements or liabilities and is offered without prejudice or commitment.

Acknowledgments

The authors gratefully acknowledge the comments made by the anonymous reviewers. These significantly improved the article.

References

Ammann P. E. and Knight J. C. (1988). *Data Diversity: An Approach to Software Fault Tolerance*. IEEE Trans. Computers, 37 4 (1988) 418-425.

Anderson T., Barrett P. A., Halliwell D. N. and Moulding M. R. (1985). *Software Fault Tolerance: An Evaluation*. IEEE Trans. Soft. Eng., SE-11 12 (1985) 1502-1510.

Brière D. and Traverse P. (1993). *AIRBUS A320/A330/A340 Electrical Flight Controls - A Family of Fault-Tolerant Systems*. In 23rd IEEE Int. Symp. on Fault-Tolerant Computing (FTCS-23), pages 616–623, Toulouse, France, 1993.

Hecht H. (1993). *Rare Conditions — An Important Cause of Failures*. In: Practical Paths to Assurance, Proceedings of the Eighth Annual Conference on Computer Assurance. (COMPASS '93) pp.81-85, 1993. IEEE.

IEC 61508-3:2010. *Functional Safety of Electrical/electronic/programmable electronic Safety-related Systems — Part 3: Software requirements*. IEC 61508-3, Edition 2. International Electrotechnical Commission. Geneva. 2010.

JSSSC. (2010). *Software System Safety Handbook: A Technical and Managerial Team Approach, Sub-section F.4, "Flight Controls Fail at Supersonic Transition"*. Joint Software System Safety Committee, US Department of Defense. Available from: https://ac.cto.mil/wp-content/uploads/2019/06/Joint-SW-Systems-Safety-Engineering-Handbook.pdf. Accessed 19th July 2023.

Knight J. C. and Leveson N. G. (1996). *An Experimental Evaluation of the Assumption of Independence in Multi-version Programming*. IEEE Trans. Soft. Eng., SE-12, 1 (1996) 96-109.

Laprie J-C., Arlat J., Béounes C. and Kanoun K. (1990). *Definition and Analysis of Hardware- and Software-Fault-Tolerant Architectures*. Computer, 23 7 (1990) 39-51. IEEE.

Lions J-L. (1996). *ARIANE 5: Flight 501 Failure*. Report by the Inquiry Board chaired by Prof. J-L. Lions. Available from: http://www.di.unito.it/~damiani/ariane5rep.html. Accessed 19th July 2023.

Namjoo M. and McCluskey E. J. (1995). *Watchdog Processors and Capability Checking*. Twenty-Fifth Int. Symp. on Fault-Tolerant Computing — Highlights from Twenty-Five Years, June 1995, 94-97.

Olson J. S. and Olson G. M. (2003). *Culture Surprises in Remote Software Development Teams: When in Rome doesn't help when your team crosses time zones, and your deadline doesn't*. Queue, 1(9), pp.52-59.

Powell D., Arlat J., Deswarte Y. and Kanoun K. (2011). *Tolerance of Design Faults*. In: Jones C. B. and Lloyd J. L. (editors). *Dependable and Historic Computing*. Lecture Notes in Computer Science, Volume 6875. Springer Nature, London.

Randell B. (1975). *System Structure for Software Fault Tolerance*. IEEE Trans. Soft. Eng., SE-1, 2 (1975) 220-232.

RTCA. (2011). *Software Considerations in Airborne Systems and Equipment Certification*. RTCA/DO-178C. RTCA Inc. Also available as EUROCAE Document ED-12C.

SAE. (1996). *Guidelines and Methods for Conducting the Safety Assessment Process on Civil Airborne Systems and Equipment*. ARP4761, December 1996. SAE International.

Siewiorek D. P., Chillarege R. and Kalbarczyk Z. T. (2004). *Reflections on Industry Trends and Experimental Research in Dependability*. IEEE Trans. Secure and Dependable Computing, 1 2 (2004) 109-127.

TF SCS. (2022). *Licensing of Safety Critical Software for Nuclear Reactors: Common position of International Nuclear Regulators and Authorised Technical Support Organisations*. Regulator Task Force on Safety Critical Software (TF SCS). Available from: https://www.onr.org.uk/software.pdf. Accessed 20th July 2023.

Tomek L. A., Muppala J. K. and Trivedi K. S. (1993). *Modeling Correlation in Software Recovery Blocks*. IEEE Trans. Soft. Eng, 19 11 (1993) 1071-1086.

TTSB. (2021). *CI202 Occurrence Investigation*. Executive Summary of the Final Report translated into English, September 2021. Taiwan Transport Safety Board. Available from: https://www.ttsb.gov.tw/media/4913/ci202_executive-summary_release.pdf. Accessed 19th July 2023.

UKMOD. (2020). *Certification Specifications for Airworthiness: Part 1 — Fixed Wing Combat Air Systems*. DEF.STAN.00-970, Issue 17, August 2020.

USDoD. (2014). *Airworthiness Certification Criteria*. MIL-HDBK-516C, December 2014.

USNRC. (2011). *Criteria for Use of Computers in Safety Systems of Nuclear Power Plants*. Regulatory Guide 1.152, Revision 3, July 2011. U.S. Nuclear Regulatory Commission.

van der Meulen M. J. P. and Revilla M. A. (2006). *The Effectiveness of Software Diversity in a Large Population of Programs*. IEEE Trans. Soft. Eng., 34, 6 (2006) 753-764.

Voas J., Ghosh A., Charron F. and Kassab L. (1997). *Reducing Uncertainty About Common-Mode Failures*. In: Proceedings of the Eighth International Symposium on Software Reliability Engineering, 1997, pp. 308–319.

Walmsley R., Anderson T., Brendish C., McDermid J. A., Rolfe M., Sultana J., Swan M. and Toms M. (2015). *NATS System Failure 12 December 2014 — Final Report*. Independent Enquiry Panel chaired by Sir Robert Walmsley KCB. Available from: https://www.nats.aero/wp-content/uploads/2015/05/Independent-Enquiry-Final-Report-2.0.pdf. Accessed 19th July 2023.

Yeh Y. C. (1988). *Design Considerations in Boeing 777 Fly-By-Wire Computers*. In 3rd IEEE Int. Symp. on High-Assurance Systems Engineering, pages 64-72, 1988.

Yeh Y.C. (2001). *Safety Critical Avionics for the 777 Primary Flight Controls System*. Digital Avionics Systems Conference, 2001 (20th DASC).

An IEC 61508 Viewpoint on the Safety Assessment of Railway Control Systems

Derek Fowler[1] and Alasdair Graebner[2]

1. Independent Safety Engineering Consultant, Reading, UK
2. Railway System Engineer, UK

Abstract

An article entitled "An IEC 61508 Viewpoint on System Safety in the Transport Sector" in the July 2022 edition of the Safety-critical Systems eJournal, proposed a way of thinking about the safety assessment of transportation systems that is based on the fundamental principles of international functional-safety standard IEC 61508. Then, in a second article (January 2023), an operational example from Air Traffic Management (ATM) was used to outline how an IEC 61508 approach to safety assessment could be applied to the ATM sector. Now, in this article, the example of a new, moving-block Automatic Train Control system, for a hypothetical Metro, is used to outline how an IEC 61508 approach to safety assessment could be applied to the safety assessment of railway control systems in general.

1 Introduction

1.1 Background

IEC 61508 — *"Functional Safety of Electrical/electronic/programmable electronic Safety-related Systems"* (IEC 2010) — is probably the most widely-accepted, international generic standard on functional safety. Although its ancestry can be traced back to process industries, the intention behind the Standard has always been to provide a solid, comprehensive basis for adaptation, as necessary, to meet the needs of a wide range of industry sectors.

In the first of three related articles, Fowler (2022) proposed 'a way of thinking' about the assessment of the various safety-related systems deployed in the Transport sector — especially commercial-aviation and rail applications — based on the key principles and safety lifecycle set out in Parts 1 and 4 of IEC 61508.

A follow-up article (Fowler and Fota, 2023) then took the example of an innovative Air Traffic Management (ATM) operational concept and used it to outline how an IEC 61508 approach to safety assessment could be applied effectively to the ATM sector, and what the results thereof might look like, starting with the concept of the traffic in the airspace being (what IEC 61508 calls) the Equipment Under Control (EUC).

This article now takes a similar approach but with the example of a new, moving-block Automatic Train Control (ATC) system for a hypothetical Metro; this is used to outline how an IEC 61508 approach to safety assessment could be applied effectively to the

Railway sector in general, and what the results thereof might look like, starting with the concept of the movement of trains around the railway being the EUC.

It is important, at this stage, to clarify five features of the article, as follows:

Firstly, it is generic in its approach and is not a case study of a particular project.

Secondly, due to the vast amount of detail that would be involved in a full system safety assessment of this kind, it is not an exhaustive, rigorous study — rather, only examples of the outputs of the relevant phases of the IEC 61508 safety lifecycle are provided, sufficient to give insights into the processes involved.

Thirdly, it is not the intention to prescribe IEC 61508-compliant processes for railway applications — rather, it is to use the lifecycle cycle model from Part 1 of IEC 61508 (IEC 61508-1) to shape thinking about system safety assessments away from a mindset that, in the past at least, "*focussed too much on system reliability and not enough on system functionality, contrary to, inter alia, the most basic principles of the international functional-safety standard IEC 61508*" (Fowler 2022).

Fourthly, in line with the approach taken in the two previous articles in this series, i.e. Fowler (2022) and Fowler & Fota (2023), it is not the intention to carry out a detailed compliance assessment of current railway safety standards and practices against IEC 61508. That said, it is worth drawing attention here to the following, rather bold, statement in the latest version of EN 50126-1 (CENELEC 2017):

> "*EN 50126 forms part of the railway sector specific application of IEC 61508. Meeting the requirements in this European Standard, together with the requirements of other suitable standards, is sufficient to ensure that additional compliance to IEC 61508 does not need to be demonstrated*",

and to the findings of Fowler (2015), which suggested that the version of EN 50126, applicable at that time (1999), fell well short of compliance with the most basic principle of IEC 61508, which is outlined in Sub-section 1.2 below. Suffice it to say that, to date, we have found no evidence to show that the CENELEC (2017) statement is justified in today's, increasingly-automated railway environment, but would be happy to hear from any readers as to how, and where, current railway standards do meet the particular IEC 61508-1 requirements presented in this paper, should that be the case.

Fifthly, whereas numerous references are made to parts of IEC 62260, *Urban Guided Transport Management and Command/Control Systems (UGTMS)*, the use of this standard (IEC 2014) is simply and solely as a convenient source of information that would otherwise have to be derived from scratch, e.g. the very large number of generic system functions described in Sub-section 3.6 above.

1.2 The IEC 61508 Viewpoint

Part 4 of IEC 61508 (IEC 61508-4) defines Functional Safety as being:

> "*that part of the overall safety relating to the EUC / EUC Control System that depends on the correct functioning of the safety-related systems and other risk-reduction measures*".

It is founded on the IEC 61508 fundamental principle that:

- where there exists an Equipment Under Control (EUC)[53], with its associated Control System[54], which is *inherently* hazardous to the environment in which it operates; then
- Safety-Related Systems (SRSs)[55] and/or Other Risk-reduction Measures (ORRMs) need to be developed, in order to *reduce*, to a tolerable level, the inherent risk presented by the EUC.

This simple principle of risk reduction is fundamental to IEC 61508 and is illustrated in the risk graph of Figure 6, which itself is derived directly from Figure A.1 of Part 5 of IEC 61508 (Fowler 2022).

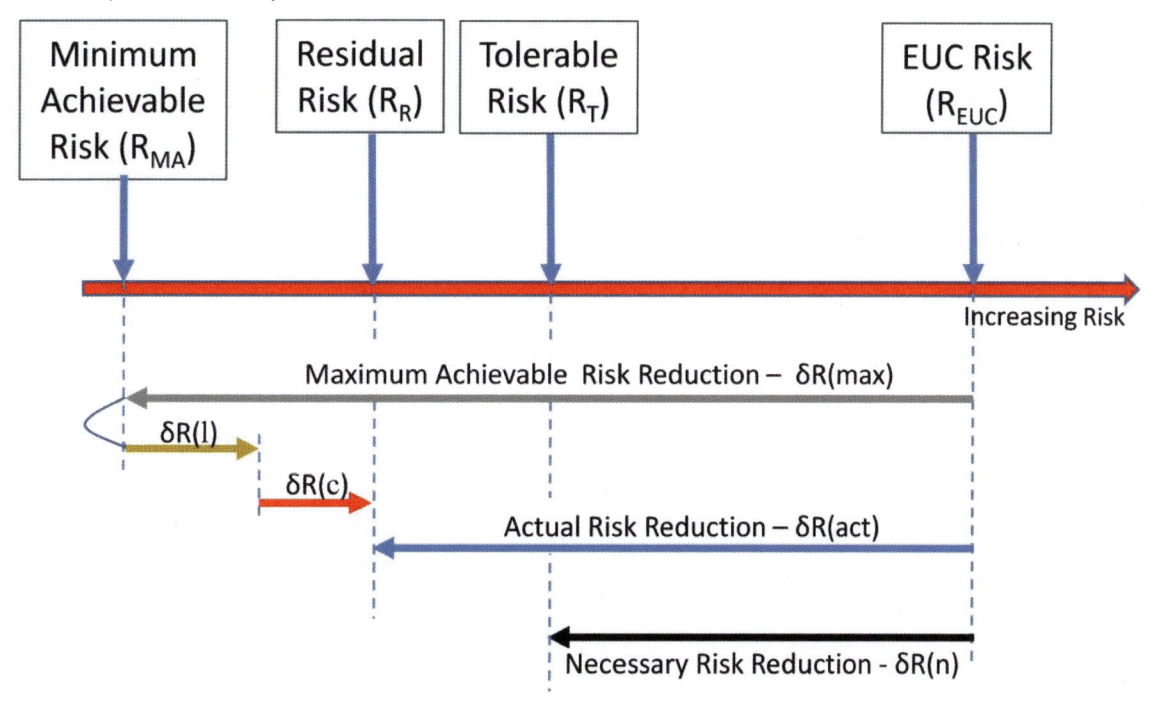

Figure 6 ~ Risk Graph

The inherent (or unmitigated) EUC Risk (R_{EUC}), provides a (usually theoretical) reference point that takes *no* account of the possible risk reduction afforded by any SRSs / ORRMs, and Necessary Risk Reduction ($\delta R(c)$) is the amount of risk reduction that must be *achieved* by the SRSs / ORRMs in order to ensure that the Tolerable Risk is not exceeded.

Residual Risk (R_R) is the risk that is *actually* achieved for the EUC, with *full* account of the risk reduction afforded by the SRSs / ORRMs now taken into account, and depends on three properties of those SRSs / ORRMs:

- their functionality and performance, which determine the maximum achievable risk reduction $\delta R(max)$, if (theoretically) the SRSs / ORRMs never failed;
- their reliability, in terms of the likelihood of their failure to function at all, and thereby reducing the achievable risk reduction by an amount $\delta R(l)$; and

---

[53] "*Equipment, machinery, apparatus or plant used for manufacturing, process, transportation, medical or other activities*" (IEC 61508-4).

[54] "*System that responds to input signals from the [EUC] ... and/or from an operator, and generates output signals causing the EUC to operate in the desired manner*" (IEC 61508-4) but without specific regard to the safety of that operation.

[55] Designated system that both: implements the required safety functions necessary to achieve or maintain a safe state for the EUC; and is intended to achieve, on its own or with other safety-related systems and 'other risk-reduction measures', the necessary safety integrity for the required safety functions (IEC 61508-4).

- their integrity, in terms of the likelihood of their operating corruptly (i.e. spuriously or incorrectly), and thereby introducing a new source of risk of $\delta R(c)$.

Hence, given that the unmitigated EUC Risk (R_{EUC}) would be *many* orders of magnitude greater than the Tolerable Risk (R_T), the inescapable conclusion is that we must first specify SRSs / ORRMs that are proven to have sufficient functionality and performance to achieve a risk *reduction* in the absence of failure ($\delta R(max)$) that is greater than what is "necessary" ($\delta R(n)$), before considering any risk *increase* caused by such failures.

That is the IEC 61508 viewpoint, on which the remainder of this article is based.

2 Scope

Like Fowler (2022), the scope of this article is limited to the initial phases of the IEC 61508 safety lifecycle, which result in the specification of detailed *functional safety requirements*[56] and *safety integrity requirements* necessary and sufficient for the subject SRSs / ORRMs to achieve a tolerable level of risk for the EUC.

The relevant phases are shown in Figure 7, overleaf, which is based on Figure 2 of IEC 61508-1 (IEC 2010), with the following modifications:

- Phases 10 and 12 to 14 have been omitted since they address requirements realisation and, therefore, fall outside the scope of this article;
- Phases 6 to 8 have been omitted as they cover only planning for the realisation phases;
- a summary of the main outputs of each phase has been added; and
- the specification of safety requirements for ORRMs, in Phase 11, falls *within* the scope of this article, even though it is outside the scope of IEC 61508 itself.

It should be noted also that IEC 61508's use of the term "*E/E/PE (System) — Electrical/Electronic/Programmable Electronic (System)*" — was felt to be too specific and limiting for the purposes of this article; therefore, the more general term "safety-related system (SRS)" is used instead herein so as to allow human and procedural elements to be included as well as (and possibly instead of) technical equipment[57].

In line with Fowler (2022), it is expected that the resulting system safety requirements would be sufficient to ensure that:

- under all *normal* operating conditions[58], a fully-functioning railway control system would be capable of mitigating all potential EUC hazards[59], such that at least a tolerable level of EUC risk would be achieved;
- a fully-functioning railway control system would be able to continue to mitigate potential EUC hazards, under all *abnormal* operating conditions[60] without a significant increase in the achievable level of EUC risk;

---

[56] The term *functional safety requirements* was coined in Fowler (2022) in preference to the (arguably ambiguous) IEC 61508 term of *safety functions requirements*; it covers safety requirements for both functionality (<u>what</u> has to be done) and performance (<u>how well</u> it has to been done).

[57] IEC 61508-1, Sub-section 1.2, Note 2 states that "…a person can form part of a safety-related system".

[58] That is all those conditions that are expected to occur on a day-to-day basis (Fowler 2022).

[59] That is, those hazards that are *inherent* in railway operations *before* any safety-related systems are provided in order to mitigate them (Fowler 2022)

[60] That is those conditions that are expected to occur less frequently but under which the ATC system is expected to continue without significant degradation of its primary functionality or performance.

- the causes and consequences of *failure* conditions, within the subject railway control system, are controlled such that the overall achievable level of EUC risk would remain at least tolerable.

As we work herein through these lifecycle phases for the subject railway operations, it might appear that some of the steps could be simplified by, for example, subsuming them into other steps. Indeed, IEC 61508 allows for this to be done, where applicable, but, for the purposes of this article, we decided to adhere exactly to the lifecycle, which was detailed previously in Fowler (2022), except where indicated otherwise in the Sections below.

IEC 61508 Lifecycle Phases — **Phase outputs**

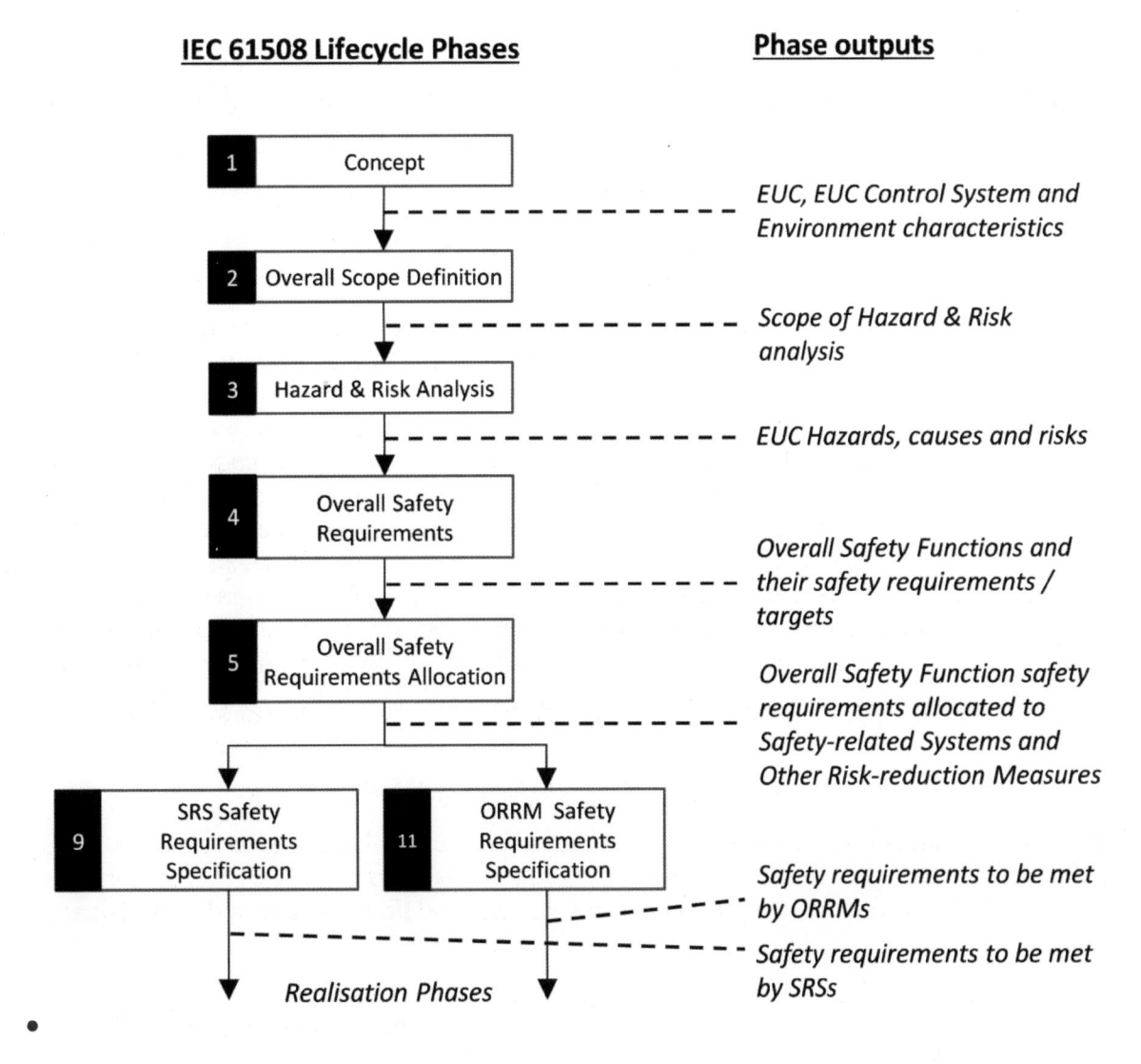

1. Concept → *EUC, EUC Control System and Environment characteristics*
2. Overall Scope Definition → *Scope of Hazard & Risk analysis*
3. Hazard & Risk Analysis → *EUC Hazards, causes and risks*
4. Overall Safety Requirements → *Overall Safety Functions and their safety requirements / targets*
5. Overall Safety Requirements Allocation → *Overall Safety Function safety requirements allocated to Safety-related Systems and Other Risk-reduction Measures*
9. SRS Safety Requirements Specification → *Safety requirements to be met by SRSs*
11. ORRM Safety Requirements Specification → *Safety requirements to be met by ORRMs*

↓ Realisation Phases ↓

Figure 7 ~ Applicable IEC 61508 Overall Safety Lifecycle

3 Operational Context

It is assumed that a new Automatic Train Control (ATC) system will replace a conventional, fixed-block signalling system (including automatic train protection), on a hypothetical existing Metro.

The ATC system will be based on the Communications-based Train Control (RailSystem 2022) concept in which real-time, train-control information (based on radio communications), and moving-block signalling principles, are used to increase line capacity (by reducing the headway between trains travelling on the same line), and to minimise the amount of trackside equipment, *without* any degradation in the safety of the railway operations.

Conceptually, railway control systems (including our ATC system) can be thought of as comprising the following:

- Automatic Train Supervision (ATS): ensures the safety of all trains by continuously detecting the presence, or absence, of trains and (where applicable) transmitting safety speed and distance data from the wayside; by applying the correct settings to infrastructure and signalling assets; and by directing both the movement and movement authority for each train formed to deliver a timetabled service as requested by ATR;
- Automatic Train Regulation (ATR): interprets the timetable and delivers the planned service; continually monitors the progress of trains, detecting when trains are running "off timetable"; and regulates the progress of a train, or trains, to bring services back in line with the timetable;
- Automatic Train Operation (ATO): receives information from the signalling system regarding movement authority and required speed profile; and causes the train to proceed when in an automatic driving mode; and
- Automatic Train Protection (ATP): continuously compares the actual train speed with the safety speed limit applicable at that time for the section occupied by the train; and causes the train to emergency brake in the event of an infringement.

In general, ATP and ATS are considered to be "vital" systems on the basis that their primary purpose is *accident prevention* and on which the safety of the railway critically depends — in IEC 61508 terms, they would fall into the category of safety-related systems. The purpose of ATO and ATR, on the other hand, is *primarily* the efficient running of the railway though, as we will see in Sub-section 4.6.6 below, ATR and/or ATO might also make some positive contribution to safety.

The level of automation for a fully-functioning, passenger-carrying train is assumed to be *semi-automated,* or GOA3, which is defined in the UGTMS standard (IEC 2014a) as follows:

> "The driver is in the front cabin of the train observing the guideway[61] and stops the train in the case of a hazardous situation. Acceleration and braking are automated, and the speed is supervised continuously by the [ATC] system. Safe departure of the train from the station is the responsibility of the operations staff (door opening and closing may be done automatically."

In effect, the control of train movements, i.e. our EUC, is fully automated whereas other areas of safety concern, such as managing the platform-train interface, are not. Even so, the choice of a GOA3 system here still presents a major challenge for this, and all similar, advanced-technology safety assessments[62]; as pointed out in Fowler (2022), regarding the introduction of *"self-driving"* cars, it would be naïve to assume that replacing ("unreliable") human operators by supposedly more-reliable computer-based systems would lead directly to fewer accidents without *first* assessing whether those systems would

---

[61] Also known as the permanent way

[62] Clearly, removing the driver from the cab (GOA4) would provide an even greater challenge; it would, however, also introduce further complexity that would be difficult to handle within this article, without adding much to its key message.

be capable of matching the traditional skills and experience of humans in equivalent transportation roles.

4 Safety Assessment

4.1 Concept (IEC 61508-1 Phase 1)

4.1.1 Aim

The aim of Phase 1 is to gather as much information about the *Equipment Under Control* (EUC), its *Environment*, and the *EUC Control System*, as is necessary and sufficient to enable the other safety lifecycle activities to be satisfactorily carried out.

It is important to note that, as an enabling activity, this would be a precursor to, but not form part of, the safety assessment *per se* and would require substantial operational and systems-engineering specialist input, relevant to each specific application. In practice, such material may be found in a typical *Operational Concept* document.

4.1.2 EUC

As with any other railway-signalling application, we can understand the EUC as being, in general, the movement of trains around the rail network, for whatever purpose. This understanding is consistent with the core IEC 61508 principle that the EUC is the main source of hazards, the mitigation of which Safety Related Systems (SRSs) and/or Other Risk-reduction Measures (ORRMs) are provided, to achieve a tolerable level of EUC risk.

The key inherent properties of the EUC that we would need for a full safety assessment are as follows:

- Train types:
    - ATC-equipped passenger-carrying trains
    - ATC-equipped engineering trains, in various formations
    - "Alien" trains, i.e. not ATC equipped;

- Passenger-carrying train properties:
    - Configuration: e.g. 7 cars, with open gangways, operating as a single unit
    - Train length
    - Tare mass
    - Power: e.g. electric 3rd rail 750V DC, running rail return
    - In service motoring and braking characteristics
    - Emergency braking capability
    - Passenger capacity;

- Railway system properties:
    - Fleet size
    - Target peak trains per hour (timetabled in each direction).

4.1.3 Environment

IEC 61508 defines the "environment" for the EUC in terms that include its physical, operating, legal and maintenance properties.

The environment properties for the subject ATC operations, which determine the functionality, performance and integrity *required* of the ATC system, usually include:

- Weather conditions, e.g. visibility and rail icing, and frequencies thereof;
- Poor rail adhesion, e.g. leaf fall on to track;
- Flood risk, which for the purposes of this article is assumed to be negligible;
- Track parameters, as follows:
    - total running length (excluding depots & sidings)
    - percentage of the track that is underground
    - maximum line (design) speed
    - number and details of stations, above and below the surface
    - number and details of depots
    - number and details of sidings
    - types and layout of demandable elements, e.g. points & controlled crossings, and non-demandable elements, e.g. diamond crossings
    - availability of secondary train detection and wayside signals for alien trains;
- Properties of individual stations, including:
    - platform lengths
    - the presence (or otherwise) of platform-screen and platform-end doors (both are assumed to be present)
    - the platform-train interface (PTI).

4.1.4 EUC Control System

Given the above interpretation of the EUC as being the movement of trains around the rail network, we can view the EUC Control System as being the functional system (comprising people, procedures and equipment), whose primary aim is to control that movement in the desired manner *and* facilitate the embarkation and disembarkation of passengers.

In its basic form, IEC 61508 generally makes a distinction between the EUC Control System and the Safety Related Systems (SRSs) that are required additionally in order to reduce the risks that are inherent in the operation of the EUC.

Fortunately, IEC 61508-1 also permits parts, or all, of an EUC Control System to be considered to be safety-related, *provided* they are subject to the appropriate requirements of the Standard (Fowler 2022) and, therefore, the need for rigid distinctions to be drawn between what is vital and non-vital is obviated.

What *is* important from an IEC 61508 perspective, is the relationship between the EUC and the EUC Control System, which is indicated in Figure 8.

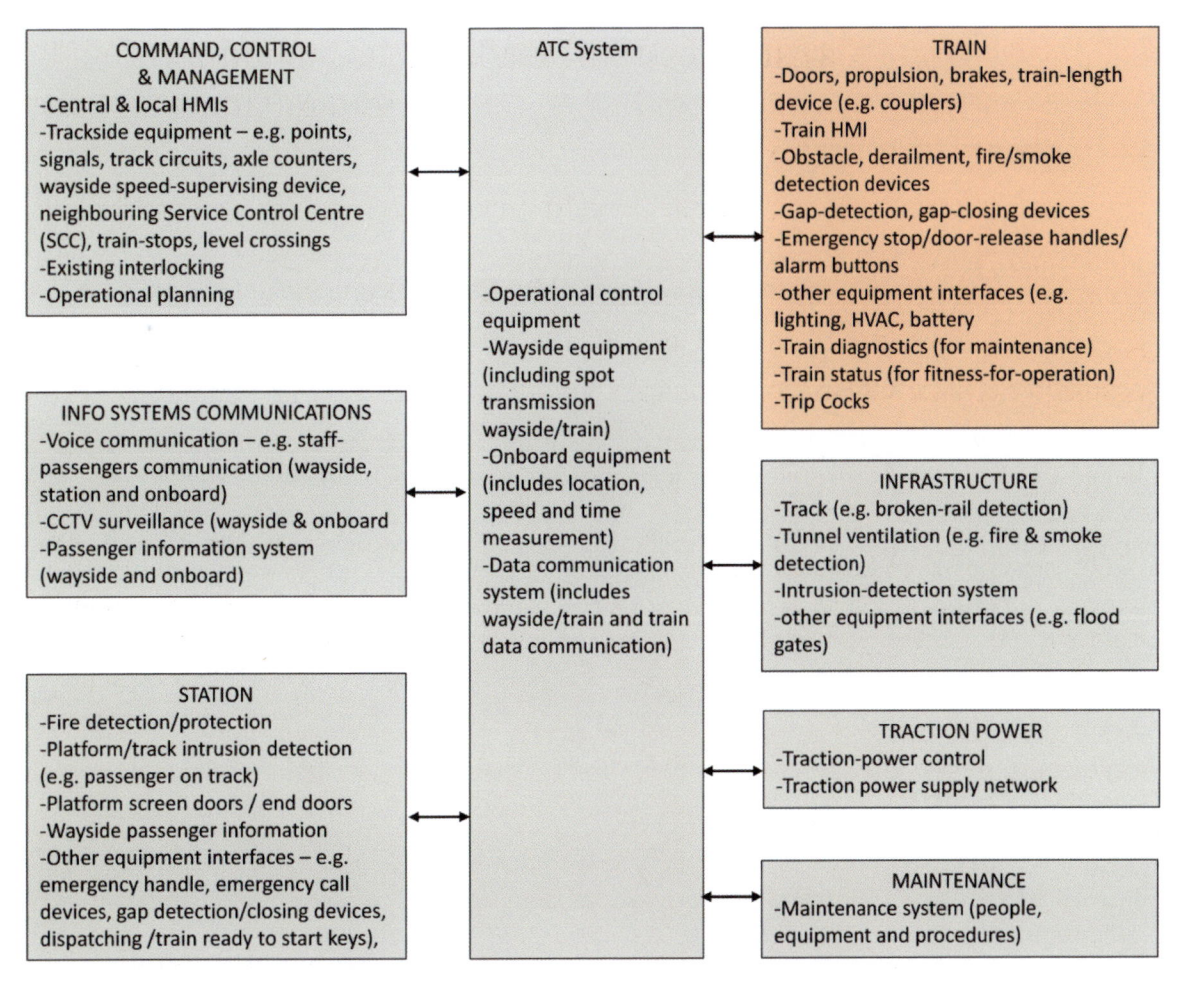

COMMAND, CONTROL & MANAGEMENT	ATC System	TRAIN
-Central & local HMIs -Trackside equipment – e.g. points, signals, track circuits, axle counters, wayside speed-supervising device, neighbouring Service Control Centre (SCC), train-stops, level crossings -Existing interlocking -Operational planning	-Operational control equipment -Wayside equipment (including spot transmission wayside/train) -Onboard equipment (includes location, speed and time measurement) -Data communication system (includes wayside/train and train data communication)	-Doors, propulsion, brakes, train-length device (e.g. couplers) -Train HMI -Obstacle, derailment, fire/smoke detection devices -Gap-detection, gap-closing devices -Emergency stop/door-release handles/ alarm buttons -other equipment interfaces (e.g. lighting, HVAC, battery -Train diagnostics (for maintenance) -Train status (for fitness-for-operation) -Trip Cocks

INFO SYSTEMS COMMUNICATIONS		INFRASTRUCTURE
-Voice communication – e.g. staff-passengers communication (wayside, station and onboard) -CCTV surveillance (wayside & onboard -Passenger information system (wayside and onboard)		-Track (e.g. broken-rail detection) -Tunnel ventilation (e.g. fire & smoke detection) -Intrusion-detection system -other equipment interfaces (e.g. flood gates)

STATION		TRACTION POWER
-Fire detection/protection -Platform/track intrusion detection (e.g. passenger on track) -Platform screen doors / end doors -Wayside passenger information -Other equipment interfaces – e.g. emergency handle, emergency call devices, gap detection/closing devices, dispatching /train ready to start keys),		-Traction-power control -Traction power supply network

		MAINTENANCE
		-Maintenance system (people, equipment and procedures)

Figure 8 ~ Logical System Relationships

Strictly speaking, Figure 8 necessarily shows only the physical attributes of individual trains whereas, the EUC is defined, at the more conceptual level of Sub-section 4.1.2, as the general *movement* of such trains around the rail network. It is important to note also that, although the allocation of the detailed items in Figure 8 to the various system elements might vary slightly, case-to-case, the following provisions always apply:

- the ATC element is the *only* one for which Safety Requirements are actually derived;
- Safety Requirements are *not* derived for any items that form part of the basic Train vehicular element[63] since it is assumed that their safety would have been established through a prior safety assessment / monitoring process of the old signalling system;
- Safety Requirements are also *not* derived for any items that form part of any *non*-ATC EUC Control System elements; however, in the event that the safety of ATC operations depends on an *assumption* of the safety integrity of any such items being more stringent than 10^{-5} dangerous failure per hour (or low-demand / on-demand equivalent) then those items must be deemed to be safety-related — see Sub-section 3.5.2 of Fowler (2022).

---

[63] *Except* for any train-mounted ATC items

4.2 Overall Scope Definition (IEC 61508-1 Phase 2)

4.2.1 Aim and Objectives

The aim of Phase 2 is to define the scope of the Hazard and Risk Analysis, which will be carried out in Phase 3.

It seeks to achieve that aim through determining the boundary of the EUC / EUC Control System and its Operational Environment and, within those constraints, specifying the scope of the Hazard and Risk Analysis.

This is particularly important when, as we are doing in this article, assessing the safety of a change to an existing railway operation and/or systems so as to identify, and exclude, the unnecessary safety assessment of those elements that are not affected by the change. It should be noted, however, that we can do this only in general terms herein because of the necessarily generic nature of the operational context for which this example safety assessment is being carried out.

4.2.2 Boundary Constraints

For the purposes of this safety assessment of ATC operations, the train movements, which constitutes the EUC, are *only* those that:

- occur *within* the specified ATC signalling-system boundary; or
- involve the *transfer* of trains to/from any adjacent signalling areas, in accordance with the required boundary conditions; or
- involve the *transfer* of trains to/from any adjacent, non-signalled areas, e.g. depots, in accordance with the required boundary conditions.

4.2.3 Scope of the Hazard and Risk Analysis

Subject to the above boundary constraints, the scope of the Hazard and Risk Analysis shall *include* all hazardous events that are *inherent* in:

- the general movement of trains under normal, abnormal and failure conditions;
- the transfer of passengers, on and off the train, at a station, from and to the platform;
- the necessary presence of maintenance staff and equipment on the track;
- the necessary presence of passengers on the track during, for example, evacuation from a train or station; and
- interactions between trains and road users at level crossings.

The scope shall *exclude* any other hazardous events, i.e. those that do not fall within the scope of the bullet list above and/or occur outside the boundaries defined in Sub-section 4.2.2.

4.3 Hazard and Risk Analysis (IEC 61508-1 Phase 3)

4.3.1 Aim

The aim of Phase 3 is to determine, and characterise, all the hazards and risks associated with the EUC[64], in the stated Operational Environment, and within the scope already identified in Phase 2.

Note: it is acknowledged that these EUC hazards (and some of the detail that follows, up to and including Sub-section 4.4.2 below), which are not specific to ATC operations, might have already been identified and documented adequately in, say, a safety case for the current (fixed-block) railway operations. For the purposes of this article, however, we will present the analysis as if no such previous work had been done.

4.3.2 EUC Hazard Identification

The objective here is to determine the hazards relating to the EUC, within the scope defined in Sub-section 4.2.

From the IEC 61508 definition of a hazard, which can be paraphrased as "a potential **source** of harm, i.e. death, physical injury or damage to the health of people or damage to property or the environment" (Fowler 2022), it follows that we must first identify the types of harmful **outcome**, i.e. accident, that fall within the signalling area's general area of responsibility and specifically within the above scope of ATC operations.

Table 13 suggests various accident types relevant to railway operations, on the subject railway and, in each case, would involve death or serious injury to one or more of those on board a train or to the workforce or members of the public on, or in the vicinity of, the track.

Table 13 ~ Accident Types Relevant to Railway Operations

ID	Accident Type	Description
A#1	Collision between trains	All collisions between trains except where preceded by derailment of at least one of the trains involved
A#2	Derailment of a train	Unintentional departure of a train from the track
A#3	Collision between train and road users	Train collides with road vehicle, cyclists and/or pedestrians on a level crossing
A#4	Collision between train and non-fixed obstacle(s) on the track	Train collides with non-fixed objects (including debris, members of the public or large animals) on the track
A#5	Collision between train and personnel on the track	Train collides with workforce (including their equipment or vehicles) or disembarked passengers who are on the track

---

[64] Strictly speaking, IEC 61508 includes "EUC Control System Hazards" here as well. We have taken the view that, for ATC, failures of the EUC Control System are among the *causes* of EUC hazards

ID	Accident Type	Description
A#6	Collision between train and fixed structure	Train collides with a fixed structure (including buffer stop), except as a result of either a derailment (A#2) or failure of such structure (A#4)
A#7	Passengers falls on board a train	Passengers injured by falling due to sudden, violent acceleration or deceleration of the train.
A#8	Passenger falls from train on to track	Passenger deaths / serious injuries due to falling from stationary or moving train, on to track
A#9	Passenger slips or trips when getting on or off a train at platform	Passenger deaths / serious injuries due to slips / trips during embarkation / disembarkation at platform, including dragging due to becoming caught in the closing train doors
A#10	Fire on board a train, in a station or trackside	Passenger deaths / serious injuries due to exposure to heat and/or smoke inhalation from a fire on a train, in a station or trackside
A#11	Fatal or serious electrical injury to passengers or workforce	Passenger or workforce deaths / serious injuries due to exposure to lethal voltages or arcing – resulting injuries include electric shock and burns from contact with live parts, or injury from exposure to arcing

The hazards derived from the above, and in relation to what are seen to be the most credible accident outcome(s), are shown in Table 14 and were adapted from the set of "core" railway hazards derived in doctoral research carried out by Ivan Lucic (Lucic 2015); all of these hazards are *inherent* in railway operations, in the stated Operational Environment, and exist *before* any form of hazard mitigation has been applied.

In the specific case of Hp#1 to Hp#12, the hazards apply directly to the EUC, i.e. the movement of passenger-carrying and engineering trains, and their mitigation places *direct* demands on the safety functionality of the ATC system.

The remaining five hazards, which have a much less direct impact on the required functionality of the ATC system, are not considered to be EUC hazards but will be addressed as part of the analysis of *abnormal* operating conditions, for which the ability of the ATC system to react appropriately will still have to be demonstrated (Sub-section 4.6.5 below).

Table 14 ~ Hazards Inherent in Railway Operations

ID	Hazard	Related Accident(s)
EUC Hazards		
Hp#1	Conflict (1) between any pair of train trajectories (2)	A#1
Hp#2	Conflict (1) between a train's trajectory (2) and track configuration	A#1, A#2, A#3
Hp#3	Train speed exceeding capabilities of the track infrastructure and/or train	A#2, A#6
Hp#4	High and/or uneven acceleration / deceleration of a train	A#7

ID	Hazard	Related Accident(s)
Hp#5	Conflict (1) between train profile and fixed structure, *except* as the result of excessive train speed (Hp#3) or damage to structure (Hp#10)	A#6
Hp#6	Conflict (1) between a train's trajectory (2) and non-fixed obstacles or unauthorised persons on track	A#4
Hp#7	Conflict (1) between a train's trajectory (2) and workforce / vehicles on track	A#5
Hp#8	Passengers attempt to exit train outside a station	A#8
Hp#9	Passenger embarkation / disembarkation at platform	A#9
Hp#10	Structural failure of track elements, tunnels, bridges etc	A#4
Hp#11	Personnel exposure to potentially lethal voltage	A#11
Hp#12	Passengers too close to, or fall/jump off, platform edge	A#4, A#11
Other Inherent Hazards		
Hp#13	Passenger evacuation outside platform	A#5, A#11
Hp#14	Train encounters adverse rail-surface conditions	A#1 to A#5
Hp#15	Conflict between a train's trajectory (2) and trackside fire	A#10
Hp#16	Station fire / other emergency on a station	A#10, A#4
Hp#17	Fire, or other emergency, on board a train	A#10

Notes:
1. For the specific meanings of "Conflict" in each case, see Appendix A
2. Conceptually, a train's "trajectory" is the path and speed profile that the train intends to follow at any point in time, and in the absence of any contrary instructions or information.

IEC 61508 requires that the sequence of events be described for each EUC hazard at this stage in the process, but to do so exhaustively would normally be impracticable for railway operations, because of the sheer number of causal factors involved. What we can usefully do, however, is to describe in general terms the precursor to each hazardous event, and this is included in the more detailed hazard descriptions at Appendix A; we then leave it to the modelling approach described in Sub-section 3.6 above, which does capture how such states are arrived at in the first place, and thus fully satisfy this IEC 61508 requirement.

Of course, what we have not said thus far is anything about the probability that each EUC hazardous event would lead to the related accident except, that the probability would, by definition, be finite. That is addressed next.

4.3.3 EUC Risks

The objective here is to determine the EUC Risks from two perspectives.

Firstly, for each accident type identified in Table 13, the *tolerable* level of EUC Risk must be identified; since the accident types would be unchanged from the previous, fixed-block operations, it is reasonable to assume, at this stage, that what are *deemed* to be relevant tolerable levels of risk would already have been promulgated.

Secondly, for each hazardous event identified in Table 14, IEC 61508-1 suggests that the *expected* value of unmitigated EUC Risk be estimated at this stage, i.e. *without* taking into account the possible risk reduction afforded by any Safety-related Systems, or any Other Risk-reduction Measures, that would be developed subsequently for that purpose.

However, as discussed in Fowler (2022), there are significant problems in estimating such values of unmitigated EUC risk for complex applications typical of the transport sector; fortunately, as explained in Sub-section 4.4 below, the determination of absolute EUC Risk is not actually necessary in practice, *provided* the associated concept of Necessary Risk Reduction is adhered to in the determination of Overall Safety Requirements.

4.4 Overall Safety Requirements (IEC 61508-1 Phase 4)

4.4.1 Aim

The aim of Phase 4 is to produce a specification of the Overall Safety Requirements for each Overall Safety Function (OSF) in order to achieve the required level of functional safety.

The specification covers both the functional safety requirements (FSRs) and safety integrity requirements (SIRs) for the OSFs although, as we will see in Sub-section 4.4.4 below, IEC 61508's use of the term *safety integrity requirements* at this level is somewhat confusing!

4.4.2 Overall Safety Function Identification

The objective here is to identify a set of OSFs, based on the EUC hazardous events derived from the hazard and risk analysis of Phase 3.

According to IEC 61508, an overall safety function is the highest-level abstraction of the "*Means of achieving, or maintaining, a safe state for the EUC, in respect of a <u>specific</u> hazardous event*"[65], whereas, for the Rail sector, the relationships between accidents and hazards (as shown above) is "many-to many", as is the relationship between EUC hazards and the OSFs that are intended to mitigate them.

However, as found in Fowler and Fota (2023) for the Air Traffic Management sector, this is not an insurmountable problem, and the set of OSFs proposed in Table 15 otherwise seems to fit the above definition of an OSF very well.

Table 15 ~ Overall Safety Functions

OSF ID	OSF Title	Related EUC Hazards
OSF#1	Establish & Protect a Safe Route for each Train Movement	Hp#1, Hp#2, Hp#5
OSF#2	Apply & Maintain Safe Separation between Trains	Hp#1

---

[65] IEC 61508 terminology can be a bit confusing here (Fowler 2022). Hierarchically, an *Overall* Safety Function can be realised as one or more Safety Related Systems and/or one or more Other Risk-reduction Measures, and a Safety Related System can be realised as one or more Safety Functions.

OSF ID	OSF Title	Related EUC Hazards
OSF#3	Enforce Safe Speed Limits for Trains	Hp#3
OSF#4	Provide Safe Passenger Embarkation / Disembarkation	Hp#6. Hp#8, Hp#9, Hp#12
OSF#5	Provide Safe Maintenance Access to Track	Hp#7
OSF#6	Ensure that the Guideway is Safe for Train Passage	Hp#6, Hp#10
OSF#7	Ensure Safe Acceleration & Braking	Hp#4
OSF#8	Ensure Safety of Traction Power Supply	Hp#11

4.4.3 Determine the Functional Safety Requirements for each Overall Safety Function

This step involves the determination of what is required functionally from each of the above OSFs. The resulting Overall Safety Requirements (OSRs) are based on *normal* operational conditions, as described in Section 2, and cover those items that are necessary and sufficient to ensure the safety of ATC operations, in the absence of *failure* and of *abnormal* operating conditions.

The properties shown in Table 16 are what is required of the respective OSFs in order to avoid, and / or mitigate the consequences of, the EUC hazards shown in Table 14.

Table 16 ~ Overall Functional Safety Requirements for Normal Operations

Requirement ID	Requirement Description	Related EUC Hazard
OSF#1	**Establish & Protect a Safe Route for each Train Movement**	
OSR1.1	A train shall *not* be authorised to enter a route unless, *and until*, the route is set and locked in a safe condition (see OSR1.2) and reserved, for *that* train	Hp#1, Hp#2
OSR1.2	A route shall be defined by: - the *route origin* (the location for which authorisation for a train to enter the route shall be given) and the *route destination* (the location at which the movement authority ceases); - all the route elements between the route origin and route destination, which are to be traversed by the train; - route elements of overlap, which are reserved for safety reasons in case of deviations from an authorized train movement; - route elements in the flank-protection area, which prevent or detect unauthorised flank movement; - the authorised direction of travel for the train.	Hp#1, Hp#2

Requirement ID	Requirement Description	Related EUC Hazard
OSR1.3	A route shall be considered as safe if, *and only if*,	
	- every requested element of the guideway is locked in the required position such that concurrent use by another train is avoided entirely; *and*	Hp#1
	- road vehicles (and other road users) are prevented from occupying a level crossing on the route, prior to, and during, train passage; *and*	Hp#2
	- every requested elements of the guideway that provide flank protection is locked in the required position	Hp#1
OSR1.4	A route element shall *not* be released and reset for another train until the previous train has cleared that element of the route	Hp#1
OSR1.5	It shall *not* be possible to route a train through or past a fixed structure whose gauge is incompatible with the kinetic envelope of that train	Hp#5
OSR1.6	The probability of a train overrunning its limit of safe route shall not exceed 10^{-9} per operating hour	Hp#1, Hp#2
OSR1.7	It shall not be possible to run a train beyond the end of route, or into an area controlled by another signalling system without permission	Hp#1, Hp#2
OSF#2	**Apply & Maintain Safe Separation between Trains**	
OSR2.1	A safe distance between following trains (see OSR2.2) shall be maintained at all times	Hp#1
OSR2.2	*Safe distance* shall be based upon the principle of an instantaneous stop of the preceding train *and* on the ability of the following train to be braked to a halt in time to avoid a collision	Hp#1
OSR2.3	The *safe distance* shall be sufficient to ensure that, under *normal* operating conditions, the probability of a train being unable to stop before colliding with the leading train shall not exceed 10^{-9} per operating hour	Hp#1
OSF#3	**Enforce Safe Speed Limits on Trains**	
OSR3.1	A train's actual speed shall not exceed its safe speed (see OSR3.2) at anytime	Hp#3

Requirement ID	Requirement Description	Related EUC Hazard
OSR3.2	The safe speed shall be the least of: - the speed above which it would not be possible to bring the train to a halt before reaching the limit of its Movement Authority, without the use of emergency braking; and - any permanent and temporary speed restrictions applicable to the track infrastructure within the train's movement authority; and - any temporary speed restrictions applied in response to degraded environmental conditions within the train's movement authority; and - any permanent or temporary speed restrictions applicable to the train itself.	Hp#3
OSR3.3	Permanent speed restrictions shall be determined on the basis of what would be tolerably safe for the train type, state and track-infrastructure geometry	Hp#3
OSR3.4	Temporary speed restrictions shall be determined on the basis of what would be tolerably safe under the actual conditions of the train, track or environment	Hp#3
OSR3.5	On approaching an area with a lower speed limit, a train shall have reduced its speed to the new speed limit prior to entry into that area	Hp#3
OSR3.6	All speed restrictions for the track infrastructure shall be applied to the whole length of the train	Hp#3
OSR3.7	The probability of a train exceeding its safe speed, by an amount sufficient to cause derailment, or other major accident, shall not exceed 10^{-9} per operating hour	Hp#3
OSF#4	**Provide Safe Passenger Embarkation / Disembarkation**	
OSR4.1	It shall not be possible for passengers to board or leave a moving train	Hp#8, Hp#9
OSR4.2	Except in an emergency, it shall not be possible for passengers to board or leave a stationary train unless the train is in a station and the door through which they embark / disembark is on the side of, and level with a section of, and adjacent to, the edge of the in-use platform	Hp#8, Hp#9
OSR4.3	Measures shall be taken to prevent embarking and disembarking passengers from becoming trapped in closing train doors or platform doors	Hp#9

Requirement ID	Requirement Description	Related EUC Hazard
OSR4.4	Measures shall be taken to prevent embarking and disembarking passengers from falling or becoming trapped between the platform edge and the body of the train	Hp#9
OSR4.5	Minimum dwell times should be maintained so as to allow less mobile or encumbered passengers to leave the train before the doors close	Hp#9
OSR4.6	Measures shall be taken to prevent passengers waiting on a platform being too close to, or falling/jumping from, the platform edge	Hp#12
OSR4.7	Except in an emergency, it shall not be possible for passengers to exit through the ends of a platform	Hp#6
OSF#5	**Provide Safe Maintenance Access to Track**	
OSR5.1	Trains shall be prevented from accessing areas of the railway that must be reserved for maintenance access (i.e. Work Zones)	Hp#9
OSR5.2	It shall be possible to move engineering vehicles into, and out of, Work Zones, *only* with the coordination of those at the worksite	Hp#9
OSR5.3	Maintenance access shall be prevented if trains are running in the proposed Work Zone	Hp#9
OSF#6	**Ensure Guideway is Safe for Train Passage**	
OSR6.1	Obstacles or unauthorised personnel within the swept envelope of the train's route shall be prevented, or shall be detected in time for emergency braking to be applied in order to avoid a collision	Hp#6, Hp#10
OSR6.2	In the event of hazardous damage to track elements or other infrastructure, appropriate action, e.g. temporary speed restrictions in, or closure of, the affected area, shall be taken in order to protect train movements	Hp#10
OSF#7	**Ensure Safe Acceleration & Braking**	
OSR7.1	Except when necessary to respond to a higher-risk situation, sudden / sharp increases or decreases in train acceleration / deceleration (jerking), sufficient to cause injury to passengers, shall be avoided	Hp#4
OSF#8	**Ensure Safety of Traction Power Supply**	
OSR8.1	Trains shall be prevented from feeding a traction power supply section that had been isolated (regenerative train braking)	Hp#11
OSR8.2	Where a traction power supply section had been cut off for on-site maintenance purposes, explicit agreement of those at the worksite shall be required prior to restoration of the supply	Hp#11

It should be noted that these requirements are objective-based (or rule-based) in that they express what the OSFs have to *achieve* rather than what they have to do; this means they form a vital link in the *rich traceability*[66] between the lower-level Safety Functions and the EUC Hazards that the functions are required to mitigate.

The need to specify interim, worst-case success criteria[67] for OSFs 1# to #3, in particular, is based on two related factors:

- the fact that they make the greatest, and most direct, contribution to what the UGTMS standard (IEC 2014b) describes as the "*safe movement of trains*" overall; and
- the reasonable assumption that the processes described in Sub-section 4.4.4 below would lead each of them being assessed as a *SIL 4* function, as defined in IEC 61508.

The key assurance question at this stage is, therefore, whether the above requirements for each OSF would be sufficient to mitigate the corresponding EUC hazard(s) — in other words, are there any conditions (*except* for failures within the OSF or *abnormal* operating conditions) that could lead to the EUC hazard occurring, at an intolerable rate.

Furthermore, the rigour of the assurance required here would depend on the Safety Integrity Level (SIL) for the OSF concerned — see the next Sub-section.

4.4.4 *Determine the Safety Integrity Requirements for each Overall Safety Function*

According to IEC 61508-1, this step involves the determination of the SIRs required of each of the above OSFs, in order to achieve a tolerable level of risk overall.

IEC 61508-1 states that the SIRs, at this level, must be specified in terms of either:

- the amount of EUC-risk reduction required in order to achieve the tolerable level of risk; or
- the tolerable rate of occurrence of the [EUC] hazardous events, in order to achieve the tolerable level of risk.

There are number of key points to note, as follows.

Firstly, the SIRs at this "overall" level are not, despite their name, properties of the OSF to which they relate[68] — they actually specify a *target* amount of EUC risk reduction that each OSF has to meet[69].

Secondly, it is reasonable to assume that in giving the choice of how to specify the SIRs, IEC 61508-1 intends that the two methods are equivalent, albeit the latter does not require knowledge of what the EUC Risk would have been *before* it was reduced. Therefore, as it is clear that the risk-reduction method depends on the functionality and performance, as well as on the failure rate, of the safety functions, so must the latter method; in other words, though it might be tempting to believe that EUC hazard-occurrence rates could be interpreted directly as OSF failure rates, that would be an entirely false deduction — for further explanation on this point see Fowler (2022).

---

[66] Traceability that embodies evidence of requirements satisfaction — in this case, evidence that the functional safety properties of Safety Functions are necessary and sufficient to reduce EUC risks to a tolerable level.

[67] For convenience, these are actually expressed a maximum probability of each function being *unsuccessful* in meeting its functional requirements.

[68] Of course, as already seen in Sub-section 4.4.3, this is true also of the *functional* requirements of the OSFs.

[69] Although we will persevere with the IEC 61508 terminology of "safety integrity requirements", such properties might be better thought of as being *safety criteria*, as used in some areas of the transport sector.

Thirdly, notwithstanding the previous point, there is a reasonably straightforward path from knowledge of the most demanding tolerable rate of occurrence of the [EUC] hazardous event, associated with each OSF, to the derivation of a SIL[70] for the OSF (Fowler 2022).

Fourthly, although not a simple mechanical process, methods of deriving tolerable rate of occurrence of the [EUC] hazardous events, from pre-defined *target levels of safety* for the associated accidents, are well documented in rail safety standards such as CENELEC (2017); therefore, since it is not important to the main message of this article to provide a worked example of failure analysis here, we will leave the discussion at this point but pick it up again in the context of lower-level SIRs derivation, in Sub-section 4.6.5 below.

4.5 Overall Safety Requirements Allocation (IEC 61508-1 Phase 5)

4.5.1 Aim

The aim of Phase 5 is to allocate, to Safety Related Systems (SRSs) and/or Other Risk-reduction Methods (ORRMs), the safety requirements, which were derived for the corresponding Overall Safety Functions in Phase 4.

4.5.2 Discussion

IEC 61508 gives prominence to the distinction between SRSs and ORRMs — partly, it would seem because, once identified, the latter measures fall outside the scope of the Standard. Whereas for, say, process industries, the identification of, and distinction between, the two categories of risk-reduction means might be quite straightforward, for the more complex transport applications it is less so.

Table 17 shows a suggested summary allocation of the OSFs from Table 16 on to what might be interpreted generically as SRSs and ORRMs, within the scope of ATC operations. For the purposes of this exercise, the SRSs have been adapted from the top-level functional elements described in the UGTMS standard[71] (IEC 2014b).

Table 17 ~ Allocation of Overall Safety Functions for ATC Operations

OSF ID	OSF Title	SRS(s)	ORRM(s)
OSF#1	Establish & Protect a Safe Route for each Train Movement	SRS#1 - Set & Protect Route Elements SRS#4 - Authorise Train Movement SRS#5 - Supervise Train Movement	
OSF#2	Apply & Maintain Safe Separation between Trains	SRS#2 - Locate Trains SRS#4 - Authorise Train Movement SRS#5 - Supervise Train Movement	

---

[70] SILs, as defined in IEC 61508-4, are also not properties of an OSF (or of a system, subsystem, element, or component thereof) – see Fowler (2022).

[71] In constructing this table, we noted that the titles of the three most critical top-level safety functions in the UGTMS standard are quite misleading — e.g. "Ensure Safe Separation of Trains" (5.1.2) actually covers only the location of trains — and so we avoided using them, preferring instead to reference the Standard's lower-level functions that addressed the full scope of the OSFs concerned.

OSF ID	OSF Title	SRS(s)	ORRM(s)
OSF#3	Enforce Safe Speed Limits for Trains	SRS#3 - Determine Permitted Speed SRS#4 - Authorise Train Movement SRS#5 - Supervise Train Movement	
OSF#4	Provide Safe Passenger Embarkation / Disembarkation	SRS#6 - Supervise Passenger Transfer	Platform Screen Doors / End Doors, Gap Fillers
OSF#5	Provide Safe Maintenance Access to Track	SRS#7 - Protect Staff on Track	Maintenance Safety Procedures
OSF#6	Ensure Guideway is Safe for Train Passage	SRS#8 - Supervise Guideway	Segregated guideway, fences, walls, bridges / subways, etc.
OSF#7	Ensure Safe Acceleration & Braking	SRS#9 - Drive Train	Train's power and braking systems
OSF#8	Ensure Safety of Traction Power Supply	-	Maintenance & Power Supply Safety Procedures Train's power and braking systems

The ORRMs include mainly non-functional, safety-related items for which separate design and development standards would normally exist but which may be related to the corresponding SRSs.

Further details of the SRSs and ORRMs will emerge during the processes described in Sub-sections 3.6 and 4.7 below, respectively.

4.6 Specification of Safety Requirements for SRSs (IEC 61508-1 Phase 9)

4.6.1 Aim

In IEC 61508, the aim of Phase 9 is to develop safety requirements for the SRSs identified in Phase 5, in terms of their FSRs and SIRs, in order to achieve the required functional safety under all *normal*, *abnormal* and *failure* conditions.

4.6.2 Overview

It is important to note here that IEC 61508-1 places great emphasis on the need for a rigorous description of the workings of SRSs at this level, including:

- a description of all the Safety Functions, how they work together to achieve the required functional safety and whether they operate in low-demand, high-demand or continuous modes of operation;

- the required performance attributes of each Safety Function — e.g. timing properties and, for more data-intensive applications than possibly envisaged by IEC 61508, data accuracy, latency, refresh rate, and overload tolerance;
- all interfaces that are necessary to achieve the required functional safety;
- all relevant modes of *normal* operation of the EUC;
- all other required modes of behaviour of the SRSs — in particular:
    - their required response in the event of defined *abnormal* operating conditions of the EUC or its environment
    - their *failure* behaviour and their required response in the event of such failure (Fowler 2022).

To that end, this Sub-section comprises four stages, as follows:

Firstly, the development of FSRs for scenarios covering the entirety of *normal* operations. This will be done (initially at least) at a relatively abstract level, without any reference to physical elements within the end-to-end ATC system[72] (see Sub-section 4.6.3 below).

Secondly, to show that the FSRs specified for the SRSs would be adequate to meet the risk-reduction required of the SRSs, in the absence of failure (see Sub-section 4.6.4 below).

Thirdly, to analyse, in a similar manner, scenarios covering *abnormal* events in order to identify any additional FSRs necessary to maintain a tolerable level of safety during such events (see Sub-section 4.6.5 below).

Fourthly, to analyse scenarios relating to potential *failures* of the ATC system in order to identify SIRs, and any additional FSRs, necessary to maintain a tolerable level of safety during such failure events (see Sub-section 4.6.6 below).

Because the first three stages are directly relevant to the "IEC 61508 viewpoint", outlined in Sub-section 1.2, and the fourth is addressed in detail in existing railway standards, most of the focus below is on the former stages.

4.6.3 *FSRs for Normal ATC Operations*

This first stage involves the identification of a set of Safety Functions for each of the SRSs in Sub-section 4.5, and the derivation of detailed functional safety requirements (FSRs) for each Safety Function that, in conjunction with the properties of the associated ORRMs, would ultimately satisfy the OSF requirements of Table 16.

It is evident, especially in the case of a fully automated railway control system, that the high number of Safety Functions (and an even-higher number of associated detailed FSRs) would be very large. Fortunately, that task is made very much less daunting by the publication, in IEC (2014b), of a comprehensive, generic functional requirements specification for UGTMS, which we can use as a starting point for our urban railway example, as set out initially in Table 18.

Table 18 shows, for each SRS derived in Table 17, a description of the Safety Functions that make up that SRS. It should be noted that these Safety Functions are limited to those that are necessary to address *normal* ATC operations and might not be sufficient for the system to specific how safely ATC must react to *abnormal* operating conditions (Sub-

---

[72] As noted in Sub-section 3.7.2 of Fowler (2022), the IEC 61508 objective here is to "*describe, in terms not specific to the equipment, the required safety properties of the SRS(s)*". This level of requirements expression respects that objective since it makes no assumptions about the technology involved in the realisation of the requirements.

section 4.6.5 below) or to provide mitigation of ATC system internal *failures* (Sub-section 4.6.6 below).

Table 18 ~ ATC Safety Functions per Safety Related System

SRS	SF ID	Safety Functions	Description
Set & Protect Route Elements (SRS#1)	SF#1.1	Reserve, Set & Lock a Route	Establishes (i.e. reserves, sets & locks) a standard route in response to a route call.
	SF#1.2	Supervise Route	Supervises that all conditions for the route are still in place.
	SF#1.3	Maintain Route Locking	Keeps the route locked against route release by manual or system input: • for an approaching train for which the movement authority allows entry into the route, or • for a train that is already within the route.
	SF#1.4	Release Route	Releases the route when all of the conditions for maintaining it locked no longer apply
Locate Trains (SRS#2)	SF#2.1	Initialise Reporting Trains Location	Initialises location of reporting trains which are: • stationary in stabling locations, • entering ATC territory, • recovering from localisation failures.
	SF#2.2	Determine Train Orientation	Determines physical orientation of train relative to defined orientation of the track.
	SF#2.3	Determine Train-travel Direction	Determines the actual travel direction of reporting trains, relative to the track.
	SF#2.4	Determine Reporting Train Location	Determines the location of all reporting trains according to the train orientation and train length.
	SF#2.5	Determine Non-reporting Train Location	Determines if a section of track is occupied by non-reporting trains based on inputs received from devices external to the ATC system.
Determine Permitted Speed (SRS#3)	SF#3.1	Determine Permanent Infrastructure Speed Profile	Determines the permanent speed profiles, based on infrastructure data, e.g. track geometry & quality, and infrastructure constraints (tunnels, bridges, platforms, etc.).
	SF#3.2	Determine Temporary Infrastructure Speed Restrictions	Sets and removes temporary speed restrictions for selected areas by operational commands or as result of system reactions.

SRS	SF ID	Safety Functions	Description
	SF#3.3	Determine Permanent Rolling Stock Speed Restrictions	Determines the maximum permitted speed for each type of rolling stock.
	SF#3.4	Determine Temporary Rolling Stock Speed Restrictions	Determines temporary rolling stock speed restrictions due to train failures and to driving modes.
Authorise Train Movement (SRS#4)	SF#4.1	Determine Limit of Movement Authority	Determines for each train its limit of the movement authority (LMA), corresponding to the first conflict point ahead of the train.
	SF#4.2	Determine Train Protection Profile	Determines the train protection profile for all trains to ensure their LMAs and authorised speeds are never exceeded.
	SF#4.3	Authorise Reporting Train Movement	Authorises train movement for reporting trains in accordance with its Train Protection Profile.
	SF#4.4	Authorise Non-reporting Train Movement	Authorises train movement by wayside signals if conditions of safe route and safe separation are fulfilled.
Supervise Train Movement (SRS#5)	SF#5.1	Determine actual train speed	Determines the actual train speed.
	SF#5.2	Supervise Safe Train Speed	Supervises actual train speed against the permitted speed with respect to the Train Protection Profile.
	SF#5.3	Supervise Safe Train Direction	Supervises movement of a train against the authorised direction of travel.
	SF#5.4	Supervise Movement-Authority Validity	Monitors validity of a train's movement authority and determines action to be taken if validity period is exceeded.
	SF#5.5	Overrun Protection	Supervises the actual position of a train against its LMA.
Supervise Passenger Transfer (SRS#6)	SF#6.1	Control Train & Platform Doors	Contains functions and requirements that are able to authorise and command the opening and closing of train doors, and platform doors, once all conditions which are required to ensure a safe passenger transfer have been met.

SRS	SF ID	Safety Functions	Description
	SF#6.2	Prevent Injury to Person between Train and Platform	Controls external devices and supervises detectors that prevent injuries to persons from falling (or detect persons falling) and becoming trapped between the platform edge and the train body.
	SF#6.3	Authorise Safe Station Departure	Authorises the train to leave the station only when all train doors and all platform doors) are closed and locked.
Protect Staff on Track (SRS#7)	SF#7.1	Protect staff on track by Work Zone	Establishes, and subsequently removes, Work Zones in order to protect staff on the track.
Supervise Guideway (SRS#8)	SF#8.1	Prevent collision with obstacles	Contains functions and requirements that are able to prevent, or detect, collisions with obstacles present in the guideway.
	SF#8.2	Prevent collisions with persons on tracks	Contains functions and requirements that are able to prevent collisions with persons who mainly could enter from platforms to track areas.
Drive Train (SRS#9)	SF#9.1	Determine Operating-speed Profile	Determines the Operating Speed Profile, taking into account ride quality, passenger comfort and the driving mode, (including service acceleration/deceleration rate), within the constraints of the Train Protection Profile.
	SF#9.2	Control Train Movement	Determines, and sends to the rolling stock, traction and braking commands to ensure that the train speed follows the train operating profile and to achieve accurate stopping.

From this point on, we run into a potential problem of developing far too much detail for this article to handle; e.g. for the 30 Safety Functions shown in Table 6, there is a total of around 350 associated Functional Safety Requirements (FSRs)! Therefore, in the illustration at Appendix B, we have shown only the Safety Functions / FSRs that apply to the three SRSs that are needed to support the overall safety function OSF#1, "*Establish & Protect a Safe Route for each Train Movement*".

4.6.4 *Adequacy of the Functional Safety Requirements*

Thus far, the SRSs, Safety Functions, and their safety requirements, have been derived purely hierarchically, and what we have yet to show explicitly is, *inter alia*:

- how the functions interact with each other, and with the elements of the wider ATC system and (what we described, in Sub-section 4.1.4 as) the EUC Control System;
- the information needed by, and produced by the SRSs and Safety Functions;
- the system states and sequence of events, during a typical "day-in-the-life" of a train;
- any additional functionality to cope with abnormal and failure events; and
- whether the requirements constitute a complete, correct and coherent set.

There is a wide range of techniques for addressing these issues, and the following are examples of a few of them.

State-transition Models (STMs): a simplified example of which is shown in Figure 9, are used to capture knowledge about system behaviour. They can be translated into other models to support qualitative analysis (e.g. Sequence Diagrams and Activity Diagrams) or quantitative analysis (e.g. Markov models). They represent system behaviour in the form of: the state space of the system in a given context; the events that cause a change of state; the transitions between states; and resulting actions (Lucic 2015).

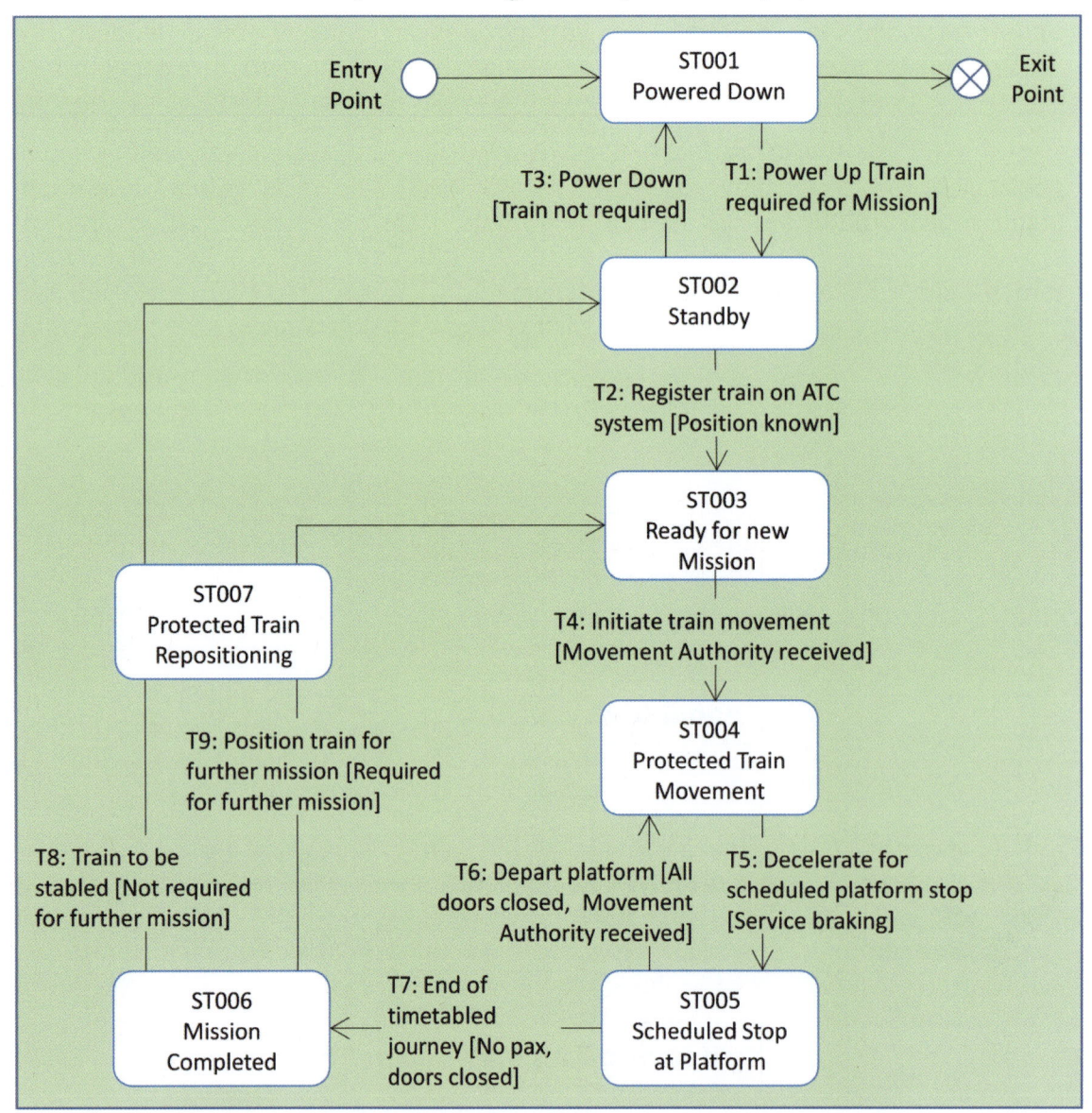

Figure 9 ~ State-transition Diagram for *Normal* Operations

The specific context for Figure 9 is our ATC-enabled railway, seen from the perspective of an ATC-capable train, for the whole of a typical day, i.e. under *normal* operating conditions[73]. The seven states are shown as rounded rectangles, and the nine permitted transitions between the states are represented by the arrows, which are accompanied by

---

[73] A more complete model would need to include, for example, states applicable to non-ATC trains, Engineering Hours & Possessions, and *abnormal* & *failure* conditions.

text signifying the trigger[74] for, and (in square brackets) any conditions or constraints[75] applicable to, the transition.

The initial state is the train powered down in a depot (ST001). When a requirement for the train to undertake a mission[76] is imminent, the train is brought to a *standby* state (ST002) in which all its systems are running as required but the train is not yet *registered* on the wider ATC system.

When the train's position is known, the train will be registered automatically leading to a state of readiness for undertaking a new mission (ST003).

Once the train has received a Movement Authority, it will move as required by its timetable, under the protection of the ATC system (ST004), until it stops at the first scheduled platform and the appropriate doors are opened (ST005). The train will then repeat states ST004 and ST005 until it reaches its final scheduled stop, all passengers having disembarked and the doors closed (ST006).

Transition T9 then provides for the train to be repositioned (ST007) to undertake further missions until ST006 applies to the final mission of the day. Finally, transition T8 provides for the train to return safely to depot at the end of the day (ST007).

We have chosen to use STMs at this high level in the system hierarchy in order to provide an overarching framework for the next level of analysis, which uses Sequence Diagrams.

Sequence Diagrams: an example of which is shown in Figure 10, is a dynamic form of interaction diagram that shows *objects* (and / or actors) whose *lifelines* run down the page, and with the interactions between them represented as a sequence of messages that are drawn as arrows from the source lifeline to the target lifeline (Sparx Systems 2022).

In this context, we use such diagrams as a method for describing *operational scenarios*, which can be thought of as:

> *"A set of actions or functions representing the dynamic of exchanges between the functions allowing the system to achieve a mission or a service". (SEBoK 2022).*

The Sequence Diagram shown in Figure 10 is for a specific operational scenario in which an ATC-capable train makes a protected journey between two stations, behind a non-ATC train.

At this level of analysis, we have chosen the functional objects to be SRSs (in blue)[77] implying that blue lifelines represent Safety Functions. There are also three actors: which represent the two basic trains[78] and various wayside devices (including demandable elements and occupancy-detection components). One of the great strengths of this technique is that, in later phases of the lifecycle, the actors and objects of the same scenarios can be redefined, at other levels, e.g. logical design, physical design and software module levels; thus, as SEBoK (2022) also notes:

> *"Operational scenarios are used to evaluate the requirements and design of the system and to verify and validate the system".*

---

[74] An event or action.

[75] Also known as "guards".

[76] A mission is *planned* journey of the train between two fixed (start and destination) points including any scheduled stops.

[77] For completeness, the SRS "Supervise Train Movement" should also have been included but has been omitted for the sake of simplicity of the diagram

[78] "Basic" means that train-borne ATC elements are not included, and is consistent with the four ATC *objects* being purely functional

In this scenario, there are:

- two trains: Train 1 is an ATC-capable reporting train and is following Train 2, which is a non-ATC / non-reporting train;
- three contiguous routes, A, B and C, in an interoperability area in which reporting trains and non-reporting trains move, under ATC control (the latter trains being controlled via wayside signals);
- two stations: the first in Route A, and the second in Route B.

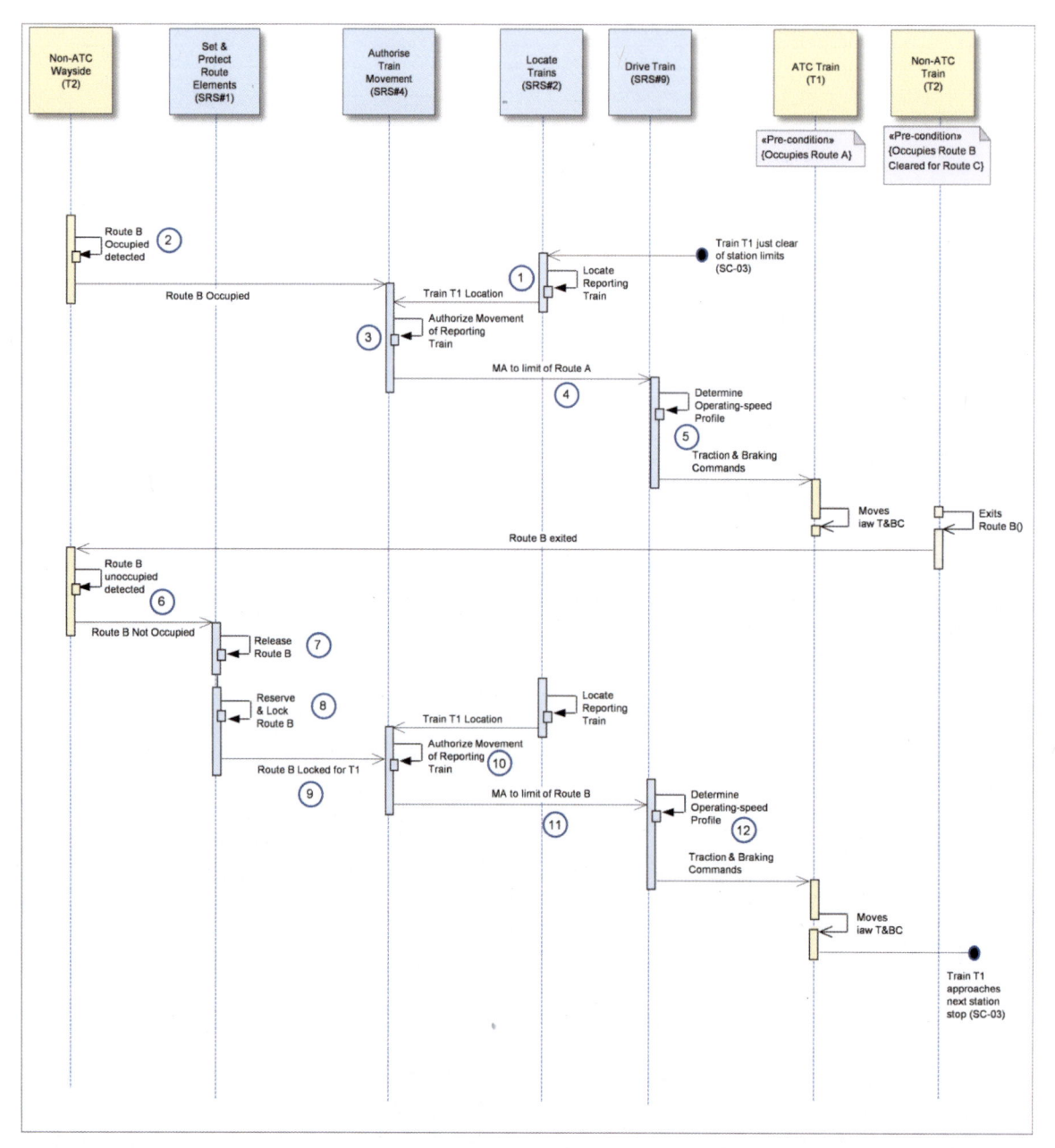

Figure 10 ~ Sequence Diagram for a Protected Movement Between 2 Stations (SC-02)

At the start of the scenario:

- Train 1 is in Route A and leaving the first station (the end of scenario SC-03[79], "*ATC Train Makes Scheduled Station Stop*"), and heading for the second station;

---
[79] See Appendix C

- Train 2 is in Route B, having departed the second station and has already been cleared for Route C.

Table 19 provides an outline narrative of the subsequent events that are numbered #1 to #12 on the diagram, together with a reference to the related Safety Functions.

Table 19 ~ Scenario SC-02 Narrative of Events

#	Description
1	Location of Train 1 in Route A is determined and reported (SF# 2.2. to 2.4) to *Authorise Train Movement*
2	Non-ATC Wayside detects, and reports, Route B as being occupied (SF# 2.5) by Train 2
3	*Authorise Train Movement* maintains the LMA for Train 1 at the safe limit of Route A (SF# 4.1. to 4.2)
4	*Authorise Train Movement* sends Movement Authority (SF# 4.3) to *Drive Train* accordingly
5	*Drive Train* determines the *Operating-speed Profile* (SF# 9.1) for Train 1 and issues traction / braking commands (SF# 9.2), to *Train T1*, for the train to continue to move in accordance with the *Operating-speed Profile*
6	Meanwhile, Train 2 exits Route B; non-ATC Wayside detects this (SF# 2.5) and reports, to *Set & Protect Route Elements*, that Route B is "not occupied"
7	*Set & Protect Route Elements* releases the Route B accordingly (SF# 1.4)
8	When Route B becomes available, *Set & Protect Route Elements* sets and locks that route (SF# 1.1 to 1.3) for Train 1.
9	*Set & Protect Route Elements* reports, to *Authorise Train Movement*, that Route B has been set and locked for Train 1
10	*Authorise Train Movement* updates the LMA for Train 1 to be at the safe limit of Route B (SF# 4.1. to 4.2)
11	*Authorise Train Movement* sends the new MA (SF# 4.3) to *Drive Train* accordingly
12	*Drive Train* determines the *Operating-speed Profile* (SF# 9.1) for Train 1 and issues traction / braking commands (SF# 9.2), to *Train T1*, for the train to continue to move in accordance with its *Operating-speed Profile* until the train approaches the next station stop (beginning of SC-03).

In effect, the Sequence Diagram for scenario SC-02 details, at a safety-function level, the interactions between the ATC SRSs in respect of state ST005 in Figure 9, as entered via trigger T9 and exited via T8. This demonstrates the role that an STM can play in deriving a complete set of Operational Scenarios for a given context; Table 22, at Appendix C hereto, gives examples of some of the Operational Scenarios that would be needed to underpin the full range of states and transitions shown on Figure 9. That said, a considerable amount of operational and technical expertise and effort would be needed to ensure a complete, correct and coherent set of Operational Scenarios is derived and analysed in practice.

It would be very important at this stage to crosscheck also the diagram and narrative against the detailed FSRs for each Safety Function, to ensure that the completeness and correctness of the relevant set of FSRs in each case.

Since the scenario analysis tells us much more about the required system dynamic behaviour than the purely textual FSRs, each scenario description should also be considered to be an FSR in its own right.

What the Sequence Diagram does not capture is the full complexity of, interactions between, and data used /produced by, each of the Safety Functions that constitute each SRS; for this, we can use Activity Diagrams.

Activity Diagrams: an example of which is shown in Figure 11, are essentially an advanced version of flow charts that model the flow from one activity to another activity.

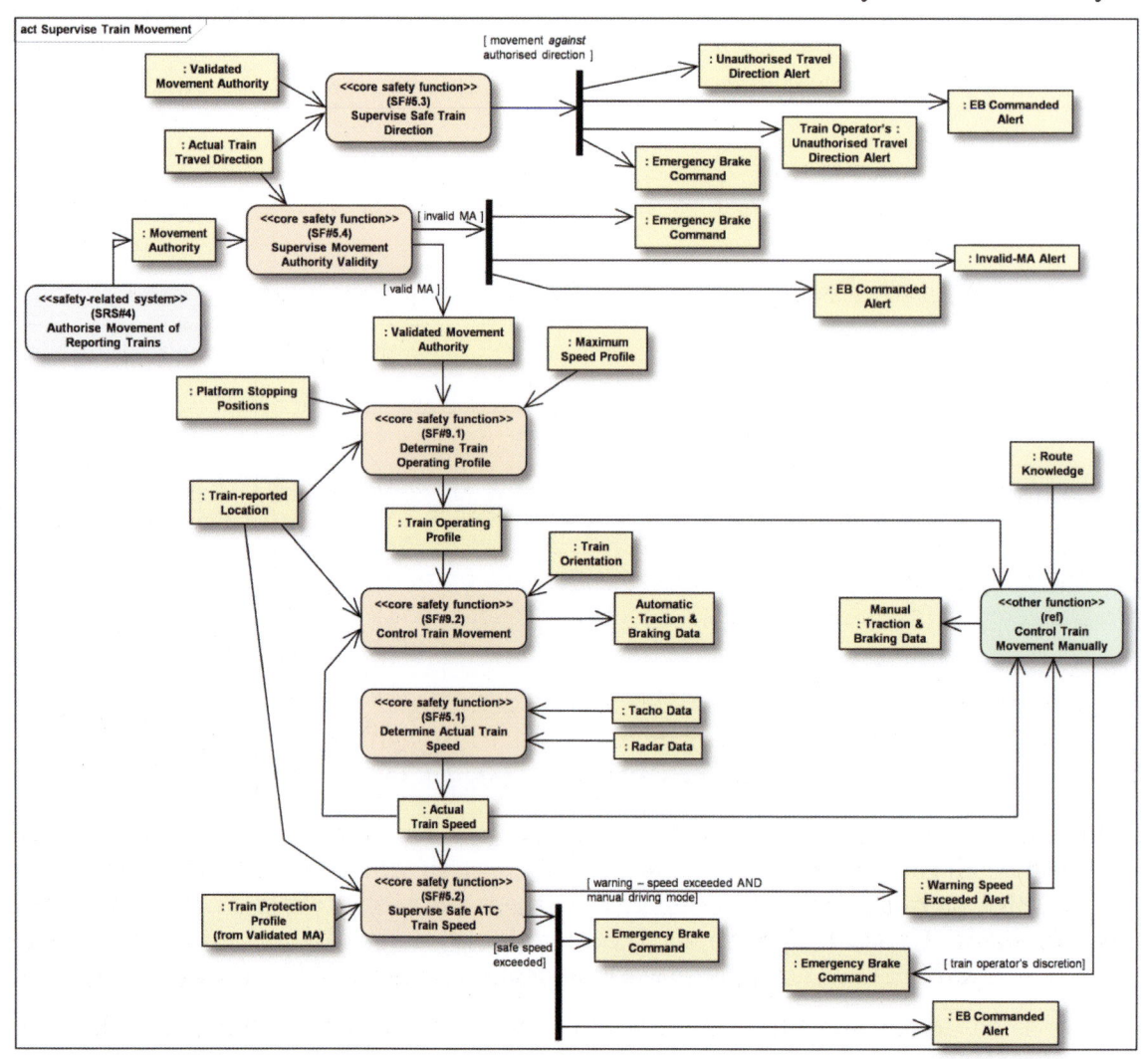

Figure 11 ~ Activity Diagram for Supervise Train Movement

This activity diagram is for the SRS "*Supervise Train Movement*", which supports each of the first three (and most safety-critical) of the Overall Safety Functions shown in Table 17. The diagram in this case is more structural than sequential, since the overall process is iterative and some of the functions might be running concurrently or asynchronously. The closely related SRS "*Authorise Train Movement*" is also shown in outline, for reference.

The activities (rounded rectangles) take the form of the Safety Functions involved, with rectangles representing the associated data, i.e. the information produced or used by the Safety Functions, and the instructions that they are required to issue or react to. The arrows indicate the required direction of flow of that data. Two possible modes of operation are covered: i.e. the train being driven automatically, or manually.

Since it would normally be impractical for purely textural FSRs to capture all the information presented in an Activity Diagram, the diagram itself should be identified as a safety requirement in its own right.

Given that we have already identified more than 30 Safety Functions, across nine SRSs, the use of a software design tool would not just help in the diagram's construction, it would also play a crucial part in in preserving the uniqueness of the functions and data, both within the full set of Activity Diagrams (covering, for example, all SRSs) and between those diagrams and the Sequence Diagrams discussed above.

Accepting that the need for some additional FSRs (or even Safety Functions) would probably be identified subsequently, in order to mitigate the effects of specific *normal*, *abnormal* and *internal-failure* events, the functional model of the ATC system, i.e. the aggregate of the Activity Diagrams, once determined, remains sensibly constant; unlike Sequence diagrams, which are very much context dependent.

Other techniques: there are many other techniques that can be used to model the system at this, and lower, levels of representation; a review of some such techniques is presented by Lucic (2015).

4.6.5 ATC Operations under Abnormal Operating Conditions

In general, *abnormal* conditions stem from two main sources:

- hazardous events in the operational environment that are not encountered on a day-to-day basis — hazards Hz#13 to 17, in Table 14, are good examples of such events; and
- failure events within the EUC Control System but *outside* the scope of the ATC system itself, e.g. a failure of a train's traction-control system.

In either case, what we are interested in, first of all, are the following:

- what effect the event would have on the continuing functioning of the ATC system and the consequences for the safe operation of the railway; and
- what actions would need to be taken to mitigate the consequences of the event, and how the functionality of the ATC system (existing or additional) could be used to support such actions.

One very useful way of modelling such events is through Operational Scenarios, based on Sequence Diagrams, as described (for *normal* operations) in Sub-section 4.6.4. First of all though, we need the equivalent of the State Transition Diagram of Figure 9, but covering *abnormal* states; this is shown in Figure 12 overleaf.

State ST008 simply provides a link to / from normal operations; the four main abnormal states are then as follows:

- ST009, Degraded Operations: a sub-optimal operational state of the railway where the train/service is able to continue with its mission, or a state where a fault or a combination of faults and external circumstances results in inability to continue under planned operation;
- ST010, Emergency Operations: response of the service/system to a hazardous event, usually external to the EUC Control System and ATC System, which requires immediate action;
- ST011, Recovery: process of returning the system to an operational state, and recovering the service to its planned operational state, following an emergency, or

degraded operation — may include rescue, involving either rescuing a train, rescuing passengers from the train, or both; and
- ST012, Mission Aborted: a mission for a train(s) has been terminated, following unacceptable circumstances.

From this analysis, Table 23, at Appendix C hereto, gives examples of some of the Operational Scenarios that would be needed to cover the full range of *abnormal* conditions.

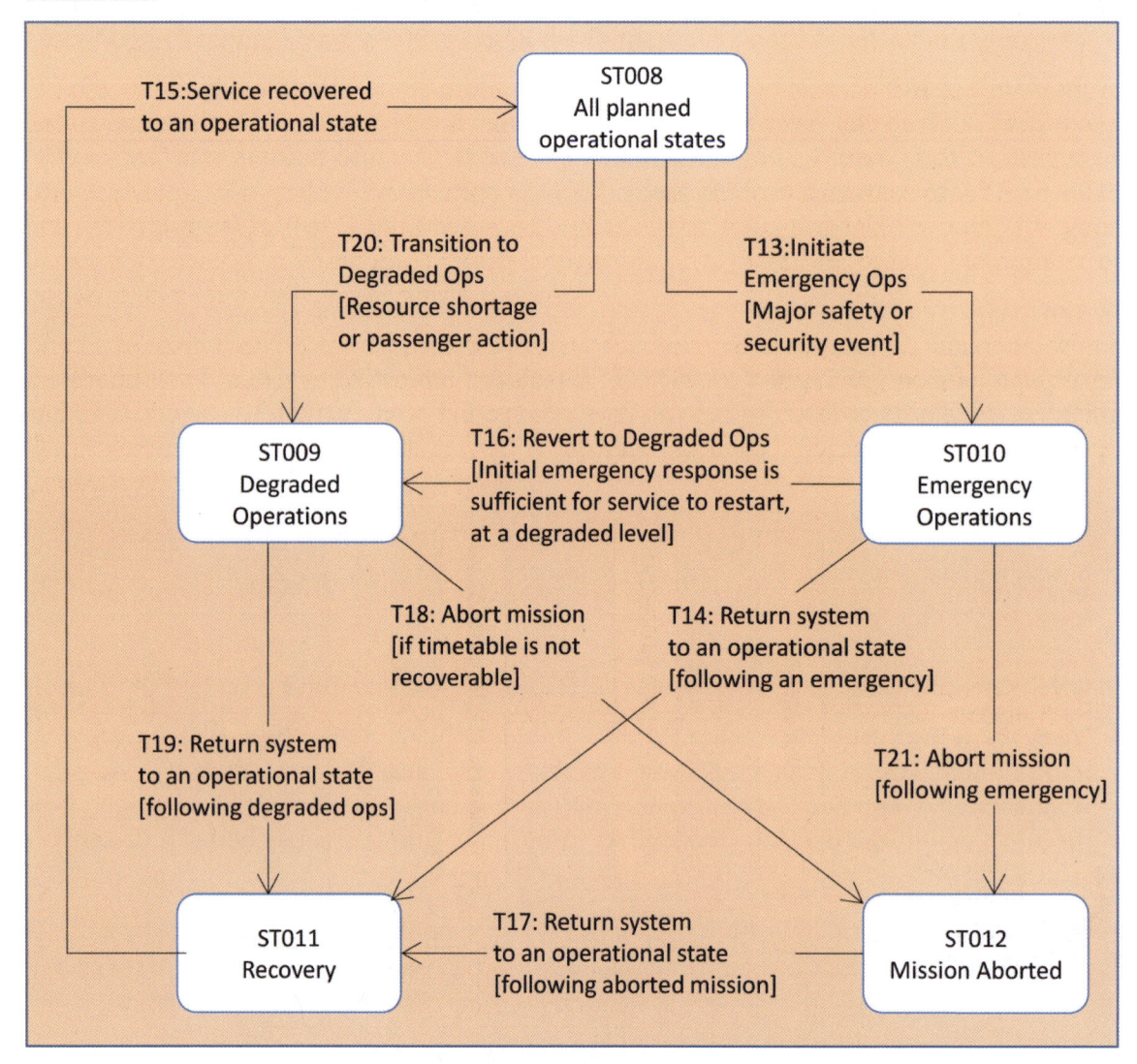

Figure 12 ~ State Transition Diagram for *Abnormal* Conditions

The final step would be to assess any additional risk that would be presented by the event, based on how effective the mitigating actions would be and how often the event is likely to occur. Therefore, in terms of the main safety requirements that might result from the analysis, the most likely would be for operational procedures and/or new *functional* safety requirements for the ATC system. This is unlike the case of failures *internal* to the ATC system, where a major, *additional* output would be safety *integrity* requirements for the ATC system, as we will see in the next Sub-section.

4.6.6 ATC Operations under Internal-failure Conditions

Finally, for Phase 9, is the specification of Safety Integrity Requirements (SIRs) for the SRSs and their Safety Functions, through analysis of potential failures internal to the ATC system. However, given that such analysis is covered comprehensively in existing rail safety standards, including EN 50126-1 (CENELEC 2017), this Sub-section is limited to addressing key principles relating specifically to the IEC 61508 viewpoint.

It is acknowledged that deriving a true "risk picture" for particular operational applications is far from easy and, in keeping with Sub-section 1.1, the following method is offered simply as a suggested approach to solving that problem.

Figure 1 in Sub-section 1.2 shows, for a single system-safety element, e.g. an OSF, a graphical representation of the relationship between its safety properties and their effect on achievable risk, according to IEC 61508. This graph is now presented in the form of a Fault Tree in Figure 13 below[80]; in this simplified example, we see how OSF#3, *"Enforce Safe Speed Limits for Trains"*, in effect acts as a potential *barrier* to the EUC hazardous event progressing through to an accident — in this case, a derailment[81].

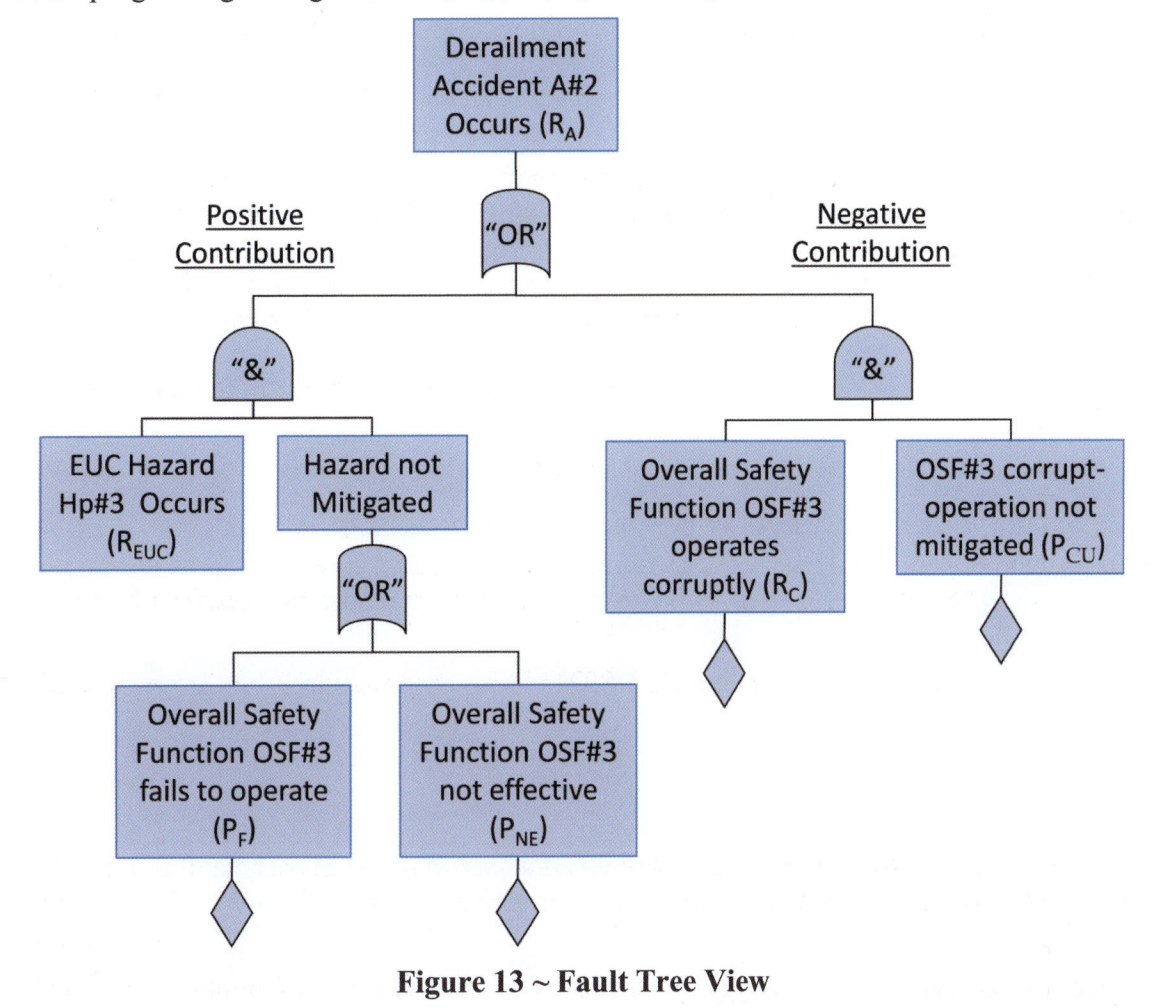

Figure 13 ~ Fault Tree View

---

[80] In mathematical terms, the fault tree applies to a safety function, in what IEC 61508-4 defines as *"a low demand mode of operation"*. However, the authors' intention here is not to detail a quantitative approach — rather, it is to present the general relationships involved.

[81] In this simple example, we have not explicitly captured the possibility of a near miss, i.e. the likelihood that a collision accident would not result even if a hazard was not mitigated, simply because of the 'geometry' of the situation, for example. It is, however, addressed in the subsequent discussion on the Barrier Model.

As we saw in Sub-section 1.2 above, whether or not OSF#3 mitigates the *consequences* of an EUC hazardous event (Hp#3) would depend on its effectiveness when working (1-P_{NE}), and the probability that it doesn't fail to operate (1-P_F). Although corrupt operation of the OSF could itself lead to a hazardous situation, the rate at which such failures might occur would always be dominated by events outside of the ATC system, i.e. failures in the EUC Control System, or abnormal conditions in the environment.

That said, there might also be means of *reducing* the rate at which an EUC hazard occurs in the first place and to illustrate this we can go to the top-level view of the ATC, described in Section 3, and set them out in the form of a Barrier Model, as in Figure 14.

On the left of the diagram is the input of unmitigated EUC Hazards that are *inherent* in railway operations. Each Barrier, acting in rough sequence from left to right, effectively "filters out" a proportion of the EUC hazards, either by removing them or mitigating their consequences. The safety contribution of ATR is less obvious than that of ATS or ATP, but the argument is that a well-designed and well-run train timetable would (for good business reasons, if nothing else) reduce congestion and, therefore, reduce the number of *opportunities* for a collision accident to occur.

The three main barriers are supported by safety functions or management functions, which are themselves implemented in the physical ATC system, comprising people, equipment and procedures. Of course, these system elements can fail to operate, effectively reducing the probability of success of the barrier, or operate corruptly, giving rise to new, *system-generated* hazards.

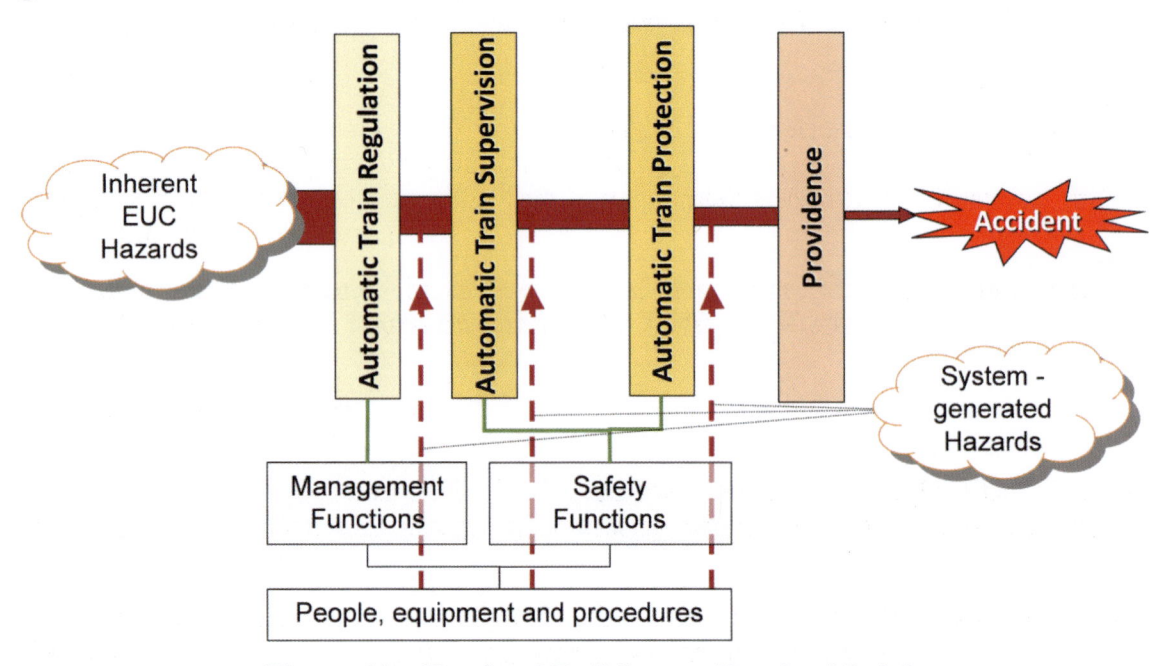

Figure 14 ~ Top-level Rail System Barrier Model

The final, Providence, barrier reflects the point that, even when all three layers of ATC have been unable to remove a hazard, there might still be a significant probability that an actual accident would not result.

In order to quantify the relationships involved, the Barrier Model can be presented in the form of the simplified, top-level Event Tree shown in Figure 15.

At the input to the tree are the unmitigated EUC hazards, which are inherent in railway operations, and which occur at frequency F_U; each barrier then has a probability of success (P_{Sn}) in mitigating the hazards at its input node (shown thus ⊗), enabling the computation of the risk of an accident (R_A) as:

$$R_A = F_U \cdot (1-P_{S1}) \cdot (1-P_{S2}) \cdot (1-P_{S3}) \cdot (1-P_{S4}) \quad \ldots\ldots\ldots\ldots\ldots(1)$$

The frequency of other, more-benign outcomes can be similarly computed, with the model capturing the net positive, as well as the negative, contributions of each barrier to the safety of railway operations, in line with the IEC 61508 viewpoint.

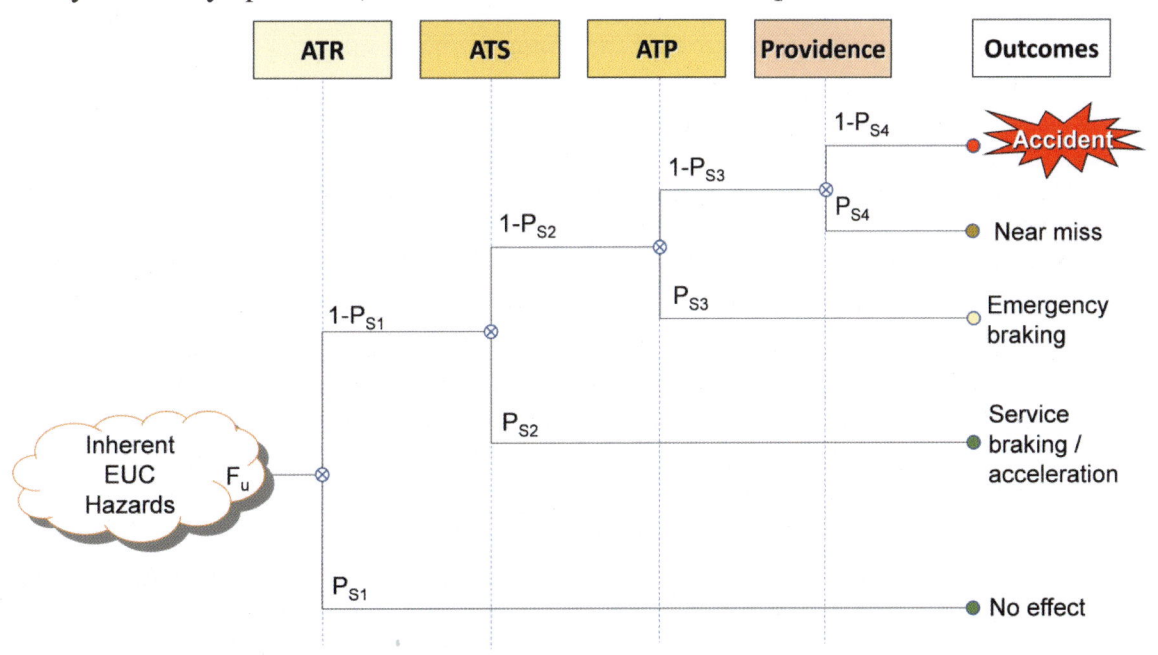

Figure 15 ~ Top-level Rail System Event-tree Model

Of course, the model, as presented here, is purely illustrative and very high-level. Nevertheless it provides a sound framework, for each accident type, and has the advantage of being able to capture multiple *end events* — unlike the Fault Tree, which has only one.

This could be done by developing such an Event Tree for each appropriate accident type of Table 13 and, for each tree:

- decomposing each Barrier into its constituent OSFs, SRSs and Safety Functions;
- constructing Fault Trees (of the form of that shown in Figure 13, but decomposed down to SRS or Safety Function level); and
- linking the Fault Trees to the relevant nodes of the Event Tree such that the top-level event in the Fault Tree represents the probability of a success outcome (P_{Sn}) for the Barrier concerned.

That, of course, raises the more difficult question as to how to get realistic estimates of the probability values for, and a sensible balance between, the Barriers. Fowler and Fota (2023) outlined how this problem had already been addressed and largely resolved, in the Air Traffic Management (ATM) sector, on the European Commission's Single European Sky ATM Research (SESAR) programme, and from which the approach outlined above was derived.

In seeking to overcome many of the shortcomings of more traditional failure-analysis techniques, e.g. hazard-severity / risk-classification schemes, discussed in Fowler (2022), the SESAR approach:

- uses real accident and incident data to populate the model with the historic probability and frequency values;
- more-accurately captures the progression of a hazardous event through to an accident;
- is capable of modelling the interdependencies between barriers, including lower-level common-cause and common-mode failures, which are implied in Figure 14;
- can be adapted so that they properly reflect the operational environment for specific applications;
- is capable of being modified so that the effects, on the historic risk picture, of the introduction of changes at the operational and/or technological level (e.g. the introduction of a new railway control system), could be assessed and, thereby, new risk models produced.

In practice, the SESAR models are used to generate easy-to-use Risk Classification Schemes that more-realistically reflect the overall safety-risk picture of the operational environment concerned.

4.7 Specification of Safety Requirements for ORRMs (IEC 61508-1 Phase 10)

As noted earlier, it has been assumed that all Other Risk Reduction Measures would already exist as part of the legacy railway infrastructure. Therefore, the specification of requirements for these items is not appropriate for such items, in this case.

5 Conclusions

Fundamentally, the IEC 61508-1 lifecycle, as outlined in the first of three articles (Fowler 2022), stems from the simple concept that where there exists an inherently hazardous *Equipment Under Control* (EUC), which presents an intolerable level of risk to its environment, so there is a need to develop and deploy *Safety Related Systems* (SRSs), and/or *Other Risk-reduction Measures* (ORRMs), in order to *reduce* that risk to a tolerable level.

True to its pan-industrial principles, IEC 61508 allows for an EUC to be anything from a nuclear reactor or a chemical process, to road traffic flows, the flow of aircraft through a block of airspace (as in Fowler and Fota (2023)), or the movement of trains around a rail network (as in this article).

Self-evidently, it is the *functional* safety properties of the SRSs / ORRMs that determine their potential to *reduce* the risks, inherent in the EUC, to a tolerable level. Only then does it make sense to consider the safety *integrity* properties of the SRSs / ORRMs, which negatively affect EUC risk in two possible ways:

- loss of function of the SRSs / ORRMs, which would lower the amount by which *inherent* EUC risk could otherwise be reduced;
- corrupt / spurious operation of the SRSs / ORRMs, which would introduce *new* EUC hazards and risks.

This is exactly what the IEC 61508-1 lifecycle does, although the scope of all three articles was limited to the seven IEC 61508 lifecycle phases that relate to the specification of safety requirements, because most of the key principles underpinning IEC 61508 take effect during these earlier phases.

The example application, herein, of the IEC 61508-1 lifecycle to a new, moving-block Automatic Train Control system, for a hypothetical Metro, has:

- provided a comprehensive set of EUC hazards, inherent to rail operations in general;
- presented a systematic way to analyse a system that results in the description of an exemplary set of SRSs[82] and a detailed specification of their constituent Safety Functions, which are required in order to provide the necessary *reduction* in the EUC risk; and
- outlined an effective method of modelling the effects of failure of the Safety Functions such that safety integrity requirements for those Safety Functions could be derived.

That said, the challenge of demonstrating correctness and completeness of the safety analysis processes should not be underestimated since, as past experience suggests, we would probably be dealing with "SIL-4" functions in most cases. A complete response to that challenge is beyond the scope of this article but the following two areas of the process presented herein go some way towards meeting it.

The first is the role of the IEC 61508 concept of "Overall Safety Functions" (OSFs), which at first seemed to be somewhat redundant but soon proved to be a vital link between the EUC hazards and the SRRs / ORRMs that are required to mitigate them. It was already realised (Fowler 2022) that the safety integrity requirements at that level are not actually properties of (but are targets to be met by) the OSFs and, by applying the same logic, we realised the need for a functional equivalent, in the form of *rules-based* requirements.

The second is the use of a hierarchical set of models that capture the required behaviour of, and interactions between, the SRSs and their Safety Functions. Not only do these prove to add an essential dynamic dimension to the rather static individual functional specifications, but they also helped identify missing, incorrect and missing requirements.

Overall, it is concluded that following the principles of the specific phases of IEC 61508 provides a considerable overall benefit of ensuring a top-down, and far more complete, approach to functional-safety assessment than might otherwise be the case. Fowler (2015) observed, *inter alia*, that European rail safety standards at *that* time were based almost entirely on a bottom-up analysis of the risks from failure of safety functions and a tacit (and totally unjustified) assumption that a tolerably safe state of a rail control system would exist provided the system were sufficiently reliable. What we believe has yet to be properly demonstrated (i.e. not merely asserted) is that the *current* set of European rail safety standards do not suffer from the same deficiencies!

Acknowledgments

The authors wish to acknowledge the considerable help, support and understanding of many colleagues (past and present) from Transport for London and beyond, without which this article would not have come to fruition. Our particular thanks go to Dr Ivan Lucic for his guidance and allowing us to make use of material from his book *"Risk and Safety in Engineering Processes"*.

The copyright holder of the quotations from published standards used for illustration in the main body of this article is the International Electrotechnical Commission, Geneva; and that of the quotation in Sub-section 1.1 is CENELEC, the European Committee for Electrotechnical Standardization, Brussels.

---

[82] No new ORRMs were identified in this case.

References

CENELEC. (2017) *Railway applications – the specification and demonstration of reliability, availability, maintainability and safety (RAMS), Part 1: Basic requirements and generic process*, EN 50126-1:2017. European Committee for Electrotechnical Standardization, Brussels.

Fowler D. (2015). *Functional Safety by Design — Magic or Logic?* In Proceedings of the 23rd Safety-Critical Systems Symposium, Bristol, UK. Available at https://scsc.uk/r129/7:1. Accessed 19th June 2022.

Fowler D. (2022). *IEC 61508 Viewpoint on System Safety in the Transport Sector: Part 1 — An Overview of IEC 61508*, in Safety-Critical Systems eJournal, Vol. 1, Iss. 2. Available at https://scsc.uk/r176.3:1, Accessed 29th December 2022.

Fowler D. and Fota O.N. (2023). *Safety Assessment of Point Merge Operations in Terminal Airspace — an IEC 61508 Viewpoint*, in Safety Critical Club eJournal, Vol 1, Iss. 3. Available at https://scsc.uk/r183.3:1#page=25, Accessed 17th July 2023.

IEC. (2010). *Functional Safety of Electrical/electronic/programmable electronic Safety-related Systems*, IEC 61508, V 2.0. International Electrotechnical Commission. Geneva.

IEC. (2014a). *Railway applications — Urban Guided Transport Management and Command/Control Systems — Part 1: System Principles and Fundamental Concepts*, IEC 62290-1:2014. International Electrotechnical Commission. Geneva.

IEC. (2014b). *Railway applications — Urban guided transport management and command/control systems — Part 2: Functional requirements specification*, IEC 62290-2:2014. International Electrotechnical Commission. Geneva.

Lucic I. (2015). *Risk and Safety in Engineering Processes*, Cambridge Scholars Publishing ISBN (13): 978-1-4438-7077-1.

RailSystem. (2022). *Communications-Based Train Control (CBTC)*, https://railsystem.net/communications-based-train-control-cbtc/, Accessed 4th July 2023.

SEBoK. (2022). *Guide to the Systems Engineering Body of Knowledge*, v. 2.7, released 31 October 2022, https://sebokwiki.org/wiki/Operational_Scenario_(glossary). Accessed 4th July 2023.

Sparx Systems. (2022). *UML 2 Tutorial – Sequence Diagram*, https://sparxsystems.com/resources/tutorials/uml2/sequence-diagram.html. Accessed 4th July 2023.

Appendix A. EUC Hazard Descriptions

Table 20 ~ EUC Hazard Descriptions

ID.	Pre-existing Hazard	Description
Hp#1	Conflict between any pair of train trajectories (see note below table)	This hazard is about the separation between trains. As a state of the railway, it exists whenever the intended movement (e.g. planned missions / perturbed running) of any two trains would result in the trains being at the same location at the same time, i.e. a **collision** would result if nothing at all were done to prevent it.
Hp#2	Conflict between a train's trajectory and track configuration	This hazard is about the relationship between the intended routing of a train and the configuration of the track elements. It exists whenever the intended movement of any train would result in the train passing through an incorrectly-configured set of points or level-crossing lights / barriers — **derailment** and/or **collision** could result if nothing at all were done to prevent incorrect route setting.
Hp#3	Train speed exceeding capabilities of the track infrastructure and/or train	This hazard is about the relationship between the speed of a train and the ability of the track elements to support it. It exists whenever the speed of any train exceeds the capability of the track, taking account of the permanent, intrinsic (e.g. curves and junctions) or temporarily-degraded characteristics of the track (e.g. buckled or broken rail) **derailment** (or **collision**, in the case of over-speed at the end of track) could result if nothing at all were done to prevent over-speeding of the train.
Hp#4	High and/or uneven acceleration / deceleration of a train	This hazard relates the effect on passengers on trains due to sudden train movement. It exists during lurching, jerking, or sudden rapid deceleration, which could result in **passenger falls** with the possibility of injury, serious injury or (exceptionally) death.
Hp#5	Conflict between train profile and fixed structure, *except* as the result of excessive train speed (Hp#3) or damage to structure (Hp#10)	This hazard covers the relationship between the intended route and speed of a train and structure gauge. It exists whenever it would be possible to route a train through, or past, a fixed structure whose gauge is incompatible with the kinetic envelope of that train (as determined by, *inter alia*, its size / shape and speed), and would result in a **collision** if nothing at all were done to prevent it. It excludes potential collisions with fixed structures arising from derailment (see other, derailment-related hazards), excessive speed of the train, and collisions arising from failure of fixed structures (see Hp#10)

ID.	Pre-existing Hazard	Description
Hp#6	Conflict between a train's trajectory and non-fixed obstacles or unauthorised persons on track	This hazard concerns the *unexpected* presence of objects, large animals or unauthorised persons on the running railway such that they could make contact with a passing train. Depending on the physical properties of object concerned, it could lead to: derailment; damage to the leading cab, with the possibility of train-operator injury, serious injury or even death; or serious injury / death to persons on the track.
Hp#7	Conflict between a train's trajectory and workforce personnel / vehicles on track	This hazard concerns the *planned* presence of workforce personnel or vehicles / equipment on the running railway such that they could make contact with a passing train if nothing at all were done to prevent it.
Hp#8	Passengers attempt to exit a train outside a station	This hazard covers the possibility of passengers falling out of a train due to: - train doors being opened too early on entry to a station; - a train departing with a door or doors open; - train doors being opened outside of a station; or - carriage separation
Hp#9	Passenger embarkation / disembarkation at platform	This covers possible incidents associated with normal entering or alighting from trains at a station. It includes: - train doors being opened on the side away from the platform leading to passengers getting off the train on the wrong side or falling out of the train on to the track; - train doors which are on the same side of the train as the platform, but which are not adjacent to the platform (i.e. the train is longer than the platform, or is not correctly berthed) being opened and passengers falling out of the train; - train doors opening at a closed station except where done deliberately (e.g. to evacuate passengers from platform or train); - a passenger being hit by closing door; - a passenger (or passenger's clothing) being caught in door of a stationary train, which then moves off, dragging the person along the platform; - slips, trips and falls associated with the gap between the train and the platform.

ID.	Pre-existing Hazard	Description
Hp#10	Structural failure of track elements, tunnels, bridges, etc.	This hazard addresses the threat of **collision** to trains (and its Passengers and on-train Workforce) from failure of structures, including: - unsound track elements; - unsound / unsecured tunnel; - unsound / unsecured under-bridge / culvert; - unsound / unsecured over-bridge. It excludes the direct effects of such failures on members of the public. It also excludes failure of other railway structural assets (e.g. signalling or electrical structures), fallen trees, etc., all of which are covered by Hp#6.
Hp#11	Personnel exposure to potentially lethal voltage	This hazard addresses the threat to people of **contact with lethal voltages** from electrical power supplies.
Hp#12	Passengers too close to, or fall/jump off, platform edge	This hazard concerns the possibility of passengers at a platform being struck or run over by a train due to passengers: - standing too close to the platform edge or otherwise infringing the kinematic envelope of the train; - falling off (or jumping of) platforms; - crossing the lines at a station (where unauthorised only).

Note: Conceptually, a train's "trajectory" is the path and speed profile that the train *intends* to follow at any point in time, in the absence of any instructions to the contrary.

Appendix B. Functional Safety Requirements - Examples

As an example, the following table lists all FSRs for the Safety Related Systems that have been derived for OSF#1, *"Establish & Protect a Safe Route for each Train Movement"*, in the analysis at Sub-section 3.6, and shows traceability back to the related OSRs set out in Table 16.

The requirements themselves have been adapted from the UGTMS standard (IEC 2014b), and represent a full list for each Safety Function, but under normal operating conditions only.

The traceability shown is to the Overall Safety Requirements (OSRs) related to OSF#1.

Table 21 ~ FSRs for SRSs for OSF#1 -
Establish & Protect a Safe Route for each Train Movement

ID	Safety Requirement	Traceability
SRS#1	**Set & Protect Route Elements**	OSF#1
SF#1.1	*Reserve, Set & Lock a Standard Route*	
FSR1.1.1	For the route to be reserved, ATC shall reserve all the route elements required based on the route origin and route destination, including elements required for flank protection, and for overlap.	OSRs 1.1 & 1.2
FSR1.1.2	The reserved status of a route element shall be provided by ATC to other functions and Service Control Centre.	OSRs 1.1 & 1.2
FSR1.1.3	ATC shall move a reserved movable route element to the desired position if it is not already in that position, not occupied by a train and not blocked against moving.	OSRs 1.1 & 1.2
FSR1.1.4	If a movable route element does not reach the desired position in a predefined time, ATC shall initiate a failure message to this effect.	OSRs 1.1 & 1.2
FSR1.1.5	ATC shall lock all route elements in a route to be set if they are confirmed in the required position.	OSRs 1.1 & 1.2
FSR1.1.6	ATC shall not set a route which would allow a train to enter a route for which it is not suited.	OSR1.4

ID	Safety Requirement	Traceability
SF#1.2	***Supervise Route***	
FSR1.2.1	ATC shall monitor the status of all route elements to confirm that they are in the required position and locked.	OSRs 1.1 & 1.2
FSR1.2.2	ATC shall provide the status of each route. to other functions and Service Control Centre.	OSRs 1.1 & 1.2
FSR1.2.3	The entrance to a route shall be prohibited by ATC in response to a safety related manual input.	OSRs 1.1 & 1.2
SF#1.3	***Maintain Route Locking***	
FSR1.3.1	ATC shall determine a train approach area in front of a route origin for which a Movement Authority has been given. The approach area shall cover an area which is longer than the operational braking distance, allowing for any human or system reaction time.	OSRs 1.1 & 1.2
FSR1.3.2	ATC shall ensure that the status "route locked by approach" prevents the immediate release of the route: • if a train is in the approach area and a movement authority has been given to the train, *or* • if a train has entered the route (with or without movement authority).	OSR 1.3
FSR1.3.3	ATC shall ensure that moveable route elements (e.g. points, etc.) that are occupied by trains are prevented from moving, regardless of whether or not the route is set.	OSR 1.3
FSR1.3.4	ATC shall ensure that the route elements in front of a train are maintained locked as soon as the train has entered the set route.	OSR 1.3
FSR1.3.5	ATC shall ensure that moveable route elements that are "blocked against switching "remain in that state until released by manual input related to the need to block the elements in the first place.	OSR 1.3
FSR1.3.6	ATC shall ensure that moveable route elements in a Recovery Route remain locked until the route has been removed.	OSR 1.3
FSR1.3.7	A moveable route element that has been locked by route-setting or manual input shall not be released until all routes / manual inputs that caused the element to be locked in the first place have themselves been released / removed.	OSR 1.3
FSR1.3.8	ATC shall not release route elements that are providing flank protection for a route until the route itself is released.	OSR 1.3
SF#1.4	***Release Route***	
FSR1.4.1	A route may be released **only** if and when **all** of the conditions for maintaining it locked no longer apply.	OSR 1.3

ID	Safety Requirement	Traceability
SRS#4	**Authorise Train Movement**	OSF#1
SF#4.1	*Determine Limit of Movement Authority*	
FSR4.1.1	ATC shall determine for each train the limit of its movement authority (LMA) based on the most restrictive of the following potential conflict points: • Limit of safe route, • Limit based on safe train separation, • Limit based on the physical infrastructure (e.g. end of track), • Zones of protection.	OSR1.5
FSR4.1.2	In the event of a loss of safe route once a movement authority has been issued, ATC shall pull back the LMA to the new limit of safe route.	OSR1.5
SF#4.2	*Determine Train Protection Profile*	
FSR4.2.1	ATC shall determine a Train Protection Profile for each train, to prevent it from overrunning its LMA, or exceeding the applicable speed limits within its LMA.	OSR1.5
FSR4.2.1	The Train Protection Profile shall be determined by the applicable Safe Braking Model — an analytical representation of a train's performance while decelerating to a complete stop, allowing for a combination of worst-case influencing factors (gradient & adhesion, etc.) and failure scenarios.	OSR1.5
FSR4.2.2	The Safe Braking Model shall ensure that an ATC equipped train will always stop within a distance not greater than that guaranteed by the Model.	OSR1.5
FSR4.2.3	ATC shall calculate the train-protection profile that results from the most restrictive of all safety-related constraints applied to the ATC-equipped train.	OSR1.5
FSR4.2.4	ATC shall enforce speed limits for the whole length of the train.	[n/a]
SF#4.3	*Authorise Movement of Reporting Trains*	
FSR4.3.1	If a Train Protection Profile with permitted speed greater than zero is established, train movement shall be allowed, up to next LMA.	OSR1.5
FSR4.3.2	Each train movement authorised by ATC shall be within the constraints of the applicable Train Protection Profile.	OSR1.5

ID	Safety Requirement	Traceability
SRS#5	**Supervise Train Movement**	OSF#1
SF#5.1	*Determine actual train speed*	
FSR5.1.1	ATC shall detect and determine the actual train speed, taking into account the effects of speed-measurement inaccuracies.	OSR1.5
FSR5.1.2	ATC shall determine the zero-speed status within the predefined tolerances of the speed measurement system.	OSR4.1
SF#5.2	*Supervise Safe Train Speed*	
FSR5.2.1	ATC shall supervise the actual speed of trains to ensure that each train remains within its Train Protection Profile.	OSR1.5
FSR5.2.2	ATC shall trigger Service braking in accordance with the warning profile in order to respect the Train Protection Profile and to avoid Emergency-brake intervention.	[n/a]
FSR5.2.3	ATC shall automatically release the Service brake during deceleration if actual determined train speed returns below the warning profile.	[n/a]
FSR5.2.4	If the determined actual train speed is higher than the speed permitted by the Train Protection Profile, ATC shall trigger emergency braking.	OSR1.5
FSR5.2.5	ATC shall provide two possibilities for automatic emergency brake release: • if, during deceleration, actual determined train speed returns below the train-protection profile provided there are no other conditions for triggering the emergency brake. • if actual train speed is determined as zero and there is no other triggering condition,	[n/a]
SF#5.3	*Supervise Safe Train Direction*	
FSR5.3.1	ATC shall detect an unauthorized movement of the train in case of travel of the train against the authorized direction of travel beyond a predefined distance,	[n/a]
FSR5.3.2	When unauthorized movement of the train against the authorized direction rollaway is detected, ATC shall apply the emergency brake,	[n/a]
FSR5.3.3	In the event that a *moving* train receives a Movement Authority that is contradictory to its direction of travel (i.e. is "behind" the train), the train shall: • emergency brake to a standstill • not accept the Movement Authority • report its inability to accept the Movement Authority, to Service Control.	[n/a]

ID	Safety Requirement	Traceability
SF#5.4	*Supervise Movement-Authority Validity*	
FSR5.4.1	In case a movement authority accepted by the train exceeds its validity period (e.g. due to data communication failure), ATC shall either: • pull back the movement authority limit to the first conflict point ahead of the train, or • stop the train immediately.	OSR1.5
FSR5.4.2	In the event that the train's Movement Authority is cancelled, the train shall emergency brake to a standstill.	[n/a]
SF#5.5	*Overrun Protection*	
FSR5.5.1	ATC shall supervise the actual position of each ATC-equipped train against its LMA and initiate an emergency braking in the event that the LMA is exceeded.	OSR1.5
FSR5.5.2	ATC shall restrict the movement authority of ATC trains that are in conflict with an unauthorised movement of any train when such an unauthorised movement is detected.	[n/a]

Appendix C. Operational Scenarios — Examples

C.1 Operational Scenarios for *Normal* Operations

Table 22 provides examples of Operational Scenarios for *normal* operations conditions, as discussed in Sub-section 4.6.4.

Table 22 ~ Example Operational Scenarios for *Normal* Operations

SC No	Description	Related Actors	Trigger In:	Trigger out:	Related States
01	Empty ATC passenger train ready to enter service from depot / siding (train berthed outside ATC signalling area	SCC, ATC Train, SRS#1, SRS#2, SRS#4, SRS#9	SCC requests Train power-up	Train registered on ATC system and position ready to exit depot / siding for first Mission of day	ST001, ST002, ST003, ST004
02	AC Train undertaking a System-protected Movement, between station stops (following a non-reporting train)	ATC Train, non-ATC Train, Non-ATC wayside SRS#1, SRS#2, SRS#4, SRS#9	Train leaves previous station limits (SC-03)	ATC Train approaches next station stop (SC-03)	ST005
03	ATC Train makes scheduled station stop.	ATC Train, SRS#1, SRS#2, SRS#4, SRS#9	ATC Train approaches next station stop (SC-02)	Train clear of station limits (SC-02)	ST006
04	Train repositions to reversing location, for next mission.	ATC Train, SRS#1, SRS#2, SRS#4, SRS#9	Train leaves final station limits (SC-03)	Doors closed. Train ready to depart reversing location (SC-02)	ST007, ST003
05	Train repositions to depot, after completing final mission of day.	ATC Train, SRS#1, SRS#2, SRS#4, SRS#9	Train leaves final station limits (SC-03)	Train powered down in depot siding	ST007, ST002, ST001

SC No	Description	Related Actors	Trigger In:	Trigger out:	Related States
06	Route setting and junction management in ATC areas	SCC, ATC Train, non-ATC Train, Non-ATC wayside SRS#1, SRS#2, SRS#4, SRS#9	Timetable implementation	Rear of train's Virtual Occupancy clears junction	ST005
07	Train exits depot to join mainline on first mission	ATC Train, SRS#1, SRS#2, SRS#4, SRS#9	Train registered on ATC system and position ready to exit depot / siding for first Mission of day	Train running according to timetable	ST004, ST005

C.2   Operational Scenarios for *Abnormal* Operating Conditions

Table 23 provides examples of Operational Scenarios for *abnormal* operating conditions, as defined in Sub-section 4.6.5.

Table 23 ~ Example Operational Scenarios for *Abnormal* Operating Conditions

SC No	Description	Related Actors	Trigger In:	Trigger Out:	Related States
016	ATC Train performs recovery of failed train.	SCC, ATC Train, SRS#1, SRS#2, SRS#4, SRS#9	Trains coupled, registered in ATC system and ready to move	Train reaches recovery location	ST011
033	Service Control applies Temporary Speed Restriction.	SCC, ATC Train, non-ATC Train, Non-ATC wayside SRS#1, SRS#2, SRS#4, SRS#9	TSR initiated by SCC	TSR in force – steady state	ST009
079	Detrainment of passengers, train not berthed in platform (taking passengers off train on foot)	SCC, ATC Train, SRS#1, SRS#2, SRS#4, SRS#9	Event necessitating detrainment	Passengers evacuated to safe location	ST010

SC No	Description	Related Actors	Trigger In:	Trigger Out:	Related States
096	Movement of non-communicating ATC trains	SCC, ATC Train, non-ATC Train, Non-ATC wayside SRS#1, SRS#2, SRS#4, SRS#9	Non-communicating ATC train needs to move	Non-communicating ATC train completes move	ST011
100	Service Control initiates unplanned station stop	SCC, ATC Train, SRS#1, SRS#2, SRS#4, SRS#9	SCC needs to stop a train at a non-timetabled station / platform	Train berthed at platform; doors ready to open if required	ST009, ST010
108	Passenger evacuation from train fire	SCC, ATC Train, SRS#1, SRS#2, SRS#4, SRS#9	Fire on train	Passengers rescued	ST010
109	Train / passenger rescue from wayside fire	SCC, ATC Train, non-ATC Train, Non-ATC wayside SRS#1, SRS#2, SRS#4, SRS#9	Fire on wayside	Passengers rescued; train recovered	ST010

This collation page left blank intentionally.

Chasing the Black Swan

Malcolm Jones

Atomic Weapons Establishment (AWE), Aldermaston, Berkshire, UK

Abstract

The term Black Swan is a familiar concept in the context of high consequence operations. There is the continual concern that there may be an 'as yet' undiscovered flaw or lack of understanding in the design of a product, process or facility that could lead to a catastrophic event. Concern lies in the potential incompleteness of understanding of any design concept, implementation and associated assessment. Given that 'absolute confidence' may never be possible, the question arises as to how best to continue to search for such a possible flaw with a view to subsequent removal or mitigation. This at first sight appears to be a process without end but the level of commitment must be balanced against the detrimental consequence that could ensue given that a Black Swan might exist. But when is 'enough-enough'? This subject is covered in the context of the ownership of nuclear warheads where the Black Swan can indeed be catastrophic should it exist. The paper is framed somewhat in terms of what can be learned from the general literature associated with Black Swan thinking.

1 Introduction

Aspects of this subject have been covered in previous papers (Jones 2016) (Jones 2017), which have taken different perspectives of an independent strength in depth approach to safety and its assessment. The first paper concentrated on organisational structures in relation to the necessary organisational levels, each having independent responsibilities for safety ensurance and assurance[83], coupled with final decision-making responsibilities and of course each having the appropriate level of technical capability and experience. The overall organisational responsibility is that of ensuring a safe product, process or facility with appropriate technical and evidential support, with the level of scrutiny proportional to the potential consequence of getting it wrong.

The first organisational layer is responsible for ensurance through making the safety case with a supporting evidence base. The second independent structure scrutinises and challenges this case for appropriate depth and completeness, including assuring that the appropriate level of expertise has been applied and that the evidence and analysis offered is complete and not flawed.

The third independent organisational layer is responsible for final decision making, having taken into account and scrutinising the ensurance and assurance evidence provided by the

---

[83] We use the term "ensurance" to mean the demonstration that a design, etc., has met its requirements; whereas "assurance" is the independent challenge of whether the ensurance is valid.

© Crown copyright (2023), AWE. This material is licensed under the terms of the Open Government Licence except where otherwise stated. To view this licence, visit http://www.nationalarchives.gov.uk/doc/open-government-licence/version/3 or write to the Information Policy Team, The National Archives, Kew, London TW9 4DU, or email: psi@nationalarchives.gov.uk.

first two layers and in turn, adding its own independent assessment based on a complementary fund of knowledge and experience. This third layer will also manage and resolve any disagreement arising from the views arising from the first two layers. Some of the fundamental competences needed for correct operation of this structure were identified in Jones (2016) together with some of the remaining difficulties.

However, our historical experience suggests this overall approach alone may not be sufficient for ensuring the absence of a Black Swan for a product such as a nuclear warhead. For this reason, a fourth layer is introduced, see Figure 16 (Jones 2016). That is a somewhat undefined layer which continues to probe into the product, process or facility with the intention of taking a 'what if' and 'expecting the unexpected' mind-set. This layer's job in essence is never finished and sets its target in the broadest sense. More is said later.

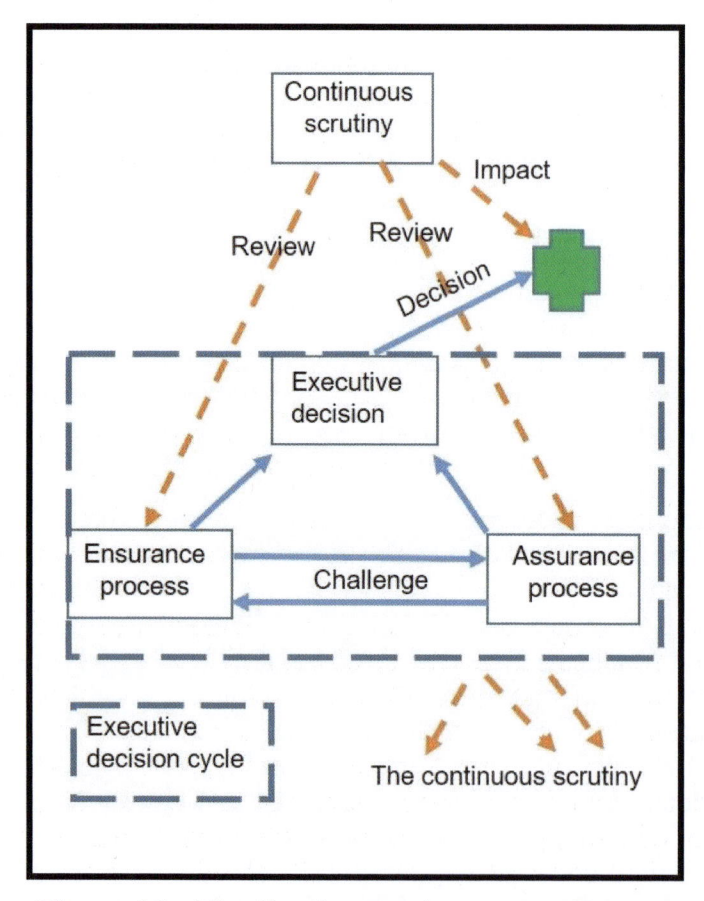

Figure 16 ~ The Continuous Assessment Process

Note that the Green Cross in the diagram is the potentially revised executive decision given what the fourth layer has unearthed as a result of continued scientific investigations; "Impact" is the impact on the executive decision given new information unearthed by the fourth layer.

The second paper covered two independent technical strategies for safety ensurance and assessment (Jones 2017). The first was based on an independent strength in depth technical analogue of the organisational structure. This is based on a deterministic approach founded on fundamental and independent levels of technical defence which is intended to include a hedge against uncertainty. The second approach complements this with a realistic, but conservative, evidential based numerical risk assessment looking for compliance with risk standards. Of course, any risk assessment will contain an element of foundational judgment for supporting such an analysis. In principle, this judgement could be in error and for this reason an acceptable level of conservatism has to be included in order to cater for any remnant uncertainty. This risk assessment relates directly to a particular (or set of) design solution as opposed to the deterministic approach which is based simply on 'how to design for safety'. The latter risk approach aims more for a demonstration of meeting acceptable risk standards given the design solution.

The two approaches have elements of fundamental difference but in concert compensate for individual potential limitations and statutory requirements. From a philosophical point of view the deterministic approach does offer the better of the two approaches for protection against the potential of a Black Swan because of its greater potential for protecting against any limits in our 'complete knowledge'. The risk assessment is necessary because of the societal demand to understand 'what the level of risk is' and whether it is tolerable in meeting accepted standards. However, the risk assessment inevitably bases its approach on an 'accepted level' of understanding with some conservatism included to cover any potential deficiency in knowledge.

There is some value in the argument that, given a history of a product or process performing satisfactorily over a given period, this adds further to the confidence that a Black Swan may well not exist. However, the value of such evidence must be set against the level of potential detrimental consequence. For example, if the requirement is that a major consequence should not have a frequency of greater than a 1 in 100 years, then a ten-year successful history only gives additional confidence that all seems well. In fact, if the frequency requirement for a catastrophic event is far more demanding, then typical design history perspectives may be somewhat less comforting. History also shows us that past success does not always support future success.

2 Historical Experience

History shows us that many, if not most, catastrophic events occur through an 'unfortunate' sequence of linked events rather than from a single technical cause. Such previously undiscovered sequences are often related to an incomplete knowledge of the range of possible states leading to the propagation of the failure sequence or, perhaps more correctly, the level of dependency between such states in such a sequence. For example, an initial technical failure will not propagate if all states potentially influenced by such a failure have been fully identified, characterised and configured through independence to terminate such a sequence. The problem arises when there is incomplete knowledge about the range of states that may be mutually or dependently influenced. So incomplete information is the enemy of safety assurance of termination of a mishap occurrence. This is often pictorially displayed in the Swiss Cheese model. In the general case the states involved may take on a wide range of types.

For example, in a simple technical product an initial analysis may appear relatively simple, i.e. that of tracking the well-known and fully-defined influenced states together with their known mitigating/independent resilience. However, the response of these states may in turn be influenced by external actors, for example environments at the time of the initial flaw and without this information the response robustness of the argument for terminating the sequence prior to the mishap will be questionable. Of course, nuclear warheads need to remain safe given a wide range of potentially severe environments. To treat any real case, it is necessary to establish, as far as possible, a complete definition of the 'system' of all states and influences. This is perhaps analogous to the goal of fundamental physics of seeking a complete understanding of all of nature's subatomic particles and forces and their potential interactions. As the 'system and influences grow' so does the difficulty of being able to fully identify and characterise the response of such states given any initiating event. In essence, complexity can become the enemy of safety and enhances the difficulty of identifying a Black Swan should it indeed exist. This complexity is perhaps best illustrated in simple form by a fictitious, but not improbable, example given in the form of a somewhat dated cinema film, "Fate is the Hunter" (Nelson 1964), shown during the 35th International System Safety Conference (2017) by John Rankin, who used it by way of example. It is paraphrased as follows:

Following an aircraft take-off one of the engines was struck by a bird which was rarely found in that part of the world — an unlikely initiator. The plane suffered a jolt due to the loss of that engine and as a result a cup of coffee, just supplied to the Captain, spilled onto an equipment box. Because the box was unsealed, coffee leaked onto the underlying equipment. The coffee was somewhat conducting in nature and as a result this interfered with underlying critical circuits, which led to the loss of the other engine. Because of aircraft congestion at the airfield at that time, the Captain took the reasonable option of landing on a nearby suitable beach. It so happened, unknown to the captain, that a pier on that beach, which had been scheduled for removal the previous week, was still in place, because of a decision by the contractor that there was no real need to hurry. Hence the fateful collision.

Although the initial verdict was judged to be human failure, careful analysis showed this not to be the case. The sequence is fictitious, but it does exemplify the need to fully understand what the 'system and the influences' really consists of and hence all of the potential interacting events given a somewhat unexpected fault initiator. Who would initially have identified the potential presence of a cup of coffee, the importance of an unsealed equipment box, congested airport conditions at the time and the continued existence of the pier that should have been absent?

Simplicity in the 'bounding of the system' is an important goal for minimising the opportunity for failing to fully characterise it. This in fact represents an important element in the safety approach to nuclear warheads: bounding the system (in the safety sense) as far as possible and aiming for simplicity, independence and clarity in the safety argument. Some of these aspects are covered in more detail later in this paper. The additional lesson learned from this fictitious example is that the sequence initiator was an abnormal environment, i.e. is an 'insult' to the technical system rather than a design flaw, although one could argue that design flaws helped the sequence to propagate. In fact, history shows that many sequences which have led to mishaps come from initial 'insult' initiators. This lesson is not lost on the strategy for minimising the opportunity of a Black Swan manifesting itself in nuclear warheads. The strategy is based on both the effort expended in both preventing such insults and the safety resilience given such an insult.

3 General Background to the Black Swan Term

3.1 Origin of the Phrase 'Black Swan'

A rare event, based on the belief widely held in England in the 1600s that swans could only be white. All swans in England at that time were white. The phrase "a Black Swan" was a metaphor for "that which could not exist". In the late 1600s, in Australia, black swans were discovered.

3.2 Current Understanding of the Phrase

An event judged through best established inductive/inferred logic to be assessed as rare — but this process does not remove the possibility of occurrence.

1. That the knowledge that we base our inductive assessment on is not quantitatively or logically correct. Its impact on risk assessment.
2. Or, more importantly that the scope of our inductive process is not complete, i.e. there are some possibilities we have not yet visualised. *Its impact on both risk assessment and defence in depth.*

The bottom line is, given the application of our best knowledge, a quantitative assessment may be broadly realistic but does not discount the possibility of an occurrence. In most cases this quantitative assessment is sufficient and the whole subject areas of 'cost benefit and insurance risks' work on this principle. However, this approach may be inappropriate if the Black Swan event has a major or catastrophic consequence. In this case there are two emerging issues:

1. The incompleteness in the quantification of the probability of mishap occurrence may be small but this delta does matter.
2. That the true nature and impact of the mishap may itself not be understood and underestimated. Although there may be a reasonable description of the mishap, the real follow-on consequences are usually less well understood, and often turn out to be of a far greater nature than first anticipated.

Hence, the context of the Black Swan is that it applies to a mishap which is assessed to be somewhat improbable, but cannot be discounted, and that its outcome can be severe or catastrophic and not fully understood. In fact, in a general sense, it might be unclear as to what the mishap itself may be and this is typified by the lessons from economic/financial traumas.

3.3 Some Terms and Definitions

Unexpected — The 'best analysis', suggests that the event has a low probability of occurrence. Such analysis cannot claim to be absolutely free of incompleteness and as such cannot assure us it cannot happen. There is often a quantitative definition of what is meant by unexpected.

Inconceivable — One cannot imagine how it can possibly happen, or believes that there is some fundamental reason why it cannot happen. This in principle is a human construct, and does not completely remove the possibility of a high consequence event.

Consequence — This relates to the range of impacts (detrimental in this case) given the event and in the case of safety this will take many forms:

- Death or harm
- Environmental damage
- Loss of asset
- Financial loss
- Reputational loss
- Political harm
- *Et cetera.*

Black Swans are generically spoken of in the context of a major detriment and, for nuclear warheads, can be associated with a major issue in relation to performance or safety. In the latter case this can be directly related to the occurrence of the worst-case catastrophic event itself, or to realisation that there may be a major flaw in the safety argument which requires urgent mitigating action. Of course, this is a key issue in the continued ownership and safety scrutiny of a stockpile of nuclear warheads.

4 Some Differing Categories of Black Swan and AWE's Culture

4.1 Known — But Not To The Degree Necessary

Knowledge about such a possibility is available but is not sufficient for correct judgement on probability and/or consequence. Of course, there is always the judgmental problem of when 'enough is enough' in relation to the depth of scrutiny which is necessary for elimination of the Black Swan's possibility.

With regards to detrimental event occurrence: The warhead programme has strived to avoid falling into this category. It has taken a very much 'what if' and 'expecting the unexpected' approach. All known possibilities are subject to in-depth scrutiny. If there is any reason why an issue has not been completely closed out, it is subject to continued scrutiny and of course this may give rise to a necessary change of design. We continue to strive to establish a more comprehensive understanding of the underlying characteristic of the known issues, whether they be of technical, human factors, implementation or governance nature. We retain a culture of assuming that we may not have reached the end of the road towards this goal and there is always more to be done — a culture of continued in depth assessment[84].

4.2 Unknowns — But Knowable Unknowns That Could Have Been Looked For Or Known By Others

The problem here is that such unknowns may have been regarded (erroneously) as being of no consequence, e.g. for safety.

With regards to detrimental event occurrence: The relevance to warhead activity follows from the comments under the last heading in the sense that there should be no assumption, without sufficient evidence, that the knowable unknowns can be discounted. If the unknowns are knowable then this gives us a direction in which to focus further effort and scrutiny with the goal of reaching a position where such unknowns are converted into 'fully characterized', and their impact determined. Included in this is the need to be aware of what's happening elsewhere in the world where similar technologies may be exercised, and where there are technology enhancements taking place which can have an advantage in enhancing our safety. Of course, in this respect one covers the whole associated subject area included in STEM (Science, Technology, Engineering, and Mathematics) where it is necessary to keep a close eye on worldwide developments in both industry and academia, which can be incorporated to our advantage. Our close collaboration with our US colleagues plays a major mutual role in this.

---

[84] Note that the fourth layer is not specifically responsible for assessing safety, but has a more open remit for probing further and further into the scientific and technical aspects that underpin nuclear science and, if something is yet to be discovered that could be a 'Black Swan', it is here that it will be found.

In addition, one needs to keep abreast of 'state of the art' developments in the range of methods for safety assessment and assurance, much of which are bound up in the general subject area of System Safety and as such where we need to be expert practitioners. Of course this again is a constantly moving and evolving activity with an acknowledgement that there will be no perfection. Any 'judgement' that we have reached a position of having identified and characterized such known unknowns is subject to constant challenge. Again the 'what if' attitude and 'expecting the unexpected' culture at AWE does provide a strong defence against this form of failure. Of course, the primary element of protection relating to 'known by others' comes through collaboration with our US colleagues and other work, particularly in the nuclear industry at large. The aim here is to establish confidence that no potential influencing subject area is left untouched.

4.3 Unknown — But Unknowable Unknowns

No absolute basis for being able to make any assured prediction for occurrence expectation or consequence — *a true Black Swan!* Nevertheless, even here 'confident' predictions may well be made but, of course, with the potential for failure due to ignorance.

With regards to detrimental event occurrence: This presents the most difficult aspect with regard to warhead safety assurance in that, if such flaws exist in our knowledge, we have little or no guidance of where to look further. The best practical protection against this uncertainty comes from the independent strength in depth approach to design, ownership and assessment both in terms of the technical and organisational aspects[85]. The best overall solution we are able to come up with in this respect, given no clear guidance of where further to look, is a continued commitment to ensure that we have a cadre of high calibre staff working at the cutting edge of all of the relevant technologies, processes and assessment methodologies and giving them sufficient freedom and encouragement 'to probe' into 'looking for the unexpected'. This activity is not solely restricted to 'in house' activity but also includes keeping a close look at developments of interest in the external world and how best to take advantage of such developments. Such unknowns are not likely to be uncovered through standard process and routine. From a business perspective, this may appear to be an untargeted, unproductive and non-cost-effective overhead — but we fail here at our peril. This Continuous Scrutiny process is identified in Figure 16. *AWE's culture strongly supports and encourages this approach.*

5 5 Lessons from the Open Literature

5.1 Nassim Nicholas Taleb

Taleb is well known for his work in this area and describes a Black Swan (Taleb 2008) in terms of:

1. It is unpredictable and as such cannot be truly sentenced as low probability;
2. It causes an extreme or catastrophic impact; and
3. It is retrospectively predictable — with the warning that there can be a tendency to simplify (possibly erroneously) the post event analysis of the cause. *There may be a telling lesson here for us in relation to the Review, Learn and Improve*

---

[85] Beware of 'groupthink' in which people strive for consensus; the claim of independence is always subject to credible challenge

actions we undertake — we need to be clear that we really do have the correct post event analysis — otherwise it can happen again.

Taleb's interest in unpredictability comes from his association with economics and the financial industries where the activity of prediction has been shown on many occasions to be unwarranted with major detrimental consequences. There may be some success in predicting the near future, but this gives no assured guidance for the longer term and the longer term may not be too extensive in this context. This aspect is somewhat like weather prediction where longer term prediction is also fraught with uncertainty. This can manifest itself via so-called Chaos Theory. In both cases predicting the future is bedevilled by the vast number of interacting contributors of, not always perfectly defined, knowledge and starting conditions. In the case of the economic and financial industries the situation is further complicated by the emotional response of people, whereas weather prediction is primarily governed by the laws of physics. *It is salutary to note that a nuclear weapon (or even a warhead) design, including its processing and ownership, is itself a somewhat complex subject area with inherent complicated relationships. However, a key lesson from Taleb's experience is that we should strive to limit complexity[86] (in respect to its relationship to safety) because of its impact on the ability to predict with confidence. As a result, we continue to strive to limit complexity and to gain as complete an understanding as possible of what we have — with the mind set of 'what if' — is it complete?*

There have been many attempts to model economic and financial futures, some based on a statistical basis, for example on the normal distribution for occurrence probability and range of consequence. In the context of financial industries, the 'well known' distribution peaks can be associated with the 'currently understood' in the relatively short term and the tails, with all their uncertainties, can be represented by the longer term 'judgements'. Because of the complex nature of the financial industries, these 'tails' often turn out to be completely misleading. Distributed approaches are sometimes applied to warhead safety assessments. Such distributions usually have far more evidential support near the peaks and less in the tails, where the low probability high consequence predictions are made and where prediction can be in significant error. This is where the Black Swans, if they exist, may lie. *The safety of warheads depends on the evidential confidence in the application of such distributions, where such distributions need to be applied.*

5.2 Taleb's View in Combatting Uncertainty

Because of the complexity associated with the financial industry, Taleb suggested that the effort expended in trying to prevent catastrophic occurrence was not well spent. He felt that catastrophes were inevitable and most effort should be best directed towards robustness in coping with Black Swan events when they do occur, rather than on predicting or preventing their occurrence. His experience was associated with economic and financial subject areas where his assumption (based on substantial historical evidence) was that these events will occur, and one should have plans in place on how to deal with them and mitigate the consequences. Given the assumption that the event will occur, Taleb's approach appears correct. *However, the priority for nuclear warheads lies firmly in the direction of preventing the occurrence and particularly in relation to the 'worst-case' occurrence of Inadvertent Nuclear Yield, rather than prioritising on the mitigation actions following such an event, if indeed this was realistically possible. For this reason, we concentrate on limiting complexity, particularly in the context of the principal safety*

---

[86] However measured

arguments, in order to enhance transparency and confidence in the evidence to support an assessment of a very low occurrence probability.

5.3 Charles Perrow

Perrow is well known for his work in accident theory (Perrow 2007). He provides another guide as to how Black Swans can arise, and what approaches should be put in place to avoid their occurrence. He has spent a great deal of his career in the field of historical accident assessment and the reasoning behind their occurrence. These have covered a wide range of subject areas, but their applicability are generally pertinent to nuclear warhead safety. The principles that clearly emerge from his work are again simplicity, clarity, and independence. These are evidenced by his observations and recommendations noted below.

   1. Complex, interconnected, and highly-coupled systems should be expected to fail

Response in warhead design: Warheads by their very nature have to be interconnected but this is different in the sense of being highly coupled in the context of safety. For example, interconnectivity in the sense of arming safety requires a unique set of authorizing actions/conditions for 'fault progression' and their absence prevents unintended fault progression. This principle also applies to other aspects of the warhead. As such in the safety sense there is limited inadvertent connectivity. The same is true for the AWE safety organizational structure in that, although there are interconnections, they are designed to be independent in the safety ensurance and assurance sense. Design also aims to minimize complexity, and this helps towards unintended (undetected) safety interconnectivity. For example, safety systems strive to minimize component counts (and particularly those that are safety-related). In addition, principal safety arguments are based on a demanding requirement to demonstrate mutual independence between safety systems including the fundamentals of principles and implementation. Coupled with this is a strategy aimed at making the principal safety argument transparent and simple, as opposed to being complex in nature. The more complex the safety argument the more challenges that can be realistically raised, and the greater the difficulty in providing the appropriate level of assurance. Both simplicity and independence minimize the opportunity for failure through unintended coupled and undetected paths. In turn simplicity and independence ease the burden of providing safety assurance given that one is always tasked to continue to look for all the 'possibilities' leading to mishap. It is certainly not a stance of taking more and more comfort from what we have achieved so far. A strong continuous probing, analysis, testing and surveillance culture is key in relation to early detection of any flaws that might exist or may be developing over time, and is supported with a commitment to maintaining a strong cadre of experts probing in the relevant technology areas.

   2. Focus on those aspects with catastrophic consequences

Response in warhead design: Although we focus on safety across the board, we nevertheless concentrate particularly on the worst-case events of Inadvertent Nuclear Yield and major radioactive material release, and consequently go to great lengths to prevent their occurrence both by way of design, associated processes and independent organizational assessment activity. Again, the prevention of Inadvertent Nuclear Yield and major release of radioactive material is based on a number of foundational safety principles, which are in turn scrutinized with respect to the probity of their underlying scientific, technical, engineering, implementation and evidential basis. This includes assurance that their implementation fully meets these principles both for normal and abnormal (accident) environments. Of course, the ownership approach also aims to minimize the occurrence of abnormal environments and the impact of human error.

3. *Strive for systems that are simple, easily understood, disconnected, and decoupled*

Response in warhead design: This is essentially a re-statement of point 1 above. We adopt this strategy for nuclear weapon design safety focusing on clarity, simplicity and strong independent arguments in the defence in depth approach. Safety is based on a limited number of very strong and independent principles, arguments and technical implementations. These, together with the clarity of their safety intent and quality of implementation, enable a clear and comprehensive challenging process to be undertaken in order to fully test and analyse for overall safety completeness and compliance. The principal arguments supporting the safety case should be simple and clear and should not arise as a result of a complex set of contributing arguments.

The strategy is based on the application of *a limited number* of clear strong and independent safety arguments and implemented safety systems based upon ensuring maximum resilience against the undermining of safety that can occur through added complexity, as the number of safety systems increases. Increasing the number inevitably leads to increasing complexity and increasing concerns about maintaining true independence between the implemented safety systems. Added complexity generally increases the difficulty of ensuring confidence of overall safety because of the multiplicity of potential sneak paths or fault sequences that can give rise to failure. In addition, a warhead design is confronted by constraints on available volume and mass and the need for the complementary requirement that these safety systems can be reliably removed when fully 'authorised' to do so, and such authorisation is based on a principle of uniqueness which effectively decouples it from the pre-authorisation safety argument.

6 Some Additional Factors

6.1 A Lesson from History — Predicting the Future based on the Past

In 1907, five years before he went down with his ship, the Captain of RMS Titanic, E. J. Smith, was quoted in a New York Times interview:

> *But in all my experience, I have never been in any accident... of any sort worth speaking about. I have seen but one vessel in distress in all my years at sea. I never saw a wreck and have never been wrecked nor was I ever in any predicament that threatened to end in disaster of any sort.*

The clear lesson here is that past history (or perceived past history), whilst it may be a guide to the future, is only a guide and so gives *no* assurance about the future. Confidence (false) was also based on the safety built into the Titanic, where all potential threats were deemed to have been considered and catered for. The ship was judged 'unsinkable' but in fact suffered a catastrophe on its maiden voyage. This resulted from a combination of failure to prevent the collision and an overestimate of the ship's capability to withstand such a collision. *This was an example of a 'Known — but not to the degree necessary'.* Similar arguments can be applied to the Columbia and Challenger tragedies where confidence was again based on 'past successes and inadequate technical assessment of known threats'.

Warnings from the past come in the form of failures and 'near misses' and, if acted upon, can improve the situation. However, near misses are not always recognized for what they are and as such there is no guarantee they are fully understood with regards to the future. AWE however scrutinizes issues of this nature to ensure that the fundamental reasons for their cause are fully understood and removed. We *may* take some comfort from the past-history of UK's nuclear weapons ownership where there have been no major safety events, but one cannot take this as assurance in respect to the future. Certainly, the number of successful weapon lifetimes in our history comes nowhere near to proving compliance with the exacting safety standards that we strive to comply with. We certainly take heed of any issues that have arisen and have acted upon them with high priority.

6.2 Human Factors and Independence

Humans are not exempt from failure. Assumptions of true independence in human actions, which is often used as a major redundancy element in preventing a failure, has a long history of being undermined; note the US Minot incident[87]. This type of failure has been noted in dual 'independent' checking processes where enhanced confidence is based on an assumption that true independence is assured in the process. Humans are seldom truly independent in this context. For this reason, the safety of nuclear warheads is based principally on scientific, technical and engineering principled foundations. Nevertheless. 'independent' checking and dual control, together with human error assessment, do have an important place in nuclear warhead safety in preventing and quantifying inadvertent actions. Of course, in the limit even safeguards based on technical principles are not absolutely free from human influence. For example, engineering-based safeguards need human actions for design, manufacture, inspection and maintenance for ensuring and maintaining design intent compliance.

6.3 Conservatism, Worst Case and Probability Function

The approach to nuclear warhead safety design and assessment is conservatively based. This conservatism is applied to combat any possible remnant uncertainty in occurrence probability and consequence and usually takes the form of a somewhat 'worst-case' rather than best-estimate approach to risk assessment. This less onerous (in application) approach is well understood and provides a sensible hedge against uncertainty, but will not always be usable. In some cases, 'worst-case' assumptions can be *too* conservative, and lead to difficulty in meeting exacting risk safety standards. Somewhat less conservative but still supportable statistical approaches, Figure 17, are then deemed more appropriate. This tends towards a more onerous approach (in application) and can carry with it a smaller conservative margin in protecting against uncertainty.

As noted previously, distributions often have greater evidential support near their peaks and far less in the tails, which typically characterise the low probability associated with potentially catastrophic events — Black Swans. The safety assessment of nuclear warheads sometimes puts us in these regions where we need to apply such tails of distributions with suitable caution and with a sound evidential base founded on substantial supporting technical and historical arguments. Such distributions are only accepted if detailed scrutiny provides the evidence noted above and that in turn this evidence stands

---

[87] An unauthorized transfer of nuclear warheads between Minot Air Force Base, North Dakota, and Barksdale Air Force Base, Louisiana, 29th — 30th August 2007.

up to independent challenge. This typically applies to assessment of explosive response to environmental challenge.

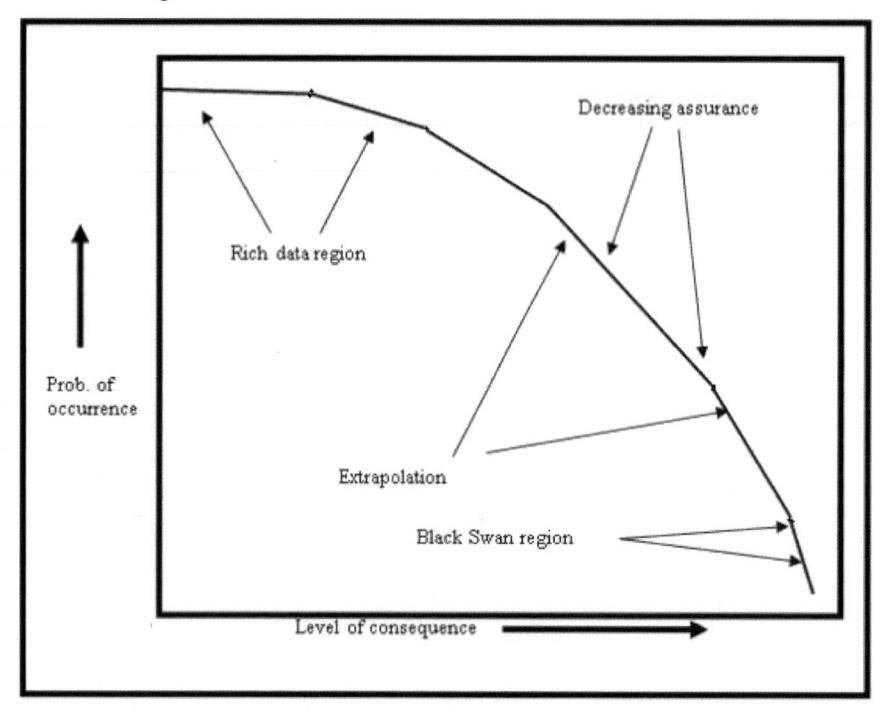

Figure 17 ~ Distribution Approach to Safety Assessment

7 The Importance of, and Achieving, Independence

The occurrence of mishaps and even Black Swans are often the result of an initiator setting off a related sequence which is not truncated. Protection against this occurrence will rely heavily on:

- A full understanding of the inventory of possible hazardous sequences leading on from any given initiator and culminating in a mishap.
- Ensuring a suitable level of independence between such events in the sequence so that the sequence is truncated before reaching the mishap stage.

Some of these aspects were covered in Jones (2017) in terms of the identification of the strength in depth of barriers or Lines of Defence (LOD) in relation to their number and strength in preventing such a mishap. In particular, the importance of independence between such LOD. The choice of LOD is based on the widest range of categories possible in order to meet the independence requirement. For example:

1. Fundamental physics or chemical properties based on the laws of nature, which directly support the LOD resilience
2. Uniqueness of response. In the sense that defeat of the LOD can only occur as a result of unique circumstances.
3. That microelectronics/firmware/software elements are clearly decoupled from the primary safety arguments.
4. Best practices engineered implementation of a concept to the extent that failure is unlikely even under challenging circumstances, e.g. accident conditions.

5. Procedure based. This relies on humans doing the correct thing at the correct time, and not doing the incorrect things at the wrong time. Examples are fully trained staff and application of the two-man checking principle.

These can be broadly categorised as having the resilience properties of: **Isolation, Incompatibility, Inoperability, Independence**. Of course, although correct procedure can have a significant influence in safety, it takes the lowest place in the hierarchy of attributes in the strength in depth argument.

The ability to deterministically make an LOD resilience case and to support the principle of LOD independence will follow this hierarchy. A structured sequence protection argument based strongly on correct LOD based procedures alone will not be acceptable. Although human LOD are least favourable in the overall choice, all LOD have some element of human involvement because of human relationship to judgement, inspection, testing, maintenance, etc.

In addition to the choice of LOD category, the overall strength in depth arguments for LOD in any particular fault sequence is enhanced by applying the following hierarchy of application for independence in as far as technical implementation allows:

1. Fundamentally different concepts.
2. Fundamentally different applications of the same concept.
3. Different engineering implementations of the same concept.
4. Application of different and differently-sourced materials in the same concepts or engineering implementation.

All of these LOD attributes form the major basis of preventing sequences propagating to the mishap conditions.

8 The Influence of Environmental Factors on Black Swan Assurance

An initiator can take the form of a design flaw (failure) or an 'insult'. The latter represents an abnormal environment (accident) and this environment could in turn be applied simultaneously to all LOD in the strength in depth strategy. As such it is important to avoid common mode failure in the application of the LOD. General historical evidence shows that many major mishaps have indeed arisen from common cause environmental based failures of this manner. The potential for abnormal environments presents the greatest challenge in ensuring that all of the sequence paths are identified for any warhead design. In turn one must show that there is sufficient resilience to ensure that such sequences, through design and testing, are truncated under these circumstances and that there is no common mode failure. Prevention of abnormal environment occurrence is of course also a major objective in the overall safety theme and every effort possible is made to prevent/limit the potential for such insults/accidents and in turn the prevention of such environments propagating to the warhead. Nevertheless, such events cannot be totally discounted and as such the safety characteristics of a warhead design must show appropriate resilience against such threats.

9 Conclusions

Hunting for the Black Swan in the context of safety can represent a somewhat uncertain activity in the sense that one may be looking for something that does not exist. One cannot prove a negative. However, there is a compelling history of disasters which evidence the existence of such Black Swans which were not identified in advance. The level of scrutiny applied to the search for Black Swans must be related to the potential consequence of failure. Of course, for nuclear warheads we are well aware of the worst-case catastrophe represented by inadvertent nuclear yield and, as a result, have established a sound culture aimed at minimising the potential for such an occurrence. In addition, we need to provide a compelling level of evidence/assurance that the probability of such a (man-made) occurrence will be less than natural catastrophes of a similar magnitude. We do this based on an independent strength in depth approach coupled with state-of-the-art application of science, engineering and technology with all of the associated requirements set by established best practice. Such designs are then subjected to an independent conservative numerical risk assessment based on a foundation of supporting evidence to demonstrate compliance with demanding national risk standards. Both fundamental design aspects and the risk assessment are in turn subject to organisational independent assurance challenge. The latter covers the fidelity and completeness of the: logic, evidence, implementation and a search for any aspects which might have been missed or not covered in sufficient depth. Both contributions are then considered at the organisational executive decision-making level where a further level of knowledge and experience is applied. These activities go a long way to eradicating the presence of Black Swans but of course this does not guarantee that one is not present. The final layer in the defence comes from the strong organisational support to a continuing probing[88] culture which applies a 'what if' and 'expecting the unexpected' mind-set. Consequently, the campaign for assuring safety never ends. This latter contribution is based on a strong and continuing organisational commitment to engaging the best brains, which continue to probe into the various science, technology and design areas with the goal of achieving even greater depths of understanding in the cause of potential Black Swan identification and early eradication before such can manifest itself. This is exercised both through direct in-house activity and through what can be gleaned from the external world. One cannot claim that this last layer leads to perfection and at times may appear to be somewhat 'undirected' in its approach. However, it is still the best way we know of with regard to tackling the demanding challenge of Unknown Unknowns. The overall strategy is hence based on:

1. A sound approach for developing a safe product and process — ensurance.
2. A sound independent scrutinising/challenging element — independent assurance.
3. A knowledgeable and experienced executive decision-making element — final accountability.
4. An organisational commitment to applying the best brains to a continuing probing approach into all of the technology and procedural areas — the last possible hiding place of the Black Swan — safety is never finished.

Disclaimer

The contents of this document represent the views of the author and not necessarily those of AWE plc.

---

[88] i.e. questioning and challenging

Correspondence Address

Malcolm Jones, Room 110, AWE, Aldermaston, Berkshire RG7 4PR UK

Malcolm.Jones@awe.co.uk

Acknowledgments

The author acknowledges the helpful, interesting and informative discussions held with members of AWE and the International System Safety Society when preparing this paper.

References

Jones M. (2016). *Organisational Problems — Potential Causes — Unintentional Consequences*. In: 34th International System Safety Conference, Orlando, Florida, USA, 8 -12 August 2016. System Safety Society, Unionville.

Jones M. (2017). *Strength in Depth and Quantitative Risk Assessment in the Context of Low Frequency High Consequence Systems*. In: 35th International System Safety Conference, Albuquerque, New Mexico, 21-25 August 2017. System Safety Society, Unionville.

Nelson R. (1964). *Fate Is the Hunter*. Arcola Pictures Corporation, Los Angeles.

Perrow C. (1972). *Complex Organizations: A Critical Essay*. McGraw-Hill, New York.

Perrow C. (2007). *The next catastrophe: Reducing our vulnerabilities to natural, industrial and terrorist disasters*. Princeton University Press, New Jersey.

Smith E. J. (1907). *Captain, RMS Titanic Quotes*. Quotes.net. Retrieved 5th May 2023 from https://www.quotes.net/quote/35858.

Taleb N. N. (2008). *The Black Swan: The Impact of the Highly Improbable*. Penguin Books, London.

This collation page left blank intentionally.

About the Safety-Critical Systems eJournal

Purpose and Scope

This is the Journal of the Safety-Critical Systems Club CIC (SCSC), ISSN 2754-1118 (Online), ISSN 2753-6599 (Print). Its mission is to publish high-quality, peer-reviewed articles on the subject of systems safety.

When we talk of systems, we mean not only the platforms, but also the people and their procedures that make up the whole. Systems Safety addresses those systems, their components, and the services they are used to provide. This is not a narrow view of system safety, our scope is wide and also includes safety-related topics such as resilience, security, public health and environmental impact.

Background

When the Safety-Critical Systems Club (SCSC) was set up over thirty years ago, its objectives were to raise awareness of safety issues and to facilitate safety technology transfer. To achieve these objectives, the club organised events, such as Seminars and an annual Symposium, and published a newsletter, Safety Systems, three times a year.

The Newsletter has, in addition to news, opinion, correspondence, book reviews, and the like, also carried articles discussing current and emerging practices and standards. The length of such articles is limited to about two and a half thousand words, which does not allow an in-depth treatment. It was therefore been decided to add a third string to our bow and supplement the events and newsletter with a journal containing longer papers. The journal is now published here, as the Safety-Critical Systems eJournal, and is to comprise at least two issues a year.

Content Sources

Sources include the outputs of SCSC working groups; solicited technical articles and topic reviews; submitted articles on new analysis techniques, discussion of standards, and industrial practice; and guidelines and lessons learned. If you wish to contribute, please see the Information for Authors[89].

Types of paper include, but are not limited to:

Technical Articles: Written by practitioners and describing practical safety assurance techniques and their industrial applications.

Integration Studies: Written by practitioners reporting upon successful (or otherwise) synergies achieved in practice with other assurance domains, e.g. systems engineering, reliability/availability/maintainability engineering, resilience, human factors, security, and environment.

Position Papers: Written by, or on behalf of, Regulators, Standardisation Organisations, or other official bodies, setting out their position on a topic, e.g. the interpretation of a particular standard or regulation.

Review Articles: Papers highlighting recent developments and trends in some aspect of safety-critical systems or of their use in a particular industrial sector.

---

[89] https://scsc.uk/journal/index.php/scsj/information/authors

Historical Articles: Papers describing the development of safety assurance in an industrial sector; how we got to where we are today.

Perspectives: The authors' personal opinions on a subject, e.g. whether to use statistical methods in particular scenarios.

Reports: The lessons learned from incidents or the outcomes of trials with a description of scenarios, or methods, and a discussion of the results obtained.

Working Group Outputs: Written by Safety-Critical Systems Club Working Groups to include discussions, underpinning theory, or guidelines.

Copyright and Disclaimer

The author(s) of each paper shall retain copyright in their work but give the Safety-Critical Systems Club permission to publish in both on-line and printed formats. While the authors and the publishers have used reasonable endeavours to ensure that the information and guidance given in this work is correct, all parties must rely on their own skill and judgement when making use of this work and obtain professional or specialist advice before taking, or refraining from, any action on the basis of the content of this work.

Neither the authors nor the publishers make any representations or warranties of any kind, express or implied, about the completeness, accuracy, reliability, suitability or availability with respect to such information and guidance for any purpose, and they will not be liable for any loss or damage including without limitation, indirect or consequential loss or damage, or any loss or damage whatsoever (including as a result of negligence) arising out of, or in connection with, the use of this work. The views and opinions expressed in this publication are those of the authors and do not necessarily reflect those of their employers, the Safety-Critical Systems Club, or other organisations.

Letters to the Editor

The editorial to the first issue of this journal said, *"You may find some of this material controversial, or you may think that it does not go far enough. Subsequent issues of this journal will have provision for readers' letters to the Editor responding to individual papers."* Such a letter should be no more than 1000 words in length (not counting title, attribution, or references). That would take up no more than two pages of the journal. Note that a letter should ideally address a single concern with few, if any, external references.

Index of Authors

Sanjeev Appicharla 13

Rob Ashmore 37

Octavian Nicolas Fota 35

Derek Fowler 35, 145

Alasdair Graebner 145

Mark Hadley 129

Malcolm Jones 195

Peter Bernard Ladkin 65

Dieter Schnäpp 65

James Sharp 13

Lou Xinxin 65

Index of Titles

About the Publisher 7

About the Safety-Critical Systems eJournal 211

About this Volume 6

An IEC 61508 Viewpoint on the Safety Assessment of Railway Control Systems 145

Chasing the Black Swan 195

Copyright and Disclaimer 212

Editorial to the 2023 Summer Issue 127

Editorial to the 2023 Winter Issue 11

Important Note 6

Letters to the Editor 212

Reducing the Risk of a Software Common Mode Failure 129

Safety Assessment of Point Merge Operations in Terminal Airspace: An IEC 61508 Viewpoint 35

The Boeing 737 MAX 8 Crashes: System-based Approach to Safety — A Different Perspective 13

The Terminological Analysis Method SemAn and its Implementation 65